Women in Muslim History

WOMEN IN MUSLIM HISTORY

Charis Waddy

Artist's impressions by Lynda Saltmarsh

Longman
London and New York

Longman
London and New York

LONGMAN GROUP LTD

London and New York

Associated companies, branches and representatives throughout the world

First published 1980

British Library Cataloguing in Publication Data

Waddy, Charis
Women in Muslim history.
1. Women, Muslim
I. Title
301.41′2′0917671 HQ1170 80–40161

ISBN 0–582–78084–5

Printed in Great Britain at The Pitman Press, Bath

Dedication

This book is written in tribute to the opening of a new century of Islam.

It is respectfully dedicated
to Her Royal Highness
Princess ʿIffat bint Aḥmad al-Thunayyan,
widow of King Faiṣal bin ʿAbdul ʿAzīz,
who, with her husband,
re-opened the gates of education
to their people, women and men alike.

Acknowledgements

My thanks are due to many friends in Muslim countries as well as in Britain whose hospitality and friendly criticism have helped me in the course of research for this book. It is not possible to name them all, but special mention can be made of Dr Esmat El-Said, Mr and Mrs Mohammed Wahby, Madame Nouha Alhegelan, Mrs In'am Mufti, Mrs Laila Tannous, Begum Tazeen Faridi, Mrs Nisa Ali and the members of the Muslim Women's Association, London. Needless to say, they bear no responsibility for the shortcomings of the author in her attempt to treat so broad and so neglected a theme.

We are grateful to the following for permission to reproduce copyright material:
Aziz Publishers (Lahore) for extracts from *Status of Women in the Muslim World* by P. S. Ali; Jonathan Cape Ltd. on behalf of Brigadier R. J. C. Broadhurst for extracts from *The Travels of Ibn Jubayr* translated by R. J. C. Broadhurst, published by Jonathan Cape Ltd.; Routledge & Kegan Paul Ltd. for an extract from *Muslim Saints and Mystics, Episodes from the Tadhkirat Al-Auliya* by Farid Ud-Din Attar, translated by A. J. Arberry (1966).

The illustrations in the text are taken from designs appearing in rugs and textiles of the Middle East.

Author's Note

A Note on Quotations from the Holy Qur'ān

The language of the Qur'ān, with its dignity, its rhythm, its range and depth of meaning, defies translation, and in the orthodox view cannot be translated. Nevertheless from early times the effort at interpretation has been essential for Muslims whose language is other than Arabic. Such "interpretations" are now appearing in languages ranging from Swahili to Russian and Chinese, including the European languages.

All passages from the Qur'ān quoted in this book have been checked with the Arabic and with the two approved English "interpretations":

Mohammed Marmaduke Pickthall *The Meaning of the Glorious Koran*, Allen and Unwin, 1939 and Mentor Paperback

Abdullah Yusuf Ali *The Holy Qur'ān – Text, Translation and Commentary*, 2 vols, Dar al-Arabia, Beirut 1965, sponsored by the *Rābiṭah al-'Ālam al-Islāmī*, Muslim World League, Mecca

In the passages quoted to me by Muslims, I have usually left the rendering as they gave it, when a slightly different turn of phrase in no way affected the meaning but helped to reach a foreign ear.

The Qur'ān is divided into chapter and verse. Each chapter (sūrah) has its name, drawn either from the subject matter (*Joseph, Mary, The Pilgrimage*, etc.) or from some word prominent near its beginning (*The Bee, The Star, The Overwhelming Event*, etc.). It is the name and not the number that enables a Muslim to place the verse. Muslim authors often give both, and I have followed this usage.

For the English reader, A.J. Arberry's *The Koran Interpreted* (World Classics, Oxford University Press, 1964) brings most dignity and beauty to the attempt to render both the meaning and something of the poetry of the original. But in this book I have throughout used the work of Muslims.

Contents

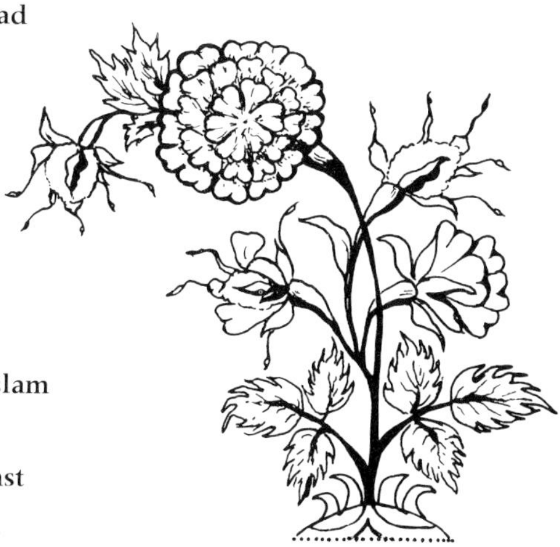

"Praise be to God, Who created the earth and the heavens . . . and gathered together the believers, men and women, and established the sacred law . . .

And the people of happiness obeyed Him and did His work, from among the dutiful men and women . . .

And when He exhorted the creatures to be obedient, He did not single out the men, but spoke of the Muslims, men and women, and the believers of both sexes and those who observed the law, men and women, and the verses dealing with this are many and are not secret."

Taqī al-Dīn al-Ḥisnī (Damascus, circa 824AH/1420AD)
Lives of Good Women

"We did not plan this book with the idea of treating its various subjects exhaustively. Rather we intended it to be a mosaic of blending material, very much like flower beds containing a variety of plants. Some of these are a pleasure to behold, some provide the enjoyment of picking the fruit and also the profit from the produce."

Al-Maʿāfirī (Damascus 581AH/1185AD)
Biographies of Famous Women

"Life in these lands has been enriched by hundreds of thousands of distinguished women, outstanding in their charm and beauty, their gentleness and wit, their elegance and perfection. How can the hidden pearls of their intelligence and their goodness be brought to light? Such women have wrestled with tyrants and overthrown them. But in the Name of God where are they today? And where is the memorial of their good deeds?"

H.H. ʿAbdul Wahāb (1353AH/1934AD)
Les Femmes Tunisiennes Célèbres

Introduction

In everything concerning the Middle East and the Muslim world there is an element of surprise. In its simplest form, this is something no traveller can fail to experience: the contrast between brilliant sunlight and cool shade, the outside and the inside of a house or a mosque.

As one steps out of the glare, the interior seems totally dark. But it is one's own eyes that have to grow accustomed to the welcome relief, and soon the seeming emptiness becomes alive with people. Slowly one is aware of the beauties of a home which, rich or poor, simple or ornate, is ready to offer a greeting to the stranger.

Into such homes one comes by invitation. To be a guest is a privilege, which involves its own duties and responsibilities. There is the grateful acceptance of the bounties offered. There is the refusal to exploit or take advantage of them. There is also the trust of the host's good name. To be made part of the family even for one meal can be the basis of a durable friendship. It is the greatest treachery to betray the loyalty this implies.

When I think of the Muslim world, and of its women, I think of the homes that have made me welcome through a lifetime of valued friendships. I remember them with joy, and with heartbreak too, for what some of them have suffered.

The first Muslim home I ever visited was one of the old houses in Jerusalem, overlooking the Ḥaram al-Sharīf, the Sacred Area, of the Mosque al-Aqsā. These houses belong to families which for centuries have carried the trust of its upkeep and its worship: Khālidīs and Ḥusseinīs, Khatībs, Nashāshībīs and Shihābs. Some claim descent from the first Arab conquerors of the seventh century AD, others from the re-establishment by Salāḥ al-Dīn (Saladin) when he took the Holy City back from the Crusaders.

I was eleven years old, and I still remember sitting with my mother in that gracious room, and being taken to the window to look out at the moonlit radiance that flooded the clear air. The Dome of the Rock shone and glittered in the brightness of the full moon – so strong a light that one could see the colours in the brilliant tiles that cover its walls.

Most of these houses are closed at present, their owners unwilling exiles from their historic trust. Fifty years later, one such family welcomed me in Amman – into perhaps the most hospitable of many generous homes I know. The cups of coffee start early in the morning as the stream of visitors begins, for enforced absence has not lessened the burden of responsibility for many human problems and hardships.

More than half a century passed between these two visits. During those years there were many, many more. Arab palaces and African villages. Weddings in Karachi and Kenton. Doctors' homes in Turkey and Tehran. A one-room hut in a refugee camp, ten-foot square and spotless, the family bedding rolled away against the walls and the water for the coffee brought from the common pump some distance away: and bungalows that house similar families who have found refuge and work half a world away in Sydney. I have spent Ramaḍān with descendants of the Prophet on the shores of the Mediterranean outside Beirut, and the ʿĪd that followed in a red-roofed house peacefully surrounded by palms and poinsettias in the heart of the now shattered city. In India I visited the widow of a President, and the wives of carpenters in the villages of Uttar Pradesh. In Asmara there was the cheerful mother of seven children – with the courage to face later the imprisonment of her husband and the scattering of her sons, across the borders or to the liberation armies of Eritrea. In Malaysia I learned to kick off my shoes so that the dust or mud of the outside world should not pollute the cleanliness of the house. In Damascus, Syria's first woman Cabinet Minister was my hostess. In Cairo I have been the guest of the pioneers of more than fifty years of women's advance, and also of some of the new generation of young women who will shape the next stage of their people's long history.

These and many more crowd into my mind. Some ask whether there is in fact among the immense variety of people in the Muslim world a tangible unity of thought and outlook. From my experience I would say yes. This unity is based on common practice and a common pride in the early history of Islam. As a background to the changing and variable scenes so hard to interpret at the present time, I have gathered together something of what women have contributed to that and to later history.

I do this partly in recognition of the completion of 1400 Years of Islam; and partly in expectation of what the next generation of women in the Muslim world are going to give.

If recent estimates are correct, some nine hundred million people – almost one quarter of mankind – profess the Muslim religion. Assuming that half of these are women, it follows that, out of every eight or ten people alive today, one is a woman directly affected by the teachings of the Qur'ān.

No intelligent observer of today's turbulent world scene can afford to ignore so large a portion of the human race, or neglect to make some attempt to understand the ideas that guide their lives and condition their response to twentieth-century changes. Numerous detailed studies have been made of some aspect or other of the life of women in a Muslim setting. There will be many more. A recent review of material now being published in this field points out the need for synthesis as well as analysis, and the great difficulties involved in reaching such synthesis. One approach is through the presentation of a common past. There is a continuity between the women closest to the Prophet and their many namesakes in the twentieth century: the Khadījahs, Fāṭimahs and 'Ā'ishahs of today. What is attempted here is a general picture of women's contribution from the time of the Prophet onwards: their contribution to the society to which they belonged, rather than their position in it.

The very size and scope of the subject is a challenge. It is like a huge tapestry stretching back into the past, a living pageant in which here and there the spotlight catches some figure, some group, in the very act of history. For those who have regarded the Muslim world as a man's domain – and they have numbered many both within and outside Muslim circles – there is an astonishing wealth of feminine character as well as charm, brilliance as well as beauty, rescued from oblivion by succeeding periods.

The subject itself is not a new one. Many authorities discuss the permissible scope of women's activities. The position of judge, for instance, was thought by many to be suitable only for men. But according to Abū Ḥanīfah, founder of one of the four schools of

Muslim law, a woman might be appointed judge and deal with all matters apart from those under the penal code. Ibn Jarīr al-Ṭabarī, whose work on the Qur'ān became a standard source for all later commentators, went further. He said that a woman might qualify for the post of judge without any restriction.[1]

An early biographical collection – the *Ṭabaqāt* of Ibn Sa'd, written in the third century of the Hijrah, the ninth century AD – devotes its final volume entirely to women of the time of the Prophet.[2] It lists numbers of otherwise unknown wives and mothers, as though to emphasise that behind the few well known personalities there were hundreds more, deserving of mention. The first book in Arabic on *Biographies of Famous Women* was written in Damascus eight hundred years ago. It was the year 1185AD (581AH), while Ṣalāḥ al-Dīn was preparing to retake Jerusalem from the Crusaders. The author was a scholar from far-off Andalusia. His work has humour as well as depth, and is no mere text-book. Already he found the subject too large to handle.

His book was selective. He wanted it to be like a garden in which his readers might find pleasure, enjoyment, and profit. They could look at the flowers, they could pick the fruit: and perhaps they could benefit from its use.[3]

I too have made a selection. This is not a history of Islam, and the women I write about are not all good Muslims. Some have encountered criticism from religious authorities, in our own day no less than in earlier times. Others are Christians, and in the climate of tolerance which the orthodox Muslim is proud to claim they too have made their mark. All of them, however, have lived their lives in societies the framework of which has been Islam. They can therefore be said to play their part in Muslim history.

Their range and diversity may help to correct some widespread misconceptions. As one Muslim writer put it recently, a change in western attitudes is needed "because for centuries people in the West have been either ill-formed or misinformed about Islam."

To give an accurate picture of Islam is essentially a task for Muslims. But the author I quote indicates that he welcomes genuine attempts from the western side to set the record straight "even though one may disagree with some views or miss some points."[4] The outstanding contemporary woman writer on the times of the Prophet, Bint al-Shāṭi', voices a similar conviction.

"It is today, we think, perfectly possible for western writers to examine the life of Muḥammad without any hostility or prejudice, and indeed the attempt demands to be made in a climate of world religious opinion that seeks to stress the similarities rather than the differences of the great faiths of the world.''[5]

Islam is an egalitarian creed. Whatever the localised social inequalities, it preaches the dignity of each human soul, man and woman alike. ''All people are equal,'' as the Prophet said, a saying which every Muslim can quote. ''They are equal as the teeth on a comb. There is no claim of merit of an Arab over a non-Arab, or of a white over a black person, or of a male over a female. Only God-fearing people merit a preference with God.''[6]

The structure of Muslim practice is also the same for all. The five ''pillars'' – creed and prayer, fasting, almsgiving and pilgrimage – are incumbent on women as on men. The fear of Judgment and the hope of Paradise are the same for both.

It is clear that women in many places are prepared to pay a high price for conserving this heritage of belief and practice. ''Liberation'' of women elsewhere in the world seems to be regarded with mixed feelings. Change in the condition and the scope of women's life in the United States and in Europe has certainly stimulated the assertion of rights given to women in the Qur'ān, and too often neglected. But it has also provoked a reaction. We in the West often forget how repulsive to the outside view much of our life has become. We tend to judge other people's societies by certain ''freedoms'' we consider important. The Muslim women I know have other criteria, other aims. The ferment of questioning, as I have seen it, is not for the most part in rebellion against Islam. It is a struggle with the dilemmas posed in every age, to one ''modern'' generation after another, by tradition on the one hand, and change on the other. People today cannot shirk the responsibility that rests on each individual, each community, to discriminate between the essence of belief, and the particular of circumstance: the unchanging commandment of God and the varying customs of men. Ways are sought to advance without failing to pass on the essentials of a great heritage. Sometimes what seems to us a backward look may be an attempt to avoid foreseeable pitfalls in the road ahead, holes into which we ourselves have fallen.

On a world scale the position of women is altering. In some countries change is just beginning. In others it is so far advanced that it is considered almost an insult to pay special attention to the woman's role. Since we are all "persons", it is said, this should be unnecessary. Yet women's movements are one of the growing points in new nations. One thing certain is that women everywhere will play a greater part in shaping the future than ever before. A shift seems to be taking place in the balance of the relationship between men and women: not in its nature, but in the balance of functions, the delicate counterpoise between the two partners. Symptoms of this change have been the removal of restrictions on what women do, and an increase in the responsibilities they carry. This process has been going on for over a century, and it is a world-wide phenomenon.

The debate on the role of women is far from ended. In the teaching of the Qur'ān women are equal – and different. What Muslim women have to say may prove a vital contribution to the debate. It is important that their voice be heard.

The vast majority of the millions of women in the Muslim world are village-dwellers, toiling in the fields of Asia and Africa. Yet however remote they may appear the tides of change are reaching them. Most of them are still illiterate. At the other end of the educational scale, women's advance in professional skills of all kinds has been rapid. Over forty universities in the Arab world alone are now sending out women graduates year by year. Every Muslim country, including the most conservative, can boast of the skill of its women doctors. They are opening up new fields into which many will follow them.

Not all, of course, of this new generation of professional women are Muslims. A general picture of women in the Arab and Muslim world cannot be one of Muslim women alone. From the beginning there has been an essential and historic interplay between different communities and different faiths, even in the setting of a dominant Muslim culture.

Mutual respect between Muslim and Christian is of vital importance in the modern world, all the more so because of the growing number of Muslims living in Europe and across the Atlantic. As Doctor Muḥammad 'Abdul-Rauf, Director of the Islamic Center, Washington, said in an editorial article in *The Muslim World*,[7] "For fourteen hundred years the minaret and the steeple have pierced the sky side by side. In view of their common heritage and a value system that shares a belief in Allah, Moses and the Torah, Jesus and the Gospel, there is no reason why they should not continue to do so – and every reason why they should.'' In the pioneer women's movements of this century, especially in Egypt, Lebanon and Jordan, Christian and Muslim have naturally worked together in all aspects of advance. The early writers and the founders of the women's unions belonged to both communities. When in 1969 and 1972, President Nasser and President Sadat honoured the original members of the Egyptian Feminist Union, there was no distinction. They had worked together for fifty years in the many social welfare societies that carried the movement forward, and in the advance into the professions.

One third of the women of Islam live in countries where Muslims themselves are in a minority. At least another third have important non-Muslim minorities as fellow citizens. Co-operation in common interests, in matters of health, education, child care, is vital. It is increasing not only within nations but in wider international spheres. What women bring with them into public life is not, says one commentator, ''self-centred claims to power'', but ''conviction of the potential collective force of women, which is available for national action.''[8]

In the mobilisation of human resources, they represent one of the great reservoirs of hope and skill. To translate wealth into health, money into human happiness, takes imagination and skill, heart power and intelligence. Untapped stores of these vital resources are waiting, under-used if not wasted.

There has been continuity in the history of Islam. There has also been another important element: surprise. From the moment when the first tide of conquest swept out of Arabia, an event wholly unforeseen by the intelligence departments of either of the two great empires of the time, there have been unexpected developments in the story.

Especially there have been sudden flowerings of civilisation: first in Baghdad, later in Spain; in Delhi and Istanbul and Isfahan. Research into women's contribution takes us into some of the great transformation scenes of history. Does such a blossoming of the spirit lie ahead now? If so, it is allowable to guess that women will make a contribution to it beyond that of any of their illustrious predecessors.

Men and Women Believers

"Men who surrender unto Allāh,
And women who surrender,
And men who believe,
And women who believe,
And men who speak the truth
And women who speak the truth,
And men who persevere in righteousness,
And women who persevere,
And men who are humble,
And women who are humble,
And men who give alms,
And women who give alms,
And men who fast,
And women who fast,
And men who guard their modesty,
And women who guard their modesty,
And men who remember Allāh much,
And women who remember –
Allāh hath prepared for them forgiveness and a vast reward."

Qur'ān, Sūrah 33: 35 The Clans

"So Khadījah believed and attested the truth which came from Allāh. Thus was Allāh minded to lighten the burden of His Prophet: Whenever he heard something that grieved him touching his rejection by the people, he had recourse unto her and she comforted, reassured and supported him."

Ibn Hishām, biographer of the Prophet

"The Prophet is closer to the believers than their own selves, and his wives are their mothers."

Qur'ān, Sūrah 33:6 The Clans

"So it befits a woman to take example from 'Ā'ishah the Faithful and Fāṭimah the Radiant, Allāh the Most High bless them both."

One Thousand and One Nights

Chapter One

The Pioneers

This is not the place for an attempt to tell once again the story of the Prophet of Islam. The following pages have a lesser theme, one which it is not so presumptuous to treat: the part played by women in the founding days of Islam, both in Mecca where Muḥammad was born and started his work, and in Medina where he completed it.

Muslim society, both past and present, has usually been regarded, in Muslim circles and elsewhere, as a man's world. Accounts of women's activities therefore usually start with a large "But . . .": exceptions are given to rules which are apparently unaffected by them. Yet as the curtain is raised on the animated scene in those cities of Arabia fourteen hundred years ago, the number of women who play prominent roles is surprising. It becomes clear that the Prophet gained the love, respect and loyalty of many women as well as men, in a society where they appear as independent individuals, outspoken in their opinions. Many took his part. The inevitable opposition which the challenge of his message provoked also had its outstanding women's voices.

Here we shall sketch the portraits of a few of the many women who take the stage, and outline certain of the scenes in which they play their part. There are riches of character and story, which have largely been hidden from view by the conventions of later societies, communities in which women were segregated to a degree unknown in the Prophet's time.

The Prophet's widowed mother, Āminah, is a shadowy figure, for she died when her son was only six years old. She had taken the boy to visit her relatives in Medina, and fell ill on the way back to Mecca. The little orphan was brought to his grandfather, an eminent member of the tribe of Quraish. Stories grew around

ʿAbdul-Muṭṭalib, not all acceptable to later authorities, but the description of the old man's care for his orphaned grandchild in his last days rings true. The first biographer of the Prophet, Ibn Isḥāq, tells us that a bed was placed for the aged ʿAbdul-Muṭṭalib in the shade of the Kaʿbah, the sacred building in the centre of Mecca. There his friends could come and talk with him. The boy Muḥammad came freely to and fro, and the uncles used to chase him away, but the grandfather liked to have him by his side.

ʿAbdul-Muṭṭalib had six daughters, so the story goes. Evidently in this family there had been none of the customary rejection of girls. According to custom, it was the women who composed and recited elegies mourning the dead. When he felt that his end was near, ʿAbdul-Muṭṭalib sent for the six girls. "You will sing for me when I am dead," he said. "I would like to hear before I die what you will say." So one by one the six daughters recited their poems. No one supposes that all the many verses given by Ibn Isḥāq in his biography of the Prophet one hundred years later are genuine. Many were probably filled in as the stories surrounding the Prophet's life were told and retold. They are nevertheless very old, and the scene itself, and the family warmth of affection, and the part the women take, are in keeping with the times.[1] One at least of these aunts of the Prophet, Ṣāfiyah, was alive to visit the dying Muḥammad and to mourn his death in another elegy nearly sixty years later.[2]

There are many contrasting threads in the pattern of the society in which Muḥammad grew up. There is a romantic side to it, represented by the Pre-Islamic poets. In a desert setting, they sang of beauty and adventure: of lovely women and well-bred horses: with all the subtlety and richness of the language which had so astonishingly developed among the tribes of Arabia. Where life was physically tough, with little margin above the level of survival, the artistic skill and sense of beauty of a gifted people found in words their vehicle of expression. In the tribal frays of the times, women often went into battle with their men, and they took part also in the contests of poetry which promoted the skills of language and verse.

It is hard to know how much the picture has been idealised, for later generations of town-dwellers never quite turned their back on the traditional values of the desert. It always stood to them for hospitality and honour, love and courage, the skills of horsemanship and hunting, the arts of horse and camel breeding, the toughness that survives privation, the lore of the stars. In Muḥammad's day, the urbanised families of Mecca used to send their children out to be nursed and hardened in the desert air. Tribeswomen suckled them, and the relationships with foster brothers and sisters remained important through life. The name of the Prophet's nurse, Ḥalīmah, is a popular one still for girls, and in one recorded conversation Muḥammad recalled those fresh-air days of his childhood. "There has never yet been a prophet who has not kept sheep," he said. "You too, oh Messenger of Allāh?" "Yes."[3] The town dwellers in the narrow streets of Mecca and Medina, men and women alike, had their memories of open air and sky in the days of their youth.

This romantic picture, however, had its reverse side. "The Days of Ignorance" is how the early Muslims characterised the era that preceded them. The expression *jāhiliyah* carries the same connotation as does the word "barbarism": uncivilised, rude, wild, uncultured. Mecca, a town at the cross-roads of caravan routes running north and south, east and west, was the seat of a flourishing commercial community. Its people were also guardians of an ancient sanctuary, a well-known centre of pilgrimage, with traditions going back to Abraham and his son *Ismā'īl*, Ishmael. The sordid idolatry, the immorality and unashamed commercialism associated with this holy place cried out for change, as did many social evils. All the Islamic historians put high among these evils the licence and barbarity with which women were treated: the unrestrained polygamy, the lack of property rights, the prevalence of female infanticide.

The instrument of change was Muḥammad. As a young man, he entered the employ of a woman of importance, the twice-widowed Khadījah, belonging to the leading Meccan tribe of Quraish. In spite of the limitations of women, in her position she was able to own and run an import-export business, send her caravans to and fro, and employ agents and managers. One of these Khadījah chose to marry. Muḥammad was twenty-five and she was forty, and their union lasted for fifteen years, until her death. She bore him six children, two sons who both died young, and four daughters, and was his first and staunchest supporter when the call came to his prophetic mission.

To the lonely orphan, who grew up without close personal

relationships with mother or sister, it is clear that family life was precious. Muḥammad had two homes: first in Mecca, with Khadījah, years older than himself, and four growing daughters; and second in Medina, in very different circumstances, amid the growing responsibilities and varied relationships of the ten turbulent years following the move from Mecca.

Some years after the beginning of his mission, and after the death of Khadījah, the opposition to Muḥammad grew so strong in Mecca that he decided to move to Medina, some two hundred miles to the north. His escape was a dramatic one, and it is from this flight or emigration, *Al-Hijrah*, that the years of the Islamic era are reckoned. It took place in 622AD. In the ten short years that followed, before Muḥammad's death in 632AD (10/632) there was hardly a moment of respite. There was armed conflict, as the Meccans attacked the small force of Muslims, who won a victory in the first encounter at Badr and were later defeated at Uḥūd. There was trouble with a number of tribes, both Jewish and Arab. And there was the return to Mecca and its capture.

In all these events women played a prominent part. Some were rejected by their families because of their new-found faith. Many lost their husbands in battle. They and their children had to be provided for. Muḥammad himself took a number of them under his protection and married them, as did others of the group who followed him from Mecca.

Mecca was taken in the eighth year after the Hijrah, and in the tenth year Muḥammad led the pilgrimage and made his final speech to vast numbers of his supporters. He died soon afterwards. In the short decade of his sojourn in Medina, the old society was swept away, the whole of the future practice of Islam was initiated or foreshadowed, and the basic legislation was ordained by which much of the Muslim world still aims to live.

Few groups of men and women in history have lived through changes as radical and as influential in history as did those around Muḥammad. Their records breathe a sense of destiny, of exhilaration in the dawn of a new era, of devotion to a cause which demanded everything and for which no privation was too great. We miss the point of the lives of these early Muslims if we fail to discern something of the same quality of fervour and hope with which the founders of other great movements of ideas have fired their contemporaries. Fallible as any other human beings they might be, often quarrelsome and revengeful. But they felt themselves to be carriers of a message that was greater than themselves. They were often humble enough to be devastatingly honest about their failures and shortcomings.

Among the many modern studies of the life of the Prophet, one famous Egyptian writer has devoted years of research to the lives of the women who shared his home. Dr 'Ā'ishah 'Abd al-Raḥmān was born in Damietta, the old port at one of the mouths of the Nile. She took as her pen-name Bint al-Shāṭi', (Daughter of the Beach), recalling her childhood memories of the seashore which had seen so many of the tides of Mediterranean history. In the 1960s she was Professor of Arabic Language and Literature in the University of Ain Shams, Cairo. Her novels reached a wide public. Having memorised the Qur'ān as a child, she became deeply interested in the life of Muḥammad, both as a father and as a husband. Every aspect of his life was recorded by his followers with meticulous attention to detail, and gathered together in early books: Ibn Isḥāq's *Life* (*sīrah*) transmitted by Ibn Hishām; Tabarī's *History*; and the authoritative compilations of Traditions: sayings of the Prophet, and recollections of his practice by his contemporaries. Much of this massive bulk of material can be traced originally to the women of his household.

Bint al-Shāṭi's research in these records bore fruit in popular books: *The Wives of the Prophet* (Cairo 1959), *The Daughters of the Prophet* (Cairo 1963), and *The Mother of the Prophet* (Cairo 1966). She gives short studies of the lives and characters of twelve women who were married to the Prophet, ten of whom outlived him. The home in Medina was a patriarchal household. The comparison has often been made with that of Abraham, Sarah and Hagar, whose stories play such an important part in Muslim tradition. Its setting was the stress of war. The young community needed to win the co-operation of its opponents, rather than to suppress them. The remarkable thing is not so much that the early Muslims felt the necessity to fight, in a land where tribal fighting was endemic. What was exceptional indeed was Muḥammad's ultimate success in turning his enemies into his friends. Several of his marriages were made with this end in view.

The place of women in Islam, and especially in its early days has been obscured rather than illuminated by an overemphasis on the number of Muḥammad's later marriages. To the faithful

Muslim, some special lesson can be drawn from each one of these: the provision for widows, for instance, or the conciliation of opponents.

No one, at the time or since, has suggested that the Prophet's household was other than exceptional. Under Islam, the prevailing polygamy was immediately restricted. While some modern authorities point out the realistic advantages of a system of limited polygamy, especially in times of war and its aftermath, many interpreters stress that the normal pattern was always meant to be one wife, with the addition of others to a maximum of four if circumstances made it desirable and the husband's means enabled him to treat them equally. "Marry of the women who seem good to you two or three or four; and if ye fear that ye cannot do justice to them then one only . . . Thus it is more likely that ye will not do injustice."[4] And again, later in the same chapter, "Ye will not be able to deal equally between your wives, however much ye wish to do so."[5] Muslims today are eager to explain that this places the emphasis on complete fair dealing. The Prophet could achieve this with a number of women, whom he married in special circumstances when times of war or stress made it needful. Other men are encouraged to keep to one wife, because they cannot possibly be fair to more. Indeed some Muslims take a still more restrictive view. If God Himself, through the Qur'ān, asserts that "You will not be able to deal equally", how can any man dare to claim otherwise?

Not many households have lived under such close scrutiny as did Muḥammad's, and few great men have been so relentlessly exposed to public view in every detail of their private lives. While he was alive, he tried to gain some privacy for his family by putting a curtain between the women and the constant stream of visitors, and he told them to cover themselves as a protection when they went out.

In view of later developments in customs connected with the veil, it is essential to note the exact words in the Qur'ān relevant to women's modesty and dress.

> Tell the believing men to lower their gaze and be modest. That is purer for them. Lo! Allāh is Aware of what they do. And tell the believing women to lower their gaze and be modest, and to display of their adornment only that which is apparent, and to draw their veils over their bosoms, and not to reveal their adornment save to their

own husbands or fathers or husband's fathers, or their sons or their husband's sons, or their brothers or their brothers' sons or their sisters' sons, or their women, or their slaves, or male attendants who lack vigour, or children who know naught of women's nakedness. And let them not stamp their feet so as to reveal what they hide of their adornment. And turn unto Allāh together, Oh believers, in order that ye may succeed.[6]

Oh Prophet! Tell thy wives and thy daughters and the women of the believers to draw their cloaks close round them when they go abroad. That will be better, that so they may be recognised and not annoyed.[7]

A previous verse (33:58) criticises "those who annoy believing men and women undeservedly". Many interpretations have been given of the words "that which is apparent", *ma ẓahara*, in deciding what a modest woman ought to conceal from view. This rendering is given in *The Meaning of the Glorious Koran*. The authoritative commentator ʿAbdullāh Yūsuf Alī expresses the meaning as "what must ordinarily appear". In notes on these two passages he says, "The rule of modesty applies to men as well as to women." "The times were those of insecurity, and the women were asked to cover themselves when walking abroad. It was never contemplated that they should be confined to their houses like prisoners." "The object was not to restrict the liberty of women, but to protect them from harm and molestation under the conditions then existing in Medina . . . where it was necessary to put down all kinds of unseemly conduct."[8] The majority of commentators are in agreement that the verse does not essentially involve the veiling of the face. Another relevant verse says, "Do not make a dazzling display, like that of the former Times of Ignorance."[9] Women were not to flaunt their charms, as had been only too general in the period of flagrant immorality out of which society was just moving.

A young Iranian musician, Mrs Taraneh Azima-Kayhan, trained in Europe and about to return to her country, made a similar comment.

I think the profound reason for the veil in Islam is that a woman should not draw the attention of others. But if deeply inside her aim *is* to draw attention to herself she will do so even by being covered. Therefore it is a question of motive. If our motive is to gain the respect of others we will do this through the way we are: our behaviour, our acts, our thoughts, what we say and what we wear.

> A woman can be a centre of attention or she can decide to give attention to others. She can be a cause of crime or a cause of creation. It depends on her deep motives.
>
> Today we talk a lot about "la femme objet", the woman as a material object and not a real human being. And we often blame men for this attitude. They may deserve part of the blame, I do not know. But we are the real cause. We must be able to attract through our character, our naturalness, our freedom from jealousy, hate and selfishness, and through what we think. Dressing in an extravagant fashion and showing our naked body must not be the test of being charming and attractive. We can change such values by rethinking our role and our place in society and in the world.[10]

Among the stories which show that the many women who came to consult the Prophet were not veiled is one from the time of his Farewell Pilgrimage. It is told on the authority of Ibn ʿAbbās, cousin of Muḥammad. Ibn ʿAbbās' brother was riding behind the Prophet on the same camel when a woman came to ask permission to perform the Ḥajj on behalf of her old father. "The Prophet allowed her to do so. She was an extremely good-looking woman and because of this the other man began to look at her. The Prophet turned his face away."[11]

This restraint in public encounters is emphasised in another saying quoted from the Prophet: "The true veil is in the eyes of the men."

Women on pilgrimage are not allowed to veil. They cover their heads, but not their faces.

Veil or no, Muḥammad's young wife ʿĀ'ishah throughout her long life always managed to play an active part in affairs. She is the source of much intimate knowledge of her husband's life and practice.

Nothing could have been in greater contrast with his former union with Khadījah than was Muḥammad's marriage to the daughter of his greatest friend, Abū Bakr. After Khadījah's death, the first wife he took was the elderly widow of one of his faithful supporters, who had died after fleeing from persecution to Abyssinia. Such women had to be provided for, and Sawdah rewarded him with faithful service to his household for the rest of his life. The second suggestion made to him was a very different one, but in keeping with the customs of the time. Girls had to be protected and provided for, and this was frequently arranged well ahead of the age of puberty, when the marriage would be consummated. Such a marriage was contracted with the little daughter of Abū Bakr, who lived in the same quarter of Mecca. The Prophet was a daily visitor in his home, and saw this lively child grow into girlhood and womanhood. He found in her a stimulating companion, full of charm and with qualities of mind and understanding – qualities that enabled her later to transmit so much of his life to future generations.

The biographer of one of the greatest women in the later history of Islam, Rābiʿah al-ʿAdawiyyah, when he feels he must defend himself for writing about a woman, voices the debt of the whole Muslim community to ʿĀ'ishah. "If it is allowable to accept two thirds of our faith from ʿĀ'ishah the Trustworthy, it is also allowable to accept religious benefit from one of her handmaids."[12]

Muḥammad himself said that she was his best beloved. He treated his other wives with scrupulous fairness and consideration, but he acknowledged that impartiality of heart was more than even he could achieve. He seems to have prized her wisdom and spiritual insight. She was the only one of his wives in whose company he used to receive his revelations. He chose to spend the days of his last illness in her room, and he died in her arms.

ʿĀ'ishah was under twenty when Muḥammad died, and she lived on in Medina for over forty years, through the period of the first four caliphs, and into the time of the establishment of the first of the Umayyad dynasty in Damascus. She died in 58/677, aged sixty-six. She was unflinchingly loyal to the memory of her husband, and her realism and honesty have preserved the record of his home, of the women who depended on him, and of his way of life. Her recollections have the mark of authenticity, not of mere eulogy. She does not hide her own reactions. When she was jealous, she says so, and when she played tricks on the other women, she says so, and when more than once her sharp tongue earned her a rebuke from her husband, she tells us that also.

She never had children, and she knew that she never replaced Khadījah in his heart. She boasted that she was the only one of his wives who was a virgin when she married him; the others were all widows or previously married. And one day she burst out, referring to her predecessor as "that toothless old woman whom Allāh has replaced with a better". Muḥammad sharply rebuked her. "No, indeed Allāh has not replaced her with a better. She believed in me when I was rejected: when they called me a liar, she proclaimed me truthful: when I was poor, she shared with me her wealth: and Allāh granted me her children, though withholding those of other women."[13]

It is 'Ā'ishah herself who tells us these things. She honestly lays open the rubs and irritations, and the jealousies and competition, with which this household of varied women plagued their busy and burdened husband. As one writer puts it, they were none of them exempt from the heritage of Eve. Their husband might rebuke them, and once he gave them a clear choice, either to stop grumbling and accept their circumstances and responsibilities, or to go. But none of those he took under his protection was divorced by him, and even this threat of divorce was even-handed, addressed to all alike. It is known as "The Verse of Choice".

"Oh Prophet! Say to thy wives: If it be that ye desire the life of this world and its glitter – then come! I will provide for your enjoyment and set you free in a handsome manner. But if ye seek God and His Apostle, and the Home of the Hereafter, verily God has prepared for the well-doers amongst you a great reward." Punishment, and reward, will be doubled for them, the Book says, and the text continues: "Oh wives of the Prophet, ye are not like any other women . . . Stay quietly in your houses, and make not a dazzling display, like that of the former times of ignorance . . . God's wish is but to remove uncleanness far from you, oh Folk of the Household, and cleanse you with a thorough cleansing."[14]

'Ā'ishah does not only state the difficulties she had in her relationships with her "sisters", Muḥammad's other wives. She pays generous tribute to them later in her life when she tells their stories. An example is Zainab, cousin of Muḥammad, who after an unhappy marriage was divorced and became his wife. 'Ā'ishah found her a hard rival to bear in his affections but, when she herself was in difficulties through a scandal she had innocently caused, Zainab stood by her. "I have not seen another woman more true of tongue or more considerate of her family, generous and of good wishes than she," says 'Ā'ishah. She pictures her former rival, the first of the wives to die after Muḥammad's death, industriously working to find money for the poor; tanning skins and threading beads to sell, "praiseworthy and powerful, a refuge for orphans and widows . . . The Prophet said she was the most generous of us."[15]

Of the faithful Sawdah, who lived to be a great age – some say a hundred – 'Ā'ishah says, "There is no one more beloved to me. I had rather be in her shoes than any others. But she is hot-tempered."[16]

The thread of reconciliation in Muḥammad's relationships, personal and political, is one which 'Ā'ishah often reveals. "Give gifts to each other," he said to her one day, "for gifts take away rancour."[17]

Another "sister" with whom she was reconciled was Umm Ḥabībah, daughter of the arch-enemy of Muḥammad in Mecca, Abū Sufyān. This woman left her father's house because of her convictions, and when her husband deserted the cause of Islam the Prophet took her under his protection. She was nearly forty at the time. When they were married, the verse of the Qur'ān was recited, "May God create affection between you and those whom you have antagonised. God is all-powerful, forgiving and merciful."[18] Reconciliation with her father did take place after the recapture of Mecca, when the Prophet treated those who had persecuted him with great generosity.

At the end of her life Umm Ḥabībah said to 'Ā'ishah, "We have nearly been like other rival wives: will you forgive me?" 'Ā'ishah did so, and in turn asked her pardon. "You have made me joyful by forgiving me," the dying woman said. "May God make you joyful too."[19]

Another marriage is an example of a union aimed at pacification of the tribes. In the sixth year after the Hijrah, news came that a certain tribe, the Banū Musta'liq, were about to move against Medina. The Prophet conducted a successful operation to subdue them. There was a bitter battle, and a number of their women were captured, including the daughter of their leader. Captives were by custom divided among the victors, and this girl, Juwairiyah, fell to the lot of one Ibn Qais. She asked for a contract of release, and appealed to the Prophet for help. 'Ā'ishah unwillingly let her in to see Muḥammad, and he wrote the contract of release, and then put forward a proposal of marriage. Her father's honour was safeguarded by the acceptance of a ransom and both he and his daughter embraced Islam.[20]

The result? The Companions of the Prophet freed those of her people whom they were holding captive, since, they said, "they are now the Prophet's relatives." About one hundred households of the Bani al-Musta'liq were thus freed. And 'Ā'ishah acknowledged, "I do not know a woman who was a greater blessing to her people than she."[21]

Two Jewesses came into the Prophet's home as captives, after the defeat of the Banū Quraizah and of the Jews of Khaibar, in perhaps the bitterest of the struggles of these years. One of them, Ṣafīyyah, became a Muslim, and like the other wives a "Mother of the Faithful". A Christian girl, Māriah the Copt, was sent with her sister as a present to Muḥammad from Egypt, by the Coptic governor, Al-Muqawqis. Alone among all the women of his Medinan home, she bore him a child, the longed-for son of his old age, Ibrāhīm. The joy of this boy's birth, and the sorrow of losing him were part of the closing drama of the Prophet's life. Thus "The People of the Book", as the Qur'an calls both Jews and Christians, played a close part in the Prophet's own household.

There are many stories of the Prophet which show his love of children. His youngest daughter Fāṭimah and her husband 'Alī, younger cousin and life-long companion to Muḥammad, were his close neighbours. Their two boys, Ḥasan and Ḥusain, and the little sister Zainab, were a joy to him. There were other children in the home, too, for an elderly Muslim later recalled a never-to-be-forgotten lesson in table manners. "I was a boy, being brought up in the care of the Messenger of Allāh, and my hand was active in the bowl, taking from every side."

"Boy!" came the authoritative voice. "Boy! Say grace (*Bismillāh*): eat with your right hand; and take the piece nearest to you." And this, said the man, had been his manner of eating ever since.[22]

The records picture a home full of vitality, but marked with more of austerity than comfort. The furnishings must have been of the simplest, and when Fāṭimah procured a curtain of figured cloth, she had to give it away if she wanted her father to continue his visits.[23] His personal habits set a high standard of personal hygiene for his followers then and since. 'Ā'ishah, always realistic, delighted to puncture the sanctimonious among the enquirers who in later years flocked to see her. "What was the first thing the Messenger of Allāh used to do when he came home?" asked one earnest seeker after truth. "He cleaned his teeth," replied 'Ā'ishah. And to another query, "What did he do at home?", she said, "He helped his wife."[24]

Other women in the family of ʿĀʾishah's father, Abū Bakr, played a prominent role in Islam. Abū Bakr, first of the caliphs and closest friend of the Prophet, was married four times. His first wife, Qutailah, did not become a Muslim, but her two children, ʿAbdullāh and Asmā, followed their father's conviction. Years later in Medina, Asmā recalled a visit paid to her by her mother. "She was an idolatress. I asked the Prophet, 'May I do good to her?' He said, 'Yes, do good to your mother.'"[25] Abū Bakr's second wife, Umm Rumān, was the mother of ʿĀʾishah and of a son, ʿAbdul-Rahmān. She followed her husband to Medina, bringing both Asmā and ʿĀʾishah. Later, Abū Bakr married the widow of one of his close friends, Jaʿafar ibn Abī Ṭālib, when the latter was killed in battle. And there was also a wife of his old age, Ḥabībah, whose daughter Umm Kulthūm was born after Abū Bakr's death, and brought up by her half-sister ʿĀʾishah.[26]

Asmā was a lively girl in her teens when her father and Muḥammad planned their escape from the plots on their life in Mecca. She slipped out of the house in the dark, and on her camel carried food for them to the cave where they were in hiding. Searchers failed to find them, and after some days they went on their way across the desert to Medina. The searchers came knocking at the house, and Asmā stoutly denied that she knew where her father was – and received a blow for her pains which knocked her earrings off. This is not the only reference to dress in the stories about Asmā; she was later rebuked by the Prophet for coming to see him in too revealing a costume.[27] She earned a nickname for her exploit in provisioning her father and Muḥammad, by tearing her girdle in half to tie up the bundles of food. Her "two girdles" stuck to her through life. Shortly after reaching Medina, she married one of the Companions: those who came with Muḥammad from Mecca. His name was Zubair ibn ʿAwwām, and their son ʿAbdullāh is said to have been the first baby born to the families that had accompanied the Prophet on the Hijrah. The last tragic scene in Asmā's adventurous life is connected with this son, ʿAbdullāh ibn Zubair, who tried to wrest power from the Umayyad Caliph in Damascus, in the year 73/692. His mother, by then very old and blind, encouraged him to fight for his convictions. He was defeated and brutally killed by the Umayyad general Ḥallāj. Asmā begged for his body for burial, and herself died soon afterwards.[28]

The gateway to the Ka'bah, Mecca

Zubaidah's reputed tomb in Baghdad

A younger son, ʿUrwah, boasted of his connection with the first ladies of Islam, not only his mother Asmā, but his maternal and paternal aunts ʿĀ'ishah and Khadījah, and his grandmother Ṣāfiyah, daughter of ʿAbdul-Muṭṭalib and aunt to the Prophet. He takes us into a new stage in the development of the Muslim community, for he tried to keep clear of both politics and war, and devoted himself to the gathering of the recollections of the early days of Islam from the followers of the Prophet. He is one of the earliest and foremost authorities on these "traditions" (*ḥadīth*, plural *ḥadā'ith*) which play such an important part in the history and the practice of Islam. He has been called the first Muslim historian. He collected his material from many sources, but especially from his aunt ʿĀ'ishah, whose company he frequented until she died. He and his much older brother ʿAbdullāh were among the chief mourners at her grave.[29]

Another relative of ʿĀ'ishah was her niece and namesake, daughter of the half-sister Umm Kulthūm, who was Abū Bakr's youngest child. The younger ʿĀ'ishah was a beautiful woman, and she strongly objected to the veil. She is said to have been very like her famous aunt, and she learned much from her, including, she said, a knowledge of the stars. ʿUrwah said of the older ʿĀ'ishah to his son Hishām, "I have never known anyone who had a greater knowledge of law, medicine, and poetry than she had." And he excused his habit of inserting poetry into his records by saying that his aunt always had some apt quotation in verse for every subject.[30] She was very generous in her gifts to charity, and very critical of the ostentation which came to Medinan society as wealth began to pour in as a result of the conquests made by the advancing armies of Islam. Clothes should be only "a traveller's provision", she said, and she kept to her husband's standards of austerity. Her sister Asmā was generous too, said ʿUrwah. But she gave spontaneously, while ʿĀ'ishah saved up and gave large sums.[31]

The lives of other women illustrate the traumatic conflicts which rent the early Muslim community. One woman among the first Meccan converts was named ʿĀtikah. She took part in the Hijrah, and in Medina she married Abū Bakr's son Abdullāh. He died of wounds received in the siege of Ṭā'if, while his father was still alive. 'Umar ibn al-Khaṭṭāb took her into his home, and he was assassinated, after ten years as Caliph, in 23/644. She then married Asmā's former husband, Zubair ibn al-ʿAwwām, and he was killed in the Battle of the Camel, between ʿAlī, the fourth Caliph, and those who disputed his succession. Her fourth husband was Ḥusain, ʿAlī's son, slain with many of his family at Kerbala. No wonder people said, "Let him who wishes to be a martyr marry ʿĀtikah." She wrote a famous elegy on the death of her third husband, Zubair, and the story of her husbands' deaths was turned into a romance.[32]

The devotion of those who followed Muḥammad in spite of poverty and persecution is matched by the fierce hatred of those who opposed him. Abū Sufyān was the leader of the Meccan opposition, and his wife Hind stood with him. She lost her father and two brothers at the first battle between Meccans and Muslims at Badr. She was determined on revenge, especially against Ḥamzah, uncle of the Prophet. At Uḥūd, where the fortunes of the two sides were reversed, she mutilated the dead Ḥamzah's body, and in a subsequent interview with Muḥammad she was anything but submissive. The terrible bitterness of civil strife, of blood feuds between close relatives, are voiced by her, in the woman's cry: "Do we bear and nurture sons, only for you to kill them in battle?"

After the capture of Mecca, both she and her husband made their peace with Muḥammad, and with their daughter Umm Ḥabībah whom he had married. Hind was forgiven her ferocity, but her spirit was no less militant, for we hear of her with the army that conquered Syria. Her son Muʿāwiyah became governor of Damascus, but his mother was dead before he seized the caliphate.[33]

Other women went out with the armies of Islam.

"We used to be with the messenger of Allah in his battles," says one of them. "We tended the wounded and gave them drink and we removed the slain to Medina."[34] At the Battle of Uḥūd, ʿĀ'ishah was one of those who carried water in leather bottles to the wounded, and Fāṭimah dressed the face-wound her father suffered.[35] Women not only nursed the wounded, they sometimes fought themselves. Forty of them are said to have taken the part of Asmā's son ʿAbdullāh ibn Zubair, in the battle in which he was killed in 73/692.[36] Umm Ḥarām, maternal aunt of the Prophet, and her husband accompanied the army that raided the island of Cyprus in the year 29/649. The attack was repulsed. Umm Ḥarām fell from the mule she was riding and broke her neck. This was near Larnaca, where the force had landed, and there she was buried, in a spot still revered by pilgrims today. After the Ottoman conquest in the sixteenth century, a mosque was built and the dome over the tomb was clearly visible from the sea. All Turkish vessels dipped their flags in homage as they passed.[37] The damage the tomb sustained during recent hostilities added to the bitter feelings between Greek and Turkish Cypriots.

The Mothers of the Faithful together with the little Ibrāhīm are buried in the cemetery of Baqī' in Medina. Other tombs far away like that of Umm Ḥarām mark the adventurous travels of women who knew the Prophet.

The Prophet's conduct at the capture of Mecca has been taken as an outstanding example of the patient statesmanship which sought to reconcile rather than crush the enemies of the nascent community. To do away with the blood feuds that dogged their lives, and to relegate acts of revenge to the pre-Islamic past were among his aims, stressed in the final summary of his message, the speech delivered at the Farewell Pilgrimage which he conducted shortly before his death.

The same thread can be followed in the stories of the Year of Deputations, following the capture of Mecca, when the leaders of tribe after tribe came to Medina to see the Prophet and make peace. A pillar in the mosque in Medina still recalls the place where he received these delegations.

A woman played a part in one of these negotiations. They are recorded in Ibn Isḥāq's *Life of Muḥammad* and discussed in a recent book, *The Prophet's Diplomacy*, by a Pakistani diplomat, Afzal Iqbal.

The Banū Ṭayyi' were a Christian tribe in the north of Arabia, near the Syrian border. When a Muslim force approached, their leader, 'Adīy ibn Ḥātim, retreated into Syria, leaving some of his people behind, including one of his sisters. She and the others were captured and taken to Medina. Captives were imprisoned in an enclosure near the door of the mosque, and when she saw the Prophet passing, she got up to meet him, for she was a courteous woman, and said, "Oh Apostle of God, my father is dead and the man who should act for me has gone. If you spare me, God will spare you." This happened three times, and then the Prophet said, "I have done so, but do not hurry away until you find one of your people whom you can trust who can take you to your country, then let me know." "The Apostle gave me clothing and put me on a camel and gave me money and I went away until I came to Syria," she says.

Her brother relates the story of her return, and his subsequent visit to Medina.

> I was sitting among my people when I saw a howdah making for us and I said, "It is Ḥātim's daughter," and so it was, and when she got to me she reviled me, saying, "You evil rascal, you carried away your family and children and abandoned your father's daughter." I said, "Do not say anything that is bad, little sister, for by God I have no excuse, I did do what you say." Then she alighted and stayed with me: and as she was a discreet woman I asked her what she thought of this man and she said, "I think that you should join him quickly, for if the man is a prophet then those who get to him first will be preferred; and if he is a king you will not be shamed, you being the man you are."
>
> I said that this was a sound judgment, so I went to the Apostle when he was in his mosque in Medina and saluted him and told him my name and he got up to take me to his house. As we were making for it there met him an old feeble woman who asked him to stop and he stopped for a long time while she told him of her needs. I said to myself. "This is no king." Then he took me into his house and took hold of a leather cushion stuffed with palm leaves and threw it to me saying, "Sit on that." I said, "No, you sit on it," and he said, "No, you." So I sat on it, and he sat on the ground. I said to myself, "This is not the way a king behaves."

Muḥammad then talked of the future: of the changes coming, from poverty to wealth, and the expansion he saw ahead when kingdoms that now seemed so powerful would fall into Muslim hands. And there would be security for all, such that a woman could cross the whole of Arabia on her camel unafraid. ʿAdīy recognised a new concept of statesmanship, made his peace and became a Muslim. And, he said later, all that the Prophet had told him came true.[38]

The women we have mentioned are only a selection among many, known by name and by character, who made their mark in the first fellowship of Islam. In each of the fourteen centuries that followed, the contribution of such women can be discerned, however restricted their public appearances may have been. For by the nature of things no society, however hard men or women try to make it so, can be other than a shared enterprise between them both.

Women in the Qur'ān

"The believing men and the believing women owe loyalty to one another, they enjoin noble deeds and forbid dishonour, they perform prayer, and pay the alms, and obey God and His Messenger. On them will God have mercy; God is All-Mighty and All-Wise."

Qur'ān, Sūrah 9:71 Repentance

"All people are equal, as equal as the teeth of a comb. There is no claim of merit of an Arab over a non-Arab, or of a white over a black person, or of a male over a female. Only God-fearing people merit a preference with God."

Saying of the Prophet

"God sets forth for an example to the unbelievers the wife of Noah and the wife of Lot . . .

"And God sets forth as an example to those who believe the wife of Pharaoh . . .

"And Mary, the daughter of 'Imrān, who guarded her chastity; and We breathed into her body of Our spirit; and she testified to the truth of her Lord and of His Revelations, and was one of the devout servants."

Qur'ān, Sūrah 66: 10–12 Banning

Chapter Two

Mother Eve and Virgin Mary

The message with which Muḥammad felt himself entrusted was revealed to him in the form of the Holy Qur'ān. The Qur'ān as a whole is addressed to everyone: to all mankind, men, women and children without exception. Far the greater proportion of its injunctions are general to the human race, as are its insights into human nature and into the value of human personality, the peak of God's creation.

In it also are numerous passages that refer to woman's special role, and historical examples of great women. "The Qur'ān speaks specifically to women," says one woman of today. "This means that we can develop freely, without a sense of rivalry with men. We are parallel with them, not competitive."

Certain passages make this explicit by using both the masculine and the feminine forms of verbs and nouns. The best known of these has already been quoted. "Men who believe and women who believe . . . Allāh hath prepared for them forgiveness and a vast reward."[1]

Other examples are:

"If any do deeds of righteousness – be they male or female – and have faith, they will enter paradise."[2]

"The Companions of the Garden shall that day have joy in all that they do: they and their wives, in pleasant shade, on thrones reclining. Theirs the fruit of their good deeds and theirs all that they ask. The word from a Merciful Lord for them is, peace!"[3]

"I suffer not the work of any worker, male or female, to be lost. Ye proceed from one another."[4]

This expression, "Ye proceed from one another", recurs a number of times in the Qur'ān. It is, a modern commentator notes, a reminder to men that women are of the same human status as themselves.[5]

Both are equally to blame when they go wrong.

"Allāh punisheth hypocritical men and hypocritical women, and idolatrous men and idolatrous women. But Allāh pardoneth believing men and believing women, and Allāh is ever forgiving, Merciful."[6]

Women pray, fast, give alms, go on pilgrimage, and are as responsible as men for fulfilling the religious duties of Islām, apart from taking part in the public prayers in mosques. This is not obligatory, and indeed not customary, though there are special places in many mosques kept apart for women.

The oath of allegiance given in the Qur'ān to be taken by women is the same as that for men, except that for men the duty of defence is added.

> O Prophet! If believing women come unto thee,
> taking oath of allegiance unto thee,
> that they will ascribe nothing as partner unto Allāh,
> and will neither steal nor commit adultery,
> nor kill their children,
> nor produce any lie that they have devised . . .
> nor disobey thee in what is right,
> Then accept their allegiance and ask Allāh to forgive them.
> Allāh is Forgiving, Merciful.[7]

Woman has a distinctive role to play, differing from that of a man, even if as human souls they are reckoned as equal.

At the same time, it is clear that man is in authority: and he bears the full responsibility for providing for his wife and family.

"Men are in charge of women, because Allāh hath made the one of them to excel the other, and because they spend of their property for the support of women. So good women are the obedient . . ."[8]

There is detailed legislation on family life in the Qur'ān, dealing with marriage, divorce and inheritance. This is the basis of the code of personal law included in the Muslim law, the *Sharī'ah*. The regulations in this personal code, and in particular the greater ease with which a man can obtain a divorce, are one of the most sensitive points today across the Muslim world. Every society faces the question of greater or lesser adaptations. While some would substitute a modern code of law, others seek interpretations which will not alter the spirit and substance of the Sharī'ah, still less of the Qur'ān, which is regarded as divinely given, but will sift out the non-essential elements of man's restrictions. It is generally admitted that custom has deprived women of rights which should be theirs according to the Qur'ān, but there is determined opposition to any actual legal changes.

Women had the right to their own property from the time of the Prophet onwards while, as many Muslims point out, for centuries women in the West could dispose of nothing of their own and were under the financial control of their husbands.

Apart from legal passages, historical characters appear in the Qur'ān as examples which raise an ideal standard of womanhood, or sound a warning of its frailty.

First of these is Eve, Ḥawā, mother of mankind. Her name is never given, but three times in different contexts the story of Satan's tempting Adam and his wife is told.

> "Oh Adam, dwell thou and thy wife in the Garden, and enjoy its good things as ye wish: but approach not this tree, or ye run into harm and transgression."
>
> Then began Satan to whisper suggestions to them, bringing openly before their minds all their shame that was hidden from them before. He said: "Your Lord only forbade you this tree lest ye should become angels or such beings as live forever."
>
> And he swore to them both, that he was their sincere adviser. So by deceit he brought about their fall. When they tasted of the tree, their shame became manifest to them, and they began to sew together the leaves of the Garden over their bodies. And their Lord called unto them: "Did I not forbid you that tree, and tell you that Satan was an avowed enemy unto you?" They said: "Our Lord, we have wronged our own souls: if Thou forgive us not and bestow not upon us Thy Mercy, we shall certainly be lost."
>
> God said: "Get ye down, with enmity between yourselves. On earth will be your dwelling-place, and your means of livelihood – for a time."
>
> He said, "Therein shall ye live, and therein shall ye die; but from it shall ye be taken out at last."[9]

There is a notable difference between this and the earlier story in Genesis. The woman is not the one who first yields to temptation. Both act together, and the responsibility is mutual. The power of choice was given to them both.

> Our first parents as created by God (and this applies to all of us) were innocent in matters material as well as spiritual. They knew no

> evil. But the faculty of choice, which was given to them and which raised them above the angels, also implied that they had the capacity for evil, which by the training of their own will they were to reject. They were warned of the danger. When they fell, they realised the evil. They were (and we are) still given the chance, in this life on a lower plane, to make good and recover the lost status of innocence and bliss.[10]

There is no scriptural authority for the Muslim to blame women for the sins of men, a theme of which certain Christian theologians have made much.

The Old Testament stories were current in the Arabia of Muḥammad's day. Often the style of the Qur'ān is allusive rather than narratory, making reference to facts well known rather than re-telling an old story. An exception is the full treatment accorded to Joseph, and his resistance to the charms of his master's wife, traditionally known as Zulaikhā. The story is told in the twelfth sūrah, which is entitled *Yūsuf*, Joseph.[11]

Other characters appear more briefly. The fate of Lot's wife is a matter of repeated warning, and Noah's wife is coupled with her. Both women are examples of individual responsibility. The wives of good men cannot rely on their husband's virtues to save them from judgment and hell.[12] Good examples are the wife of Pharaoh, and the Virgin Mary. Pharaoh's wife, known by tradition as 'Āsiyah, saved the life of the infant Moses when he was picked up from the river.[13] Her prayer is for faith in the midst of the evil world in which she lives, whereas Mary "guards her chastity" apart. These two, with Khadījah, first wife of the Prophet, and Fāṭimah, his daughter, are known by tradition as the four perfect women.[14]

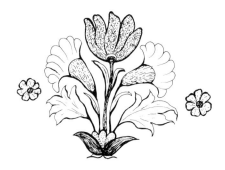

Three times the story is told of the visit of angels to Abraham to promise the birth of Isaac in his old age: and his wife's incredulous laughter at the news.[15] Sarah's name is not actually mentioned. Nor, surprisingly, is that of her rival Hagar (Hājar), whose banishment and abandonment in the desert, on the site of the future Mecca, plays so great a part in Arab tradition, pre-Islamic as well as Muslim, in the story of the Ka'bah and the ritual of the Pilgrimage, the Ḥajj.

The ritual is well described by a woman pilgrim in a recent article.

> One of the most important pillars of Islam is Pilgrimage. That is why millions of people from all round the world go to Mecca, walk seven times round the Ka'abah in the House of the Lord, and then walk seven times between Ṣafā and Marwah. These are two hills about a mile and a half away from each other. Hagar, in despair, once walked between them in the burning desert because Abraham had left her, with her son Ismā'īl, in the desert, without water. She walked and walked until she found water. Millions of Muslims, men and women, walk seven times between Ṣafā and Marwah asking forgiveness and paying tribute to a woman whom God helped when man deserted her.[16]

The Queen of Sheba, Bilqīs, provides the only reference in the Qur'ān to a woman exercising political power. This she did in her own right, and she ruled well. The narrative recounting her visit to Solomon and her conversion to the true faith is delightful.[17] It is a bird which brings news of her to Solomon. His wisdom extends to a knowledge of the language of birds and even of the lowly ants. At a muster of birds, the hoopoe is missing, but soon appears. This lovely bird still inhabits the mountains of Yemen. It is indeed, as a commentator notes, a royal creature, light and graceful, with elegant multicoloured plumage and a yellow crest. Solomon uses his force of birds as a mobile arm, light on the wing: they fly everywhere and see everything, like efficient scouts.[18]

Says the hoopoe, "I have compassed territory which thou hast not compassed, and I have come to thee from Sabā with tiding true. I found a woman ruling over them and she has been given abundance of all things, and hers is a mighty throne." The fault found with her is not that she rules, but that her faith is false. "I found her and her people worshipping the sun instead of Allāh." No objection is raised to her position and authority as a woman.[19]

Women who became rulers in the Muslim world were always compared with her.

Far outshining any of these women is Mary, mother of Jesus, *Sayyidatnā Maryam*. "The angels said, O Mary, Allāh hath chosen thee and made thee pure, and hath preferred thee above all the women of creation."[20] Her story is one of the recurrent themes in the Qur'ān. Jesus and Mary are closely linked, as a demonstration of the power of God. Jesus is 'Isā ibn Maryam, Jesus son of Mary. "And We [Allāh] made the son of Mary and his mother to be a sign."[21] "We breathed Our spirit into her and made of her and her son a sign for all peoples."[22]

Numerically, there are more references to Mary in the Qur'ān than there are in the Gospels, and one chapter is named after her. The theme of her story runs through from the early Meccan revelations to those of Medina. Less than five years after the beginning of the Prophet's mission certain of his followers fled from persecution to Abyssinia. Its capital was the city of Axum, high in the mountains above the Red Sea. There they talked with the Christian king, the Negus. He asked for an example of the revelations that this new prophet was receiving, and they recited to him the story of the birth of Jesus. The Sūrah of Mary must have been among the early portions of the Qur'ān that they took with them. The other account is in the Sūrah of The Family of 'Imrān, Mary's father, and this belongs to the Medinan period, at least ten years later. The later passage tells the story of Mary's own miraculous birth to aged parents and her childhood in the temple.

The narrative continues with Mary living in the *miḥrāb* of the Temple, and in this niche or sanctuary her guardian, Zakariah, finds that she has received food. "He asked, Mary, whence cometh unto thee food? She replied, It cometh from God. Truly God giveth beyond measure to whom He will."[23] This verse is inscribed on the *miḥrāb* – the niche which shows the direction of prayer – in many mosques, notably that in the Santa Sophia in Istanbul, Justinian's famous church which was turned into a mosque after the Ottoman conquest in 857/1453. It shows that the change from church to mosque did not discontinue the honour of Mary.[24]

The key phrase, "Truly God giveth beyond measure", occurs many times in the Qur'ān, including the climax of the powerful verses on the subject of Light, "God is the Light of the heavens and the earth."[25] A comparison may be drawn between the song of Mary in the Gospel of St Luke, the Magnificat, with its vision of the conquering power of humility, and the Quranic reiteration of God's power and generosity. In the Christian Gospel Mary sings, "My soul doth magnify the Lord, and my spirit hath rejoiced in God my Saviour. For He hath regarded the lowliness of His handmaiden . . . He hath exalted the humble and meek . . . He hath filled the hungry with good things . . ."[26] Compare this with the Qur'ān: "Thou exaltest whom Thou wilt, and Thou abasest whom Thou wilt; in Thy hand is welfare . . . Thou givest sustenance beyond measure to whom Thou wilt."[27]

The Annunciation and the Virgin Birth are both present in the Quranic story of Mary and Jesus.

> The angels said: "Oh Mary, God giveth thee glad tidings of a Word from Him: his name will be the Messiah Jesus, the son of Mary, held in honour in this world and the Hereafter and of the company of those nearest to God; he shall speak to the people in childhood and maturity. And he shall be of the company of the righteous."
>
> She said: "Oh my Lord, How shall I have a son when no man has touched me?" He said: "Even so: God createth what he willeth: when He hath decreed a plan, He but saith to it 'Be' and it is! And God will teach him the Book and the Wisdom, the Law and the Gospel, and appoint him an apostle."[28]

The story of the birth of Jesus in the shade of a friendly palm tree is beautifully told, and is a universal favourite. In Ramaḍān, as people wait for the sound of the gun which marks the end of the day's fast, radio broadcasts will often include it among other well-known passages in the Qur'ān. So will readings at the many parties where families and neighbours gather to break the fast (*ifṭār* – literally break-fast). Muslim mothers tell their daughters the story of Mary. "We can learn much from her. A girl can be pure and virgin until she is married – dedicated, as Mary was."

From the earliest days, when some of the first Muslims made a bridge of understanding to the Negus in Abyssinia by reciting her story, a common reverence for Mary and the gift of her son has been a link between Muslim and Christian.

The lunar cycle of months brings round the feasts of the Muslim calendar at different seasons. Sometimes, therefore, Christmas will coincide with one of the big Muslim feasts. In one such year, on Christmas Eve, a well-known writer in Lebanon, Dr Hassan Saab, published an article in the journal *L'Orient*.

> We observe Christmas with as much joy as we do the Birthday of the Prophet.
>
> For Islām, Jesus is the son of Mary rather than the son of God. But he is the prophet of God whose life embodies a series of miracles – Proofs. In the Qur'ān, Jesus is the Spirit, the Word, and the sign of God for the universe.
>
> Islam, authentic and rigorous expression of Semitic monotheism, cannot admit either the divinity or the crucifixion of Christ, but it confers on him a special position among prophets and men.
>
> We put forward this Quranic image of Jesus today to show that Christmas has spiritual significance for Muslims, as it does for Christians: also to recall once again that in the teachings of our two religions, the points that unite us are at least as profound as those that separate us. We need to become increasingly conscious of our points of encounter, as well as of our differences. A clear perception of these is a necessary condition for true brotherhood whether spiritual or national.[29]

Christians, too, can find something to touch their hearts in pondering the narrative as presented in the Qur'ān. A group of teachers in Britain discussing this found three points from which they could learn. They noted the Virgin's submission to the will of God, her complete and utter obedience, which made her a vehicle for the miracle of the spirit of God. Such submission is, of course, the essence of Islām, the meaning of the word itself. They were struck also by the suffering of Mary. At the time of the birth she was alone, without a human protector, and when she brought her baby back it was to puzzled and critical people who did not at first understand. And they saw, in the reverence shared by those who ponder Mary's experience, a starting point of reconciliation and healing where relationships between Muslim and Christian have been difficult.

Many places in the Middle East have taken Mary to their hearts and feel she belongs to them. In Bethlehem, Muslim pilgrims visit the Church of the Nativity, alongside their Christian brothers and sisters. In Jerusalem, the ancient church over the tomb of the Virgin had for long its own *miḥrāb* where Muslims could pray.

When the Muslim conquerors came to Syria in the seventh century, there were already many such sanctuaries honouring the

Virgin. One of these was the convent of Saidnaya, north of Damascus, founded by the Emperor Justinian. Like the later Lourdes, Saidnaya became the resort of thousands of pilgrims. They came for healing, and especially for a cure for sterility. Muslims honoured the Virgin and her shrine, and there are many stories of healings connected with them. One ruler of Damascus, a thirteenth-century pilgrim tells us, had his sight restored. The first thing he could see as he rose from his knees was the light of the sanctuary lamp, and he promised regular supplies of oil for it, a gift that went on for seven centuries, till the last years of the Ottoman sultans in Istanbul. Salāḥ al-Dīn's brother was cured of an illness there, and his sister was a benefactress. The Virgin's birthday, September 8th, was widely celebrated as a holiday for Christian and Muslim alike.[30]

Turkey treasures the home where the Virgin is said to have lived in her old age. Tradition says that St John, instructed by Jesus to care for his mother, took her in later years to Ephesus. On a wooded mountainside above the ruins of the ancient city, the traces of a First Century house have been found, and round them a small church built. The place itself was only discovered a hundred years ago, through the dream of a German nun. But the tradition that the Virgin lived in some such spot in this area is a very early one, and the peaceful house and garden and spring hold something of her spirit. Muslims honour it, and by the altar are written passages from the Gospels, the Muslim traditions and the Qur'ān, in praise of the Mother of Jesus. A tradition from Bukhārī's collection is quoted: "O Jesus, O Mary, From birth you have been free from Satan's touch."

The flight of the Holy Family to Egypt, from Herod's persecution, is a living tradition in that country. The tree where they rested on arrival, and the places where they sojourned, are part of the nation's heritage. There are echoes of their presence in the neighbourhood of Cairo, in Wadi Natroun, and far up the Nile. Muslim and Christian alike are glad that their people sheltered Mary and her son and Joseph. When in the 1960s there were rumours of appearances of the Virgin at one of her ancient shrines, the stir among Muslims was almost as great as among Christians.

There is a note of tenderness in the Quranic story of Mary, which breaks through a barrier of resistance, of non-comprehension, in the stranger's difficult approach to the Qur'ān. The Qur'ān comes to the Westerner stripped of so much of its essential beauty. In the course of interpretation into foreign tongues the majestic resonance of language has gone. Also its visual quality has been largely lost, and the vivid pictures it raises in the mind of a desert-dweller do not evoke an immediate response in a western reader. The Qur'ān has an artistry of expression, depicting the worship of God in every aspect of His creation. In attempted translation, its symphony of sound and sight comes through in a weak and colourless form. The awe-inspiring rhythm of sun and moon and stars, the thunder of tempest by sea and by land, the fresh shoots of green that follow the blessing of rain on parched land, all these can pass unnoticed, along with the flight of birds, the clatter of hooves, and even more the tenderness of love, and the delicacy of human relations.

It is the spirit of the Qur'ān that is vitally important, as well as its rules. From women who take it as the guide to their lives one gains a picture of a way of life rather than a code, though a code of law is based on it.

The refrain of kindness runs through all that is said about personal relationships: love and patience, generosity and gratitude between parents and children, husbands and wives. In the most intimate relationships, the Prophet is quoted as saying that there must be consideration for each other, never a selfish exploitation of the other partner.[31]

"Show kindness to parents . . . Lower to them the wing of humility out of tenderness." "Speak kindly to them," (orphan children). "Consult together in kindness," (husband and wife). And when a question of divorce arises, "A woman must be retained in honour or released in kindness."[32]

There is thunder and lightning in the Qur'ān, and judgment and hell fire may indeed await those who stray, as death haunts those who lose their way in a scorching desert. But there is also grace and companionship, pity and peace. On the Straight Path life is full and free, and men and women walk it together.

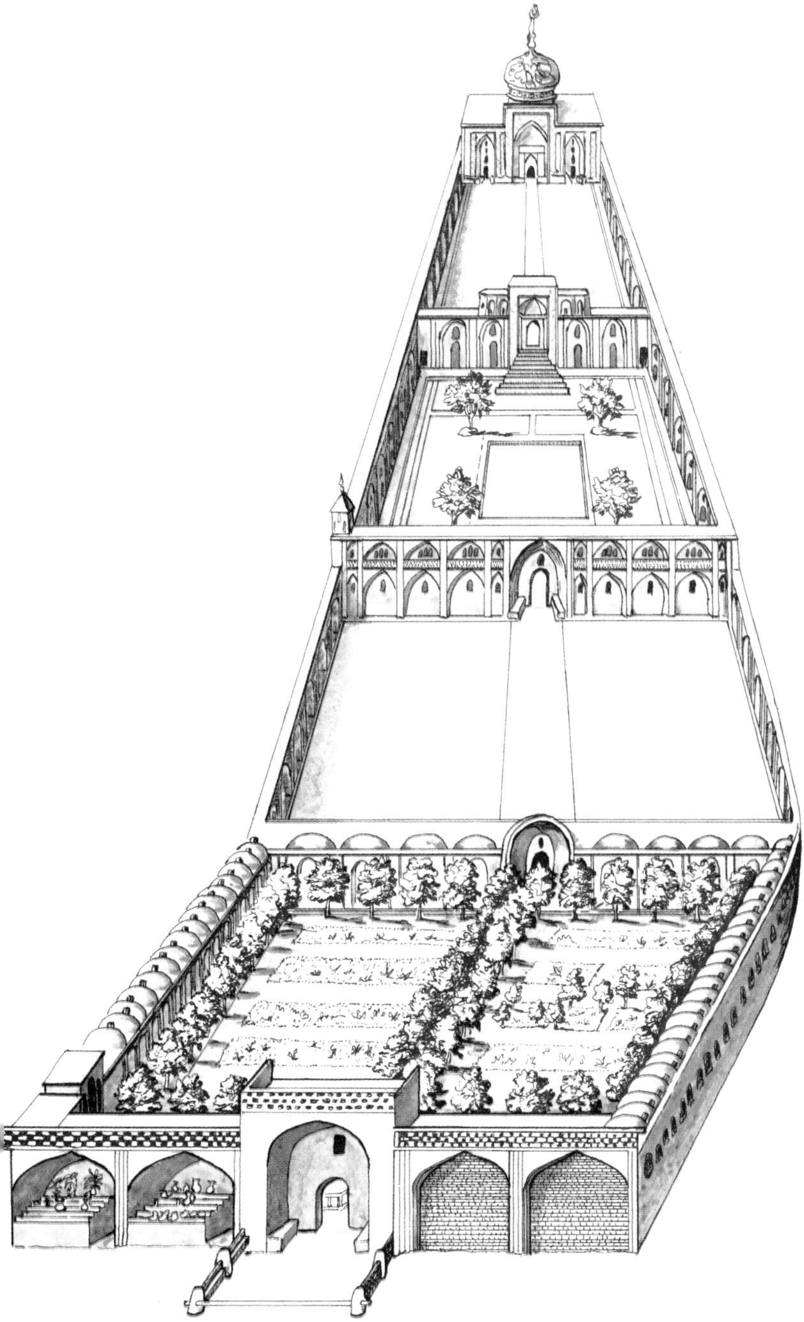

The shrine of Sayyidah Fāṭimah al-Ma'sūmeh in Qum

Queen Sayyidah's mosque in Jiblah, Yemen

Three Women at the Court of Hārūn Al-Rashīd

Khaizurān: mother of the Caliph
Zainab: senior Abbasid princess
Murayyah: Umayyad widow

Ibrahīm ibn al-Mahdī relates:

I went into the presence of Khaizurān, mother of Al-Rashīd. She was reclining on an Armenian carpet. In the foremost part of the carpet sat Zainab bint Suleimān. The other cushions were occupied by the mothers of children of the Caliphs Al-Manṣūr, Al-Mahdī and Al-Hādī.

A woman came in, and standing on the edge of the carpet she saluted the company and went on to say, "I am Murayyah, widow of [the Caliph] Marwān. I have fallen on evil days, my steps have faltered and Time has reduced me to borrowing even the clothes I stand in."

Now Zainab saw that Khaizurān's eyes were filling with tears. So she cut short Murayyah's speech and said, "Oh mother of the Commander of the Faithful, beware lest any compassion for this accursed woman penetrate your heart." She turned to Murayyah and said, "May you instead remain in your present condition. You seem to forget the time I visited you [when your husband was Caliph]. You were seated on this very rug. I stood then on the spot where you now stand. You looked at me with a scowl on your face and said, 'What have women to do with the affairs of men?' Then you rudely ordered my dismissal."

Murayyah said, "What she has related about me is true. It is that behaviour which has placed me in this position. Fortunate is he who learns from the experience of others." So saying she left.

Khaizurān, after the departure of Zainab, sent for Murayyah. She treated her kindly and was so generous to her that she was better off than in the time of the Umayyads.

Chapter Three

Three Queens

It was quite possible for those who saw the birth of the Abbasid dynasty and the founding of Baghdad to have known people who themselves knew the Prophet of Islam. Many families who moved into the new city will have had elderly relatives who could recall the tales their mothers and grandmothers told of Mecca and Medina while the Prophet was alive.

To second and third – and even fourth – generation Muslims, the memories were still green of the early years of struggle, and also of the bitter internecine strife that soon afflicted the young community. Abū Bakr, first successor of Muḥammad, died in peace and was buried in his daughter ʿĀʾishah's room, beside her husband the Prophet. The second Caliph, ʿUmar, fell to an assassin's dagger, and the disputes over the succession between the supporters of ʿUthmān and ʿAlī, third and fourth Caliphs, led in the end to violent deaths for them both.

The active participation of women in all these events, as well as the desolation and bereavement involved, stand out in the narratives of the historians. Nāʾilah, young wife of ʿUthmān, lost the fingers of a hand as she strove to protect her aged husband from his assailants.[1] The always difficult relationship between ʿĀʾishah and Fāṭimah, youngest and much-loved daughter of the Prophet, had its part in the early rifts in the Islamic community. Nor was ʿĀʾishah on good terms with Fāṭimah's husband, ʿAlī, who succeeded ʿUthmān as Caliph. She was enraged by the murder of ʿUthmān, and although ʿAlī disclaimed any part in it she went into battle against him.

The engagement was known as the Battle of the Camel – so named because ʿĀʾishah herself watched the battle from the back of a camel. Here Muslim first faced Muslim on the field of war. ʿAlī won: but his family were to be involved in a long and tragic struggle with that of Abū Sufyān, the Umayyad clan. Mu'āwiyah, son of Abū Sufyān and Hind, whose story we recall during the opposition to Muḥammad in Mecca, was established in Damascus. The transference of the Caliphate to these Umayyad rulers in Syria was at the cost of a division between Sunnī and Shī'ī which has persisted ever since. The quarrel culminated in the massacre at Kerbela of 'Alī's son Ḥusain and most of his family, on 10th Muharram 61/10th October 680. Its anniversary has been widely observed as a day of mourning ever since.

Half a century later, when the vigour of the Umayyads was declining, the struggle with the Prophet's family was renewed, this time with the descendants of his uncle 'Abbās, strongly entrenched in Iraq. The year 132/750 saw the overthrow of the last Umayyad to rule in Damascus. Four years later his supplanter, Abul-'Abbās al-Saffāḥ, handed on his newly-won power to his son Al-Manṣūr, perhaps the greatest of the long succession of Abbasid caliphs.

It was Al-Manṣūr who planned and built the new city of Baghdad. His purpose was strategic, and what he planned was an entirely new town, purpose-built to be the capital of the new and still expanding empire. It was to be called "The City of Peace".

One hundred thousand men, we are told, built Al-Manṣūr's Round City, in only four years.[2] It must have been one vast building site, and the Caliph moved in with his family almost before the dust had settled. Two thirds of the central core of the town were occupied by the Royal Palace and the buildings connected with it. By the end of the second century of Islam, the Abbasid family were to be thirty thousand strong, and they occupied many other palaces up and down the river Tigris. They were a powerful element in the life of the city.[3]

There have been many new cities in history, but few which have so swiftly become the centre of a great renaissance. The flowering of learning and culture that took place during the reigns of Al-Manṣūr's sons and grandsons is one of the major intellectual awakenings not only in Arab history but in world history.

The part that women played in this sudden growth of civilisation can be traced in the numerous records that have been preserved from the period.

The move to Baghdad marked an increase in the influence of Persian custom which had grave consequences for women. The

Persians, like the Byzantines, and earlier the Assyrians, were accustomed to protecting their women by the wearing of a veil. During the Umayyad period, Arab tradition was dominant and the life of women comparatively free. It was in Baghdad that their movements became severely restricted, and the organisation of the harem, with that sad and sinister figure the eunuch to guard it, dates from this time. The changes were gradual and they did not prevent certain outstanding women from making their mark.

Three famous queens graced the courts of the caliphs during the first century of Baghdad's existence.

First of the three was Khaizurān, who by her beauty and her wits won her way from slavery to be the wife of Al-Manṣūr's son Al-Mahdī, and mother of the two subsequent caliphs Al-Hādī and the famous Hārūn al-Rashīd.

Second was Zubaidah, of royal birth, married to her cousin Hārūn al-Rashīd. She was the mother of his son and short-lived successor Al-Amīn, and step-mother of the brother who replaced him, Al-Ma'mūn.

Third was Burān, daughter of a fabulously wealthy minister of Al-Ma'mūn, who married her at a wedding that became proverbial for splendour.

All three were influential in the affairs of their time, were patrons of the arts and generous benefactresses. Khaizurān was the most politically ambitious, and Zubaidah the best remembered, for her provision of fresh water supplies on the pilgrim road and in Mecca. Every pilgrim thankfully drank of the well she sank on the Plain of 'Arafāt. Both of these women exercised their greatest power when their sons were ruling. Burān never became queen-mother, so that her period of influence was shorter, but she survived her husband Al-Ma'mūn for over half a century, and was part of Baghdad society during the reigns of eight of his successors.

It was Al-Manṣūr's sharp eye that discerned the quality in the slave girl Khaizurān and introduced her into the household of his son, the future caliph Al-Mahdī. In some sections of Muslim society, the system of employing slave girls supplemented the institution of marriage with its legal maximum of four wives. In a few places, this custom persisted even into this century. These girls might be captives taken in one of the constant wars on the borders of empire, or they might be driven on to the slave market in Mecca or Baghdad or other cities by poverty or unfortunate family circumstances. The birth of a son to their master made their position more secure, and the man might then free them and take them as a legal wife. The most promising boys and girls on the slave market were selected for training, especially in the arts of music, and there were well-known schools for this purpose.

Khaizurān, when her prospective buyer, Al-Manṣūr, first questioned her as to her origin, said she had no family. Later, when she was well established, she brought some relatives to court, where they gained good positions.[4]

Khaizurān was not only beautiful and clever. She was lucky. For she quickly presented her husband with two sons. There was also a little daughter, Banūqah, "the Little Lady", and there was much grief and public mourning when the child died. After his accession in 158/774 Al-Mahdī married Khaizurān. He told her to model her behaviour on that of a senior Abbasid princess, Zainab, who had seen the establishment of the dynasty and was an honoured figure at the Baghdad court. This lady is first heard of at the time of the last Umayyad caliph, and was still influential at the time of Al-Ma'mūn, after both Khaizurān and Zubaidah had had their day.[5]

The education of the two boys, like that of all the Abbasid princes, was a matter of close attention. The older boy, Mūsā, was outstripped by the younger, Hārūn, and the first serious strife among the Abbasid royal family arose between these two brothers, the future caliphs Al-Hādī and Al-Rashīd. As her husband grew older, Khaizurān's political influence increased. In the short troubled period of her elder son's rule she over-reached in her attempts to control the chaotic course of events. Al-Hādī bitterly reproached her for this, and there are stories of attempted poisoning on both sides. The early historian Ṭabarī says, "Khaizurān, in the first part of Al Hādī's reign, used to settle his affairs and to deal with him as she had dealt with his father before him in assuming absolute power to command and to forbid."[6] The father died in 169/785 in a hunting accident, on the way to bring the rebellious Al-Hādī to submission. The younger son Hārūn was in Khurasan, at a safe distance. The clash between the brothers lasted less than two years, for by the end of 170/786 Al-Hādī was dead, and Hārūn Al-Rashīd on his way to enter Baghdad and take over the caliphate. His mother lived for another few years.[7]

It was a wet day in the autumn of 174/790 when Khaizurān's funeral procession passed through the streets of Baghdad. At its head the Caliph himself walked barefoot through the mud, in honour of his mother. But his wife Zubaidah had already taken her place as the leading lady in Baghdad.

Zubaidah was brought up in very different circumstances from those of the slave girl Khaizurān. The first glimpse of her is a chubby little girl playing with her illustrious grandfather Al-Mansūr, who nicknamed her "Little Butterball" – Zubaidah. She married her cousin Hārūn, and they were deeply in love, so much so that Hārūn was distracted from the affairs of state that were supposed to occupy his attention. For some years she had no children. Then a son was born to her, the future caliph Al-Amīn. But a few months previously, while Zubaidah was pregnant, another son, the eldest, was presented to the caliph by a Persian slave, who died in giving him birth. Zubaidah cared for the older baby, as she did for her own child, and the two boys grew up together. Here again were seeds of serious strife, for the twice-royal Al-Amīn could not compete with his more able step-brother.

This rivalry was not Zubaidah's only trouble. Her husband Hārūn was a man of violent passions. She kept his love, but had to share his passion with many other women. Fear was never far away in that gay and brilliant court, and many are the tales of sudden death for favourites who aroused the Caliph's suspicions. To Hārūn is attributed a famous "crime of honour". It was rumoured that his sister 'Abbāsah had paid with her life for a liaison. Sentence of death would be executed not by the law but by the family. Many could keep such a thing secret, but when it came to the Caliph's sister, the matter could not remain hidden.[8]

When Hārūn Al-Rashīd died there was war between his two sons. This brought fire and destruction to Baghdad, only sixty years after its founding.

Zubaidah, who loved both men, tried unsuccessfully to mediate. She stayed faithfully by the side of her own son Al-Amīn, but she was no blind partisan. An army was sent to fight Al-Ma'mūn, and she talked to its general. "The Commander of the Faithful is my son, the exclusive object of my affections. But for Abdullah al-Ma'mūn I have much sympathy on account of the wrongs which have befallen him. My son, the king, has disputed with his brother over his sovereignty: but you should recognise Abdullah's rights as a son and as a brother. Do not affront him in speech, for you are not his peer; nor treat him roughly as you would a slave; nor demean him by fetters or chains . . . Hold his stirrup when he mounts, and, if he speaks ill of you, be patient with him."[9]

In the event, it was the general and not Al-Ma'mūn who was captured. Al-Ma'mūn's troops advanced on Baghdad, and Al-Amīn was killed in an attempt to escape. Al-Ma'mūn was held responsible for his brother's death. But Zubaidah would have nothing to do with revenge. "What have women to do with avenging blood and taking the field with warriors?" she said. She took no part in the attempt to install a son of Al-Mahdī, Ibrāhīm, as caliph, in rivalry with Al-Ma'mūn's claims, but she retired into deep mourning.

Al-Ma'mūn wrote to her, assuring her that he had had nothing to do with the killing of his brother, and promising to be a son to her. The mother's reply was a great-hearted one: "If I lost a son who was Caliph, I now have a son who is Caliph. No mother is bereft who holds you by the hand. There is a day when you two will meet again, and I pray Allāh that he will forgive both of you."[10]

Her magnanimity may have contributed to Baghdad's recovery and to the brilliance of the reign of Al-Ma'mūn. For some years he stayed away from Baghdad, living in Persia. When he returned, he married the daughter of his treasurer, Ḥasan ibn Sahl. The betrothal had taken place when the young Burān was only eight years old. Now she was eighteen, and the wedding-party her father provided surpassed all previous limits of splendour. Zubaidah bestowed on her a large estate and an historic heirloom: the jewelled jacket of the Umayyad princess 'Abdah. It was a sleeveless coat with a row of large rubies down the front and the back, and it had already graced the wives of two caliphs in Damascus before it came into the hands of the wife of the first of the Abbasids. In time it came into the possession of Zubaidah.

In the midst of glowing descriptions of the gifts, the feasting, the showers of pearls, one poignant scene is depicted. The bridegroom came to greet the bride in her home. He placed on her lap a golden tray with a thousand pearls. He said, "What more do you ask?" She had two requests, the first a surprising one. It was pardon for the uncle Ibrāhīm who had been put up to oppose him, and who had been in hiding ever since. This Ibrāhīm was a popular figure, son of an African slave girl, poet and musician, with a fine singing voice. In younger days, he had not been regarded as a good influence on his nephews, Hārūn Al-Rashīd's sons, and once got a thrashing for taking them to too gay a musical evening. Al-Ma'mūn forgave his rebellion. The expensive menu, including "fishes' tongues", of the dinner which Ibrāhīm subsequently gave to the new Caliph is preserved in the records.[11]

So the conciliatory role of a woman had its place in settling the affairs of Baghdad. Burān's second plea was that Zubaidah be allowed to go once more on pilgrimage. Since Al-Amīn's death she had been living in seclusion. This, her sixth journey to Mecca, was her last public appearance. She had done much in her lifetime to create and enrich the life of Baghdad's palaces, famous for their wonderful gardens, their sumptuous decoration and their exquisite furniture. But she was equally at home on the road to Mecca, on that pilgrim journey which was and is so much part of the Muslim experience.

From Kufa, in southern Iraq, to Mecca is nine hundred miles. Nine or ten sites of inns founded by her are known, each with a well or a cistern. They lie between the older ones, because they were meant for those who had to make the long journey on foot. In the time of Hārūn al-Rashīd there were serious droughts in Mecca, and Zubaidah determined to improve the water supply. She increased the depth of the well Zamzam and dug a well on the Plain of ʿArafāt. An aqueduct was planned to bring water into the city from springs twelve miles away. This and other work was in progress, and she was able to complete it on this final visit.

A contemporary writer, the first historian of Mecca, says, "The people of Mecca owe their very life to her, next to Allāh." And another a few years later reckons her as one of the great personalities among "the excellent and jovial company round the caliph Hārūn", none of whom surpassed his wife, "the most desirous of the good, the swiftest to perform pious deeds, and the readiest in benefactions. She, among her other benevolences, brought water to the sanctuary, after the supply had failed."[12] The cry of "God bless Zubaidah" has been heard in Mecca ever since, for more than eleven hundred years. Her care for travellers was recorded in guest houses far afield from the pilgrim road, as far away as the Oxus, and several cities were named Zubaidiyah after her.

Zubaidah returned to Baghdad, and she died in the year 216/831. She had no son to lead the mourners, and her step-son Al-Ma'mūn was away in Persia. If rain fell on her funeral procession, as it did on that of Khaizurān, perhaps it reminded her mourners of her lasting legacy, where water cool and pure still flows in desert places for those who follow her along the pilgrim road.

Two years later Al-Ma'mūn died, while travelling near Tarsus. His wife Burān was at his side. She lived on in Baghdad until she was eighty, and died in 271/884. The records sing her praises as "a most accomplished lady of wit, charm and romance".[13]

Motherhood

"We have enjoined on man kindness to his parents: In pain did his mother bear him, and in pain did she give him birth."

Qur'ān 16:15 Wind-curved Sandhills

"Be kind to parents . . . And out of kindness, lower to them the wing of humility and say: My Lord! bestow on them Thy Mercy even as they cherished me in childhood."

Qur'ān 17:23–24 Israelites

"Paradise lies at the feet of mothers."

Saying of the Prophet

"One day, in the rashness of youth, I spoke harshly to my mother. She sat in the corner and with tears in her eyes said: 'You forget the days of infancy. Can you recall those days when you would cling to my bosom helplessly and would not dare to speak to me loudly? Now you are powerful as a tiger and formidable as an elephant only because I am an old woman.'"

Sa'dī Shīrāzī

"She took my hand in hers, and leading
Me on, with loving talk
She taught me how to walk.
While I have life, be this my pleading:
Since she my being bore,
I'll love her evermore."

Īraj, Iranian poet, d.1925

Chapter Four

Fāṭimah and her Namesakes

The gentle Fāṭimah, youngest daughter of Muḥammad and mother of his grandsons Ḥasan and Ḥusain, died shortly after her father. Venerated by all Muslims, she has been especially revered by the Shīʿī followers of the house of ʿAlī, her husband. Innumerable Muslim girls, Sunnī and Shīʿī alike, are named after her.

Fāṭimah typifies the woman whose life is spent, and whose personality is fulfilled, in service to her family; whose greatness consists not in what she does herself but in nurturing the faith of those around her. Her short life covered the period of her father's mission. Born before his call, she died within a few months of his decease, still in her twenties.

She was born in Mecca, into a household watched over by her mother Khadījah and including her elder sisters and a boy cousin, her future husband. ʿAlī was brought up by Muḥammad, was devoted to him, and became his first disciple after Khadījah.

The first scene in a life of many crises shows her father comforting the sobbing child after her mother's death. Three years of unpleasant persecution followed, experiences which must have borne hardly on a sensitive girl. The one recorded incident in which she figures shows plenty of courage. One day in the Kaʿbah her father was set upon as he bowed in prayer, and was pelted with refuse. Young Fāṭimah cleaned the dirt off him and shouted at the offenders. When the Prophet made his escape to Medina he soon sent an escort to bring his two younger daughters to join him, and Fāṭimah's betrothal and marriage to ʿAlī took place shortly afterwards. Like most of the newly established community they were poor. They lived very close to the Prophet's house and saw him constantly.[1]

Legend has embroidered the story of Fāṭimah with imaginary

and miraculous detail. But the picture that emerges from the early records is of a hard-working housewife, doing her best for her family in straitened circumstances, often short of food yet sharing what she had with those who came hungry to the door. She was passionately devoted to her father and to the message he preached. What she and her husband learned from him she taught to her friends and to her children.[2]

When life became easier and there was more to eat, the household would still sometimes go without for a day, and give the food to those worse off. This is an early example of the importance of fasting in Muslim training. Those who are better off learn what it means to be hungry, and to be alert to the needs of others. Fasting is also valued as a way of teaching the discipline of self-control: to be able to say no to one's own desires and therefore not to be the slave of any lust or habit.

Fāṭimah bore two sons and two daughters to 'Alī. Muḥammad enjoyed the company of his grandchildren: the two boys, Ḥasan and Ḥusain; the elder girl Zainab, who was to play a major role in the tragedy of her brother Ḥusain's death; and the little Umm Kulthūm, named after her mother's sister.

According to Muslim tradition, there have been only four perfect women, and Khadījah and Fāṭimah are two of them.[3] Both were mothers of families, with practical experience, fulfilling responsibilities common to their sex. Fāṭimah is pictured passing on what her father taught her in the midst of an over-busy life; with blistered hands from grinding corn, pacifying the children with one hand while keeping the grindstone turning with the other; unwilling to ask help from the neighbours; occasionally impatient with her husband, and often confiding in her father. When 'Alī wanted to marry a second wife, Fāṭimah sought her father's support in objecting. "We are part of each other," said Muḥammad. When he and 'Alī returned from the battle of Ūḥud, where the Muslims suffered a severe reverse, Fāṭimah tended the wound her father had received and cleaned both their swords.[4]

When the time came for Muḥammad to die, supporters of 'Alī maintained that he was the only rightful successor (*khalīfah*, caliph), because of the Prophet's own choice, expressed shortly before his last illness. However, during that illness it was Abū Bakr who led the public prayers in the Prophet's place, and his daughter 'Ā'ishah claimed that it was he whom Muḥammad designated as successor. By general agreement, at a gathering held before the Prophet's funeral and not attended by ʿAlī, the choice fell on Abū Bakr.

Fāṭimah was greatly distressed at this, and the breach with Abū Bakr and his family widened when she was refused a share in property which she felt should have come to her under her father's will. When she fell ill a few months later she did not want to see ʿĀʾishah or any other member of Abū Bakr's family, nor to have them attend her funeral. But a bridge was built by her sister-in-law Asmā bint ʿUmais, who was by this time married to Abū Bakr. She it was who cared for Fāṭimah at the end.

This Asmā's life illustrates the close pattern of mutual care between the families who surrounded the Prophet. She was a very early convert to Islam in Mecca and was married to ʿAlī's brother Jaʿfar. He led the group of Muslims who took refuge from persecution in Abyssinia and won the support of the Negus. After their return, Jaʿfar was killed, and Muḥammad himself came weeping to break the news to his widow and children. It was Abū Bakr who took her into his home, and she bore him a son. The difficulties between Abū Bakr and Fāṭimah did not come between Fāṭimah and Asmā, who, years later after Abū Bakr's death, was to marry the widowed ʿAlī and give him two sons.[5]

When Abū Bakr died, first ʿUmar and then ʿUthmān succeeded him. ʿAlī became the fourth caliph. He himself accepted these honoured predecessors, though he is said not to have paid allegiance to Abū Bakr until after the death of the grief-stricken Fāṭimah.

The sharp division between Sunnī and Shīʿī can be traced to these events at the time of the death of the Prophet. (The word *sunnī* means one who follows the *sunnah*, or practice, of the Prophet. The word *shīʿī* means one who belongs to the *shīʿah*, division or party, which maintains that the Prophet himself appointed his cousin and son-in-law ʿAlī to succeed him.) After the violent deaths of ʿAlī himself at Najaf in Iraq, and of his son Ḥusain, murdered at Kerbela in 61/180, the rift between Sunnī and Shīʿī was never healed. The story of the family of ʿAlī, and of the rivalry between Sunnī and Shīʿī, is interwoven at every stage with the developing pattern of Muslim history. Shīʿah Islam became the dominant form in Iran.

Ḥusain was killed by emissaries of the Umayyad caliph Yazīd, together with all but one of his male relatives. It was the women of the family who escaped the massacre at Kerbela. The heroine of the story is Ḥusain's sister Zainab, who was with her brother to the end. Her courage and energy saved the life of one of his sons, who was very ill at the time. Two of her own sons were among the slain. She shepherded the sad procession of captives who, with the head of the murdered Ḥusain, were taken to Damascus. There she persuaded the caliph to allow not only Ḥusain's daughters but also the surviving son, ʿAlī Zain al-ʿĀbidīn, to return to Medina.

The children Zainab rescued were to play a notable part in history, for ʿAlī Zain al-ʿĀbidīn continued the line of the Prophet's family, through the famous succession of Shīʿī Imāms and other descendants of Muḥammad, Fāṭimah and ʿAlī. Claimants to this honourable ancestry are to be found today in many Muslim lands.

ʿAlī Zain al-ʿĀbidīn and his sisters lived on for many years in Medina. One of them, namesake of her grandmother, Fāṭimah, was as well known for her piety as was her brilliant sister Sukainah for her beauty and her wit. Sukainah's real name was Āminah, after her great-grandmother, mother of the Prophet. "She had an intelligent mind, an independent spirit and a very lively sense of humour, with a fondness for playing practical jokes. When taken to task for not being pious like her sister Fāṭimah, she said, 'You named her after our grandmother, and me after a woman who never did embrace Islam.'"[6]

Their brother ʿAlī Zain al-ʿĀbidīn was greatly respected for his learning and his goodness. The title of *Imām* was used of him and his successors, and came to denote religious leadership, with always the possibility that it might also imply a claim to political authority, vested in the caliphs.

With the Abbasid dynasty, the family of the Prophet regained the political leadership, but the new caliphs were descendants of the Prophet's uncle ʿAbbās, not of ʿAlī. The succession of Shīʿī Imāms continued. There was from the first a close connection between the followers of ʿAlī and Ḥusain and the Muslims of Iran. Reaction against the Arab conquerors focussed on the acceptance of Shīʿī ideas and loyalties.

Honour was shown for ʿAlī, his wife Fāṭimah and his descendants, rather than for the ruling caliphs. The tombs of ʿAlī and Ḥusain in Iraq, at Najaf and Kerbela, were widely honoured and visited. To these two shrines were shortly to be added three more:

one, Al-Kāẓimain, in Baghdad itself, and the other two in Iran, at Mashhad and Qum. At all of these, year by year on the tenth day of the first month, Muḥarram, renewed mourning for the death of Ḥusain roused deep feelings, as it still does.

One attempt was to be made to heal the rift between Alid and Abbasid, Shī'ī and Sunnī. Its author was the Caliph Al-Ma'mūn, and it was doomed to failure, but it left an enduring mark on the history of Iran. It is in connection with this that another Fāṭimah of the family of 'Alī is still remembered. She was known as Fāṭimah al-Ma'sūmah, and she is buried in the city of Qum.

Qum lies on the road between Isfahan and Tehran, mediaeval and modern capitals of Iran. The golden dome of Fāṭimah's shrine dominates a landscape of fertile orchards. In mediaeval times the town was famous for its red grapes, its pistachio nuts, and for the leather goods and exquisite materials its craftsmen manufactured. It was early known as a centre of Shī'ī support.[7]

The story of Fāṭimah al-Ma'sūmah begins with her father, seventh in the line of Shī'ī Imams, Mūsā al-Kāẓim. Events in his immediate family circle were to have enduring consequences, for it is his elder brother Ismā'īl that one section of the Shī'ī world follows to this day: the Ismā'īlīs, led by the Agha Khan. Ismā'īl was, however, passed over by his father in favour of the younger Mūsā, whose title Al-Kāẓim means "one who restrains his anger". This control of passion is said to have been shown in his dealings with his opponents, whom he won over by kindness. Ibn Khallikān, in his biographical dictionary, gives examples of Mūsā's generosity: "Being informed that a man had spoken ill of him, he sent him a purse of a thousand dinars." Ibn Khallikān also describes how afraid were the Abbasid caliphs in Baghdad of his possible rivalry. First Al-Mahdī, and then Hārūn al-Rashīd, brought him from Medina to Baghdad and put him in prison, though three times they released him. Both caliphs are said to have been woken by anxious dreams about him, and the long-suffering official summoned in the middle of the night by the worried Hārūn al-Rashīd protested, "Shall I liberate Mūsā al-Kāẓim for the third time?" Nevertheless he died in captivity, in the year 183/799.[8] Later, his grandson, the ninth Imām, was buried alongside him, and the double shrine, Al-Kāẓimain, (the two Kāẓims), has been a well-known landmark in Baghdad ever since. The first reference to the burial place of Queen Zubaidah, who died a few years later, places it near Al-Kāẓimain.[9]

The effect of this series of imprisonments on his numerous children – he is said to have had thirty-seven of them – is not recorded. Hārūn al-Rashīd's son Al-Ma'mūn adopted a very different policy towards Mūsā al-Kāẓim's son, the eighth Imām, ʿAlī al-Riḍā (Persian: Reza).

The tension between the Arab and the Persian elements in the empire of Islam was a matter of constant concern to the caliphs. Hārūn al-Rashīd died while on a campaign in the eastern province of Khurasan, near the city of Tus. His son Al-Ma'mūn, himself the son of a Persian mother, stayed on in the east. After the death of his brother Amīn in Baghdad, and his own accession as caliph, he decided to enlist the support and loyalty of his Iranian subjects by appointing as his successor the Shīʿī Imām of the time, ʿAlī al-Riḍā. This was in the year 201/816.

ʿAlī al-Riḍā was a much older man than Al-Ma'mūn. He was known for his piety and his scholarship and had no taste for politics. Unwillingly he accepted the appointment. The Shīʿīs were jubilant, the Abbasid family in Baghdad were furious. Imām ʿAlī himself is said to have pointed out to Al-Ma'mūn the strength of the opposition he had aroused, while his Persian chief minister was concealing it.

ʿAlī al-Riḍā's sister Fāṭimah al-Maʿsūmah set out to join her brother in Khurasan in the same year. She reached Qum, and there she died. Two years later her brother was about to travel to Baghdad with Al-Ma'mūn, when he too died suddenly. It was suspected that both had been poisoned.

Imām ʿAlī was buried with much ceremony next to the tomb of Hārūn al-Rashīd. His tomb became so popular a place of Shīʿī pilgrimage that the city was re-named Mashhad, place of witness or martyrdom. Meanwhile the people of Qum rose in rebellion against the Caliph and refused to pay taxes. Al-Ma'mūn put down the rebellion and destroyed part of the city. Qum, already known as a fanatically Shīʿī stronghold, rebelled again a few years later against the Caliph Al-Muʿtazz (252/866-255/868).[10] It was not the last time that its people were to find themselves in religious opposition to political authority.

Al-Ma'mūn returned to Baghdad and made up his quarrel with the Abbasid family, and with his step-mother Zubaidah. The attempt to bridge the gap between Arab and Persian had failed.

One feature of Shī'ah Islām is the veneration of the tombs of holy men and women – suspect to the strict Sunnī, since it carries a danger of giving to men a respect which belongs to God alone. The "shrine" cities of Iran have held an importance which has persisted while the political capitals have changed.

The tombs of Hārūn al-Rashīd and Imām 'Alī al-Riḍā stood alongside each other for centuries. One among many beautifiers of the shrine was the daughter of Sultan Maḥmūd of Ghaznah, conqueror of India. In 512/1118 Princess Tërkën Zumurrud provided in the tomb chamber a border of the famous lustre tiles made in Kashan, after her father had reconstructed the sanctuary and crowned it with a lofty dome. Some of these tiles are still in place.[11] They are mentioned by the traveller Ibn Baṭṭūṭah, who visited the place in about the year 733/1332. He found "a large town with abundant fruit trees, streams and mills. The noble mausoleum is surmounted by a great dome of elegant construction, the walls being decorated with coloured Kāshānī tiles." He adds, "Opposite the tomb of the Imām is the tomb of Caliph Hārūn al-Rashīd . . . When a Shi'ite enters to visit it he kicks the tomb of Al-Rashīd with his foot, and pronounces a blessing on Al-Riḍā."[12] Hārūn al-Rashīd's tomb has disappeared, but that of Imām 'Alī draws thousands of pilgrims every year.

At every stage of development in the glories of Persian architecture and art, attention was paid to the twin sanctuaries of Mashhad and Qum. Often the same craftsmen would work in both places. Round the tomb of Fāṭimah al-Ma'sūmah clustered other graves: one authority mentions no fewer than four hundred and forty-four tombs to be visited. These later included a number of the Safavid dynasty, who claimed descent from Mūsā al-Kāẓim through another brother of Fāṭimah al-Ma'sūmah and 'Alī al-Riḍā.[13] The tomb of yet another of Mūsā's children is in Western Iran. Sitt Zeinabar's little shrine stands in a remote mountain valley near Alamut, with a "spring of healing" beside it.[14]

More important than the memories of the past have been the schools and colleges in Mashhad and Qum, which have given a lengthy and thorough theological training to succeeding generations of students, the equivalent for Shī'ī Islām to that of the great Sunnī University of Al-Azhar in Cairo. As centres of religion and learning, the two Iranian cities have maintained a fraternal link as close as that of the brother and sister they commemorate.

Prayers of Rābi'ah Al-'Adawiyyah

"O my Lord, the stars are shining and the eyes of men are closed and every lover is alone with his beloved, and here I am alone with Thee."

"Real resignation consists not in bowing down under the Will of God but in rising up into it."

"Rābi'ah used to pray all night, and when the day dawned she allowed herself a light sleep in her place of prayer, until the dawn tinged the sky with gold, and I used to hear her say, when she sprang up in fear from that sleep, 'O soul, how long wilt thou sleep and how often wilt thou wake? Soon wilt thou sleep a sleep from which thou shalt not wake again until the trumpet call of the Day of Resurrection.'"

"Celebrate the praises of thy Lord ere the rising of the sun and ere the going down thereof. And glorify Him some hours of the night and at the two ends of the day, that thou mayest find acceptance."

Qur'ān 20:130 Ṭā Hā

Chapter Five

Servant of God Alone

A broken jug. An old rush mat. A brick for a pillow. Such were the possessions of a woman living in a back street in Basrah, while the walls of Baghdad were rising.

A friend who describes the little house was grieved at such deprivation, but Rābiʿah would accept nothing more. Her poverty was self-chosen, a vehicle for a message proclaiming complete submission and dependence on the God she served.[1]

Rābiʿah's hut was near the Tigris. A few hundred miles away lived Khaizurān and Zubaidah in their palaces. No greater contrast in life-style could be drawn. Past the little house in Basrah flowed the ever-increasing traffic of the empire. The date of Rābiʿah's birth is given as 95/713 or 99/717, and she was in her thirties when the city of Baghdad was built. During the remaining fifty years of her lifetime the boats went to and fro in an endless procession: carrying bales of silk from China, bundles of spices from India, slaves from Africa, and the outward traffic from the capital, from Persia and from Syria in the far north. The money which paid for these goods went far afield. Hoards of Islamic coins have been found in many parts of Europe. In Rābiʿah's lifetime a king of Mercia, Offa, minted in England a gold coin modelled on the Islamic dinar.[2] This was some years before Charlemagne sent envoys to his contemporary Hārūn al-Rashīd in Baghdad.

The Tigris carried a golden stream, surging with the world's riches and toil. Only a few paces from it, and yet so far apart, lay a different world.

It was not just the obvious difference between rich and poor, sharp there as in many another society ancient and modern. To Rābiʿah and her associates poverty was not the enemy. They were asserting another scale of values. Austerity and simplicity had marked the life of the Prophet and his companions. Muḥammad himself had just one cushion in his room, stuffed with palm leaves, and gave it to his guests while he sat on the floor.

The sudden wealth which came with success made possible for some a very different standard of living. Expansion and experiment were the mark of the generations who followed the first Muslims, and they enjoyed many of the good things of life that had been unknown to their fathers. And this was approved. Islam has always laid emphasis on the rightful enjoyment and use of wealth, and encouraged the work which will acquire it. But many reacted against the flamboyance of riches, and the way in which values of money or of power could put God's service in second place. There was a growing preoccupation with the world, with the complications of business and of statecraft, and nowhere more so than in the prosperous cities of Iraq.

Here and there, faithful Muslims sought to maintain the high ideals of the early Companions of the Prophet. In the first and second generations the emphasis was on the gathering of traditions, the recollections of what the Prophet said and did. In Abbasid days, the transmission and study of these memories of the Prophet continued. Besides this, little groups of men and women encouraged each other in lives of total concentration on the service of God. They aimed to maintain and transmit not only the words but the practice of the dedication and sacrifice of the early days of Islam, in challenge to the growing secularism of the society in which they lived.

Rābi'ah al-'Adawiyyah was one of such a group in Basrah, at the time of the change-over of the dynasties and the early Abbasid Caliphs.

"That woman on fire with love and ardent desire . . . consumed with her passion for God."[3] This is how her biographer describes her. Farīd al-Dīn 'Aṭṭār, Persian poet and mystic, wrote the lives of many of these early ascetics, the fore-runners of the later Ṣūfī orders.[4] He himself belongs to the thirteenth century, the seventh of the Hijrah, when the Mongol threat was advancing from the east and the destruction of a declining Baghdad was near.

The message of these men and women seemed relevant to his own troubled times. Whatever the conflicts and queries about certain developments of Ṣūfī doctrines, these early pioneers shine out as a challenge to the evils of their day, courageously maintaining the values and practices of the Faith, and bringing them before their contemporaries in an uncomfortable and often dangerous way. 'Aṭṭār's "Lives" are not without their humour. The stories that went around about these holy men and women had an edge to them, and were a distinct and thorny element in the life and thinking of the community. Exaggerated their actions might be, and often outrageous. But they raised awkward points and called the dubious into question: acting in some ways as the conscience of their day.

Many of the stories told of Rābi'ah are of this type. She had frequent visitors, distinguished scholars and men of God. Her dealings with them were direct, her conversation salty and shrewd. People looked up to these men, but they had their faults and she dealt with them. Once she was ill, and a number of recorded incidents concern what she gave to those who came to console her. Three friends, like Job's comforters, tried to say the right thing. To the first she retorted, "What you say stinks of egoism." And to the others, "You will have to do better than that." Another sat by her bedside and reviled the world. "You love the world very dearly," said Rābi'ah. "You talk about it so much." Another leading scholar talked to her about prayer, and she soon reduced him to silence. So he said, "Since one cannot speak about your situation, will you say something about mine?" "You are a good man, but for the fact that you love the world," Rābi'ah replied. "You love reciting traditions." The man was deeply moved, and started praying that God might be satisfied with his work. "Are you not ashamed," cried Rābi'ah, "to seek the contentment of One with Whom you yourself are not content?"[5]

This man was one among a number who had dealings with the caliphs, to whom they spoke as forthrightly as Rābi'ah did to them. Hārūn al-Rashīd and others sought out such men, from whom they could expect an honesty and directness denied them by the sycophancy of the court.

In the recorded lives of these ascetics women play a great part: their mothers, their wives, their sisters. Some were saintly in their own right, as Rābi'ah was. She was outstanding, but not unusual, in her role as a dedicated woman. It was generally admitted that women could be as saintly as men, though this view always seemed to need explanation and defence. The great reformer Al-Ghazālī, who owed much to Rābi'ah's life and teaching, says to his male readers:

"Consider the state of the God-fearing woman and say to your own soul, 'O my soul, be not content to be less than a woman, for a man is contemptible if he comes short of a woman, in respect of her religion, and her relation to this world.' So we will now mention something of the spiritual state of the women who have devoted themselves to the service of God . . ."[6] He then cites several well-known women saints as examples of attainment in the spiritual life.

A Damascus writer, Taqī al-Dīn al-Ḥisnī (died 830/1426), wrote a whole book about women saints, and found no lack of material. This was in spite of his low opinion of women in general in his own day: "The most double-faced of mankind are women, because of the weakness of their intellect and their religion and their convictions, and therefore their faith fails." In his introduction he begins with God's creation and His sending the Prophet and the Qur'ān. He continues: "When He exhorted the creatures to be obedient, He did not single out the men, but spoke of the Muslims, men and women, and the believers of both sexes and those who observed the law, men and women, and the verses dealing with this are many and are not secret."[7]

Farīd al-Dīn 'Aṭṭār himself defends his inclusion of Rābi'ah. "If anyone says, 'Why have you included Rābi'ah in the rank of men?' my answer is that the Prophet himself said, 'God does not regard your outward forms.' The root of the matter is not form but intention, as the Prophet said, 'Mankind will be raised up according to their intentions.' Moreover if it is proper to derive two-thirds of our religion from 'Ā'ishah, surely it is possible to take religious instruction from a handmaid of 'Ā'ishah's. When a woman becomes a 'man' in the path of God, she is a man and one cannot any more call her a woman."[8]

He tells the story of Rābi'ah's life in the following terms:

> The night when Rābi'ah came to earth, there was nothing whatsoever in her father's house; for her father lived in very poor circumstances. He did not possess even one drop of oil to anoint her navel; there was no lamp, and not a rag to swaddle her in. He already had three daughters, and Rābi'ah was his fourth; that is why she was called by that name.
>
> "Go to neighbour So-and-So and beg for a drop of oil so that I can light the lamp," his wife said to him.
>
> Now the man had entered into a covenant that he would never ask

any mortal for anything. So he went out and just laid his hand on the neighbour's door, and returned.

"They will not open the door," he reported.

The poor woman wept bitterly. In that anxious state the man placed his head on his knees and went to sleep. He dreamed that he saw the Prophet.

"Be not sorrowful," the Prophet bade him. "The girl child who has just come to earth is a queen among women, who shall be the intercessor for seventy thousand of my community. Tomorrow," the Prophet continued, "go to 'Isā Zādhān, the governor of Basrah; write upon a piece of paper to the following effect: 'Every night you send upon Me a hundred blessings, and on Friday night four hundred. Last night was Friday night and you forgot Me. In expiation for that, give this man four hundred dinars lawfully acquired.'"

Rābi'ah's father on awaking burst into tears. He rose up and wrote as the Prophet had bidden him, and sent the message to the governor by the hand of the chamberlain.

When the governor had read the letter he said, "Give two thousand dinars to the poor as a thank-offering because the Prophet had me in mind, and four hundred dinars to that Shaikh and say to him that I desire that he should come before me that I may see him, but it is not fitting that such a person as he is should come to me, but I will come and rub my beard on his threshold."

The man took the gold and purchased what was necessary.

When Rābi'ah had become a little older, and her mother and father were dead, a famine came upon Basrah, and her sisters were scattered. Rābi'ah ventured out and was seen by a wicked man who seized her and then sold her for six dirhams. Her purchaser put her to hard labour.

By day she continually fasted and served God, and by night she worshipped standing until day. One night her master awoke from sleep and, looking through the window of his apartment, saw Rābi'ah bowing prostrate and praying.

"Oh God, Thou knowest that the desire of my heart is in conformity with Thy command, and that the light of my eye is in serving Thy court. If the affair lay with me, I would not rest one hour from serving Thee; but Thou Thyself has set me under the hand of a creature."

Such was her litany. Her master perceived a lantern suspended without any chain above her head, the light whereof filled the whole house. Seeing this, he was afraid. Rising up, he returned to his bedroom and sat pondering till dawn. When day broke he summoned Rābi'ah, was gentle with her and set her free.

> "Give me permission to depart," she said.
>
> He gave her leave, and she left the house and went into the desert. From the desert she proceeded to a hermitage where she served God for a while.
>
> Then she determined to perform the pilgrimage, and set her face towards the desert. She bound her bundle upon an ass. In the heart of the desert the ass died.
>
> "Let us carry your load," the men in the party said.
>
> "You go on," she said. "I have not come putting my trust in you."
>
> So the men departed, and Rābi'ah remained alone.
>
> "O God," she cried, lifting her head, "do kings so treat a woman who is a stranger and powerless? Thou hast invited me to Thy house, then in the midst of the way Thou has suffered my ass to die, leaving me alone in the desert."
>
> Hardly had she completed this orison when her ass stirred and rose up. Rābi'ah placed her load on its back, and continued on her way.
>
> The narrator of this story reports that some while afterwards he saw that little donkey being sold in the market.[9]

The most renowned of Rābi'ah's friends was the saintly Ḥasan al-Baṣrī. Born in Medina, and brought up in Basrah, he is said to have belonged to the household of the Prophet's secretary Zaid ibn Thābit, and to have known many of the Companions of the Prophet. He was a jewel merchant before his conversion, and he became one of the most prominent figures of his generation, known for his uncompromising condemnation of worldliness in high places.[10] He must have been much older than Rābi'ah, but he constantly appears in stories about her. There seems to be a certain delight in telling tales in which she takes the great man to task. He it was whose egoism she rebuked from her sick bed. Another time he was leaning out of the window weeping when Rābi'ah passed his house. "Master," she said, "this weeping is a sign of pride of self. Guard your tears . . ." Many ascetics thought it proper to spend much time in weeping over their sins. Rābi'ah too felt deeply the evil of sin, and the separation it brought between the soul and God. She also wept with contrition, but she went on through repentance to gratitude, and her prayers are full of thanksgiving and joy.[11]

Miracles were attributed to these holy men and women. Walking on water was one attainment, and a further one was levitation. There is another story told of her and Ḥasan al-Baṣrī. Ḥasan threw his rug on to the Tigris, it is said, and challenged

Rābiʿah to join him in prayer on the water. "Ḥasan," said Rābiʿah, "you are showing off." She tossed her prayer rug up into the air. There Ḥasan could not follow her, and after she had prayed she said, "What you did, fishes also do, and what I did, flies also do. The real business is outside both these tricks. One must apply one's self to the real business."[12]

"The real business" of life was a total concentration on the love of God. Gratitude, so strong a note in her life, must be for the Giver, not the gift. She rebuffed anything that could distract her, and her refusal of any form of comfort is ascribed to this motive. One day she was persuaded to replace the rags she wore, and sent a servant to buy a piece of cloth. The man turned round as he went and asked, "What colour?" This was too much, and Rābiʿah snatched back the dirhams and threw them in the Tigris. "How did colour come into the business?" she said.[13]

The greatest tribute to Rābiʿah's teaching is to be found in the works of the philosopher and reformer Al-Ghazālī, three centuries after her death.[14]

Since Rābiʿah and her fellow ascetics had challenged the excesses of the early caliphs, a spectacular decline had occurred. In a classic passage the historian Philip Hitti analyses the causes of this decadence.

> If anything parallels the astounding rapidity with which the sons of the desert conquered in the first Islamic century most of the civilised world, it is the swift decadence of their descendants' domination between the middle of the third and the middle of the fourth centuries [of Islam].

As well as external factors leading to this decline, there were internal divisions, both religious and political, and there were social and moral forces of disintegration, in which a deterioration in the position of women played its part. Hitti continues:

> Arab stamina and morale broke down. Gradually the empire developed into an empire of the conquered. The large harems, made possible by the countless numbers of eunuchs, and the girl and boy slaves, who contributed most to the degradation of manhood; the unlimited concubines and the numberless half-brothers and half-sisters in the imperial household with their unavoidable jealousies and intrigues; the luxurious scale of high living with the emphasis on wine and song – all these and other similar forces sapped the vitality of family life and inevitably produced persistently feeble heirs to the throne . . . National economic decay naturally resulted in the

curtailment of intellectual development and in the stifling of creative thought.[15]

The arrival of the Saljūqs in Baghdad in 447/1055 restored public security, established good administration and once more gave encouragement to a vigorous intellectual life. Niẓām al-Mulk, powerful minister to more than one Saljūq sultan, established observatories and colleges, including the famous Niẓāmiyah. To his court, Al-Ghazālī came as a young scholar. He was given a teaching post in the Niẓāmiyah.

The framework and the patronage for a revival of Islamic thought were present. It took a tremendous upheaval, a radical re-direction, in one man's spirit to make of this opportunity a major revival of the deepest message of Islam.

Al-Ghazālī's passionate search for truth, and his impatience with the hair-splitting arguments into which contemporary learning had fallen, led to a personal crisis which was to be the turning point in the thinking of his age. Unable to continue teaching, he withdrew from Baghdad. Nine years of wandering resulted not only in the recovery of his health but also in the writing of books which are still classics of Muslim thought. It is in one of these that he quotes Rābi'ah; "The Revival of the Sciences of Religion", *Iḥyā 'ulūm al-dīn*, an encyclopaedic work which in many books or sections deals with the whole range of thought and knowledge, giving a world view of man and society, God and creation.

One section of the *Iḥyā* is "The Book of Love and of Passion". It is here that Al-Ghazālī draws on Rābi'ah's thought and experience. On the mystic "way" there are many stages, and it is on the stage of love that he considers her views most important. He quotes her, and accepts her teaching as at least equal in authority to that of any of the great shaikhs.

"The Book of Love and of Passion" has been called one of the greatest analytical essays on love. In a recent study of Al-Ghazālī's thought, *The Concept of Man in Islam in the Writings of Al-Ghazālī*, Dr Ali Issa Othman emphasises the importance of the heart, as well as the intellect, in man's search for a nearness to God. "Al-Ghazālī's genius and his contributions to Muslim thought lie in his discovery of the limitations inherent in the *intellect* as a tool of knowledge, and the central importance of the *heart* as the seat of all knowledge and experience." The heart makes contact with reality through both the intellect and the body. In seeking truth and God, self-discipline is as important as learning.[16]

Al-Ghazālī quotes Rābi'ah's most famous verses:

I have loved Thee with two loves, a selfish love and a love
that is worthy of Thee.
As for the love which is selfish, I occupy myself therein with
remembrance of Thee to the exclusion of all others.
As for that which is worthy of Thee, therein Thou raisest the
veil that I may see Thee.
Yet there is no praise to me in this or that
But the praise is to Thee, whether in that or this.[17]

Al-Ghazālī comments,

> She meant by the selfish love, the love of God for His favour bestowed and for temporary happiness; and by the love worthy of Him the love of His beauty which was revealed to her; and this is the higher of the two loves, and the finer of them. The delight arising from the Beauty of the Lord is that which the Prophet of God explained when he said, speaking of his Lord Most High, "I have prepared for my faithful servants what eye hath not seen nor ear heard and what has not entered into the heart of man,"[18] and some of these delights are given beforehand in this world to the one who has wholly purified his heart . . . He who knows God knows that all joys, save only sensual delights, are included in this joy.[19]

Al-Ghazālī also quotes the answer Rābi'ah gave when she was asked about Paradise. She cited the proverb, "First the neighbour, then the house", meaning that what she desired was not the delights of Paradise but the Lord of Paradise Himself.[20]

She gave a similar reply one spring morning when her servant called her to come out and "see what the Maker has wrought." "Do you rather come in, and see the Maker. The contemplation of the Maker pre-occupies me, so that I do not care to look upon what He has made."[21]

Yet there are other stories of the open air, and of a comradeship with the animal creation, akin to the spirit of St Francis. A bird flew in, 'Aṭṭār tells us in his biography, and dropped some much-needed onions into her pan.[22] And another day, "Rābi'ah had gone into the mountains. She was soon surrounded by a flock of deer and mountain goats, ibexes and wild asses which stared at her and made to approach her." The ubiquitous Ḥasan al-Baṣrī came on the scene, and the animals made off, to his chagrin. "Why did they run away from me, and associate so tamely with you?" "You eat them, so why not?" Rābi'ah remarked. She herself was a vegetarian.[23] Even a flight of locusts left her corn alone.

Al-Ghazālī, in his discourse on love, describes that kind of love which is expressed in joy in nature. If something is loved for its own sake, and not to gratify a selfish desire, such love is real. "You should not think that the love of beautiful objects is not conceivable except when the gratification of some lust is involved. The gratification of lust is a different kind of pleasure. Beautiful objects such as water, greenery, beautiful sights, flowers, birds and geometrical figures may be loved for their own selves, not for the utility they may serve. Man is relieved from his worries and depressions merely by looking at such things without any expectation of using them."[24]

Al-Ghazālī himself sought to restore the original spirit of Islam, when bitter debates between theologians had darkened it. He considered zealotry, fanaticism, one of the great barriers in the search for truth: the self-righteousness that accused of heresy or disbelief all those who did not follow one particular school of thought. Such men "narrow down the boundless mercy of God, and limit salvation to a small circle of theologians."[25] According to the true spirit of Islam, God is the only Judge of sincerity. If a person professes the unity of God men can never assume any authority to deny the honesty of his belief.

Between Rābi'ah's poor hut and Ghazālī's lecture room in the Niẓāmiyah there is a long span of time and experience. The seed she sowed lay dormant, to flower again in the teachings of one of the greatest of Muslims. Rābi'ah's profound experience of the love of God made its contribution to the resurgence of Islam at a moment of historic importance. For in Al-Ghazālī's time began the period of Islam's second great impact on the West. The first conquests had swept through the Mediterranean to Spain. The twelfth and thirteenth centuries were to see contacts of a different kind: not only the military clashes of the Crusades, but more important the encounters of scholarship and trade, through Spain and Sicily and the great Mediterranean ports.

It is tempting to try to trace the effects in history of such lives as those of Al-Ghazālī and Rābi'ah. But perhaps her greatest impact is still in the easing of the path for souls who tread the difficult ways of life and pain and death.

"When the time came for her to die," 'Aṭṭār tells us, "many pious folk were sitting round her and she bade them 'Rise and go out; for a moment leave the way free for the messengers of God Most High.' All rose and went out, and when they had closed the door, they heard the voice of Rābi'ah making her profession of faith and they heard a voice saying, 'O soul at rest return to thy Lord, satisfied with Him, giving satisfaction to Him. So enter among My servants and enter into Paradise.'[26]

"There was no further sound heard, they returned and found that her soul had departed."[27]

Rābi'ah's prayers still sift the motives and purify the intentions of the souls of both men and women.

> O God, my whole occupation and all my desire in this world, of all worldly things, is to remember Thee, and in the world to come, of all things my desire is to meet Thee. This is on my side, as I have stated; now do whatsoever Thou wilt.

For the most part her faith was radiant with joy, but once, we are told, she was overwhelmed with a dread of God's judgment. She prayed, "Oh my God, wilt Thou burn in hell a heart that loves Thee?" She heard an unseen voice speaking to her inner consciousness, "O Rābi'ah, We shall not do this. Do not think of Us an evil thought."

Her best-known prayer shows that her fear was overcome.

> Oh God, if I worship Thee for fear of hell, burn me in hell, and if I worship Thee in hope of Paradise, exclude me from Paradise, but if I worship Thee for Thy own sake grudge me not Thine everlasting beauty.[28]

Throughout her life, the slave girl whom her master saw at prayer used to spend her nights on the roof-top. As the dawn appeared, Al-Ghazālī tells us, she would pray:

> O God, the night has passed and the day has dawned. How I long to know if Thou hast accepted my prayers or if Thou hast rejected them. Therefore console me for it is Thine to console this state of mine. Thou hast given me life and cared for me and Thine is the glory. If Thou wert to drive me from Thy door, yet would I not forsake it, for the love that I bear in my heart towards Thee.[29]

The Story Tellers

"Now the Wazir had two daughters, named Shahrazad and Danyazad, of whom the elder had perused the books, annals and legends of preceding kings, and the stories, examples and instances of bygone men and things: indeed it was said that she had collected a thousand books of histories relating to antique races and departed rulers. She had perused the works of poets and knew them by heart; she had studied philosophy and the sciences, arts and accomplishments; and she was pleasant and polite, wise and witty, well read and well bred."

One Thousand and One Nights

"Lal Bibi was virtually a walking volume of Arabian Nights. She was a born story-teller and knew how to get the best response from her audience. She would never tell us a story while daylight lingered and, as she had always left off her story the previous evening at the most critical stage, she kept us on tenterhooks for the whole of the next day. Even after the fall of dusk, she would not start the story straightaway; she would take her time over her dinner . . . while we hovered around her like chickens. Our impatience had no effect whatsoever on her. At last, she would seat herself comfortably on a low stool, take the favourite among the children on her knees, and begin the story . . . In short, she did everything possible to whet our appetites."

Begum Shaista Ikramullah

Chapter Six

A Window on Baghdad

From the moment of the city's founding there began in Baghdad an exuberant growth of culture and scholarship. The appetite for knowledge was insatiable. Translators set to work, making available in Arabic the main texts of both Greek and Indian learning. Calligraphy, which was to play so central a part in Islamic art and architecture, was developing: more than one Quranic manuscript has survived from the period. Poetry was abundant, and music also, as well as the studies which built up the body of tradition and law.

The Caliph Al-Ma'mūn himself added one important feature to the scholastic structure of Baghdad: the *Bait al-Ḥikmah*, House of Wisdom, an academic institution with a large library and a wide-ranging translation bureau.[1]

The unprecendented growth in literary production was aided by the spread of paper. The art of paper-making came from China. To make, procure and sell it, for the benefit of Baghdad's thousands of scholars, was a major trade. The trade name of Baghdad's many book-sellers was *warrāq*, papermaker: they were stationers as well. In one quarter alone, just outside the Basrah Gate of Al-Manṣūr's Round City, one hundred such shops were to be found. They were salons where scholars gathered and talked and discussed the new books of the day.[2]

From one of these, an unexpected window on the life of the times is opened. Its catalogue has survived, expanded by the author into an encyclopaedia of the literature available in his day. Those who visit Istanbul's Book Market, among its extensive bazaars, may savour an atmosphere somewhat akin to that of the mediaeval street, with its hundred bookstalls, in which Ibn al-Nadīm compiled his booklist, *Al-Fihrist* (index or catalogue), expanding it year by year with new titles, and interpolating anecdotes and points of interest about the authors he names.

He finished it about the year 378/988, a century later than the death of the Caliph Al-Ma'mūn's queen, Burān. It is a date that takes us forward to a time when the supremacy was slipping from Baghdad; to the age of the rival Fatimid caliphs in Cairo, and the founding of the University of Al-Azhar. The first great chapter in Arabic literature and scholarship was complete and the books with which Ibn al-Nadīm was acquainted summed it up.

Ibn al-Nadīm's encyclopaedic catalogue contains many references to women, and throws some shafts of light on their place and part in Abbasid society.[3]

It must be said that no major work by a woman is recorded. There are a number of categories in which women's names appear.

First, the poets. It was in this sphere that women most made their mark, both in pre-Islamic times and later. *Al-Fihrist* lists most of its women poets as having written only "a few sheets", rather than a full collection, *dīwān*, but Abū Nuwās, one of the leading poets of the time of Hārūn al-Rashīd and boon companion of his son Al-Amīn, is said to have memorised the dīwāns of fifty women poets, in the course of perfecting his poetic and linguistic education.[4]

The skill of improvisation was highly prized. Quick wits and a mastery of poetic form produced a flow of verse suitable to the day and the occasion. Poems came spontaneously, and only a small part of what was produced in the sparkling contests of wit found its way into compilations under the better-known names.

The most famous of women poets was Al-Khansā', contemporary of the Prophet. She is one of those whose lives bridge the old days and the coming of Islam. She was an independent character, chose her own husband, bore six children, and had already written most of her poetry before she came with a delegation of her tribe to Medina to embrace Islam. Muḥammad could not but be hostile to much of the work of the poets of his day, for they were the chief promoters of the pagan ideals he had come to replace. He is said, however, to have liked the verse of Al-Khansā'. Women's special genre of poetry was the elegy, and grief for the dead was something the Prophet felt deeply. 'Ā'ishah recounts catching a glimpse of his face through a door when he had just received news of the death of three devoted friends. It was ravaged with grief.[5]

The most famous poem of Al-Khansā' was an elegy on her brother Sakhr. She took part in the poetic competitions of the day, and held her own with the men. At one of these competitions, a rival said, "We have never seen a better woman poet than you." She replied, "Don't you want to say that I am the best poet, male or female?"[6]

Her poetry, along with that of other early Arab poets, was popular in Baghdad. So also were the verses and songs of contemporary women, among whom *Al-Fihrist* mentions 'Ulayyah, sister of Hārūn al-Rashīd, singer, musician and poetess. She was a close friend of Zubaidah, and her songs and her wit delighted her brother.[7]

Another category is "the passionate lovers": those about whom there are books, during the pre-Islamic period and the period of Islam, followed by others from elsewhere in the world. The list enumerates many girls loved and sung by poets, and mentions the tragic tales of ill-starred love: the Romeos and Juliets of the Arab World, the best known being Lailā and Majnūn. The popular romance of Ablah and 'Antar belongs to a later period.

Al-Fihrist has a section headed "the loving and the fickle". Among the "loving" about whom books had been written figured several of the Prophet's family: his wives Khadījah and Umm Salāmah, and his daughter Ruqayyah; Sukainah and Rabāb, daughter and wife of Ḥusain; and many other honoured names. 'Ā'ishah only appears with the mention of "some books about the Battle of the Camel" – her unsuccessful intervention at the beginning of the Caliphate of 'Alī. There are two works about Fāṭimah.

Women's role as patrons stands out. Queen Zubaidah gains mention in connection with her secretary, an author named 'Alī ibn Da'ūd, "a master of eloquent literary style" and a collector of animal stories. He also wrote a book on singing entitled "Using a Loud Voice". Another patron is a woman named Lailā, granddaughter of an early Islamic hero. As the Arab empire expanded captives were brought to Damascus and Baghdad and shared out among the victors. One of these prisoners, a man from Iran named Sābūr, was given to Lailā by her father, and remained in her service for fifty years. His son Ḥammād grew up under Lailā's patronage and became very popular as a "quoter of historical traditions, poems and genealogies". He is credited with the collection of the famous seven odes by pre-Islamic poets, the *Mu'allaqāt*, though Ibn al-Nadīm – as often, both critical and tolerant towards his authors – says he "may have made mistakes about one thing after another."[8]

Al-Fihrist names women with a varied range of skills. Two are grammarians – a much respected branch of knowledge, related to the use of the full range of excellence of the Arabic language. There was a woman scholar of Arab dialects, "whose origin was among the tribes", and another "acquainted with tribal legends and colloquialisms". A third wrote a book entitled "Rare forms and sources of verbal nouns".[9] Aspiring poets, like Abū Nuwās, used to spend time with the desert tribes to perfect their knowledge of pure Arabic. In a different field, Arwā, "a woman known for her wise sayings", wrote a book about "sermons, morals and wisdom".

An Indian woman, Rūsā, was the author of a book on the medical treatment of women, listed among Indian works on medicine available in Arabic. Māryah al-Qibṭiyyah, an Egyptian woman of the first century AD, wrote on alchemy, and finds her place among books by savants, alongside works on Cleopatra and Bilqīs, Queen of Sheba. One woman authority on the traditions of the Prophet is noted, Fāṭimah bint al-Mundhir, who lived in Medina and died about 145/763. She was the wife of Hishām, son of 'Urwah who gathered so many traditions from his aunt 'Ā'ishah.

The making of astrolabes, a branch of applied science of great repute, was practiced by one woman, 'Ijlīyah bint al-'Ijlī al-Asṭurlābī, who followed her father's profession in Aleppo and was employed at the court of Saif al-Daulah (333/944–357/967), one of the powerful Hamdānid dynasty in northern Syria who guarded the frontier with the Byzantine empire in the tenth century AD.

In the development of the art of calligraphy, one woman at least took part. Thanā' was a slave in the household of the tutor to one of Al-Manṣūr's sons. This tutor, Ibn Qayyumā, seems to have been a dedicated teacher, for the young slaves in his household benefited as well as his royal pupil. Of the two whom he sent to be trained by the leading calligraphist of the day, Isḥāq ibn Ḥammād, one was the girl Thanā'. His pupils, says Ibn al-Nadīm, "wrote the original measured scripts never since equalled."[10]

All these women appear in the pages of *Al-Fihrist* because they wrote, or were the subject of, books. They do not represent a list of even the best-known scholars. For one author named in the field of the study of Traditions, for instance, a later list includes at least twenty respected scholars and teachers. This is Al-Khatīb's massive *History of Baghdad*, in fourteen volumes, a biographical dictionary listing no fewer than seven thousand, eight hundred and thirty scholars, covering three hundred years of history. In a special section at the end he names twenty-nine women: not a large number, but a significant inclusion. He confines himself to those who lived in Baghdad.[11]

When after thirty years' work he completed his history, he went on pilgrimage in 445/1053. In Mecca he found a woman scholar and spent a week reading through with her Bukhārī's authoritative collection of Sayings of the Prophet, *Al-Ṣaḥīḥ*. Karīmah al-Marwaziyah, who died in Mecca in 463/1070, must have had a high reputation, for so great a master to sit at her feet.[12]

Such weighty studies were, however, the exception. There are indeed stories of versatile young slave girls at the court of Hārūn al-Rashīd passing stiff examinations in various branches of learning. "What branches of learning have you followed?" "First, that which Allāh has commanded in His Book. Then that which engages the people's mind in poetry, language, literature and historical narration."[13] But there is a lighter side to the literature of Baghdad which reveals much about the character and status of its women.

In the secular field, the lively *Kitāb al-aghānī*, Book of Songs, compiled in the fourth century of Islam, the tenth century AD, contains a wealth of anecdote and biographical detail on musicians and others, men and women, depicting vividly the life of the Baghdad court, as well as giving many stories of earlier figures in the history of Arabia.[14] The art of the story-teller, *al-rāwī*, who recounts tales old and new, played a great part in Abbasid life, as it did in later periods. Recent researchers are turning to such sources as *The Thousand and One Nights* for light on society outside the range of the more formal chronicles.[15] Ibn al-Nadīm himself, for all his scholarship, was not above dealing with popular fiction. He takes us out into the bazaars and side streets of the city, and his lists include works on travel, on magic and erotica.

A clear distinction is maintained between the popular and the serious. Separate lists are given of works by serious writers and by "those who converse in the evenings and are tellers of fables". Books on "passionate lovers" are distinguished in this way, and under "those whose traditions enter in to the evening stories" come tales of humans who loved djinns and djinns who loved humans, of sexual adventures and magic journeys. There are books on fools and on sorcery, and books on the wonders of nature. One such popular selection had thirty tales, ten each on the wonders of land, dawn and ocean. These "evening stories and fables", told in the streets and market-places, were the equivalent of modern movies and television, and whiled away the hours of darkness during which bad lighting restricted other forms of entertainment.[16]

Many of the stories later collected in versions of "The Thousand and One Nights", were already circulating. Sindibād al-Ḥakīm's adventures appear in *Al-Fihrist*, which also mentions a Persian collection, "The Thousand Stories", *Hazar Afsan*. This introduces the filibustering feats of the indefatigable Shahrāzād, though Ibn al-Nadīm thought it "truly a coarse book without warmth in the telling".[17]

All this popular stuff was, and is, ill regarded by the critics, but it is not irrelevant to the study of attitudes towards women, any more than is the later humour of the Turkish Nasreddin Hoça, and his Egyptian counterpart Goha. Vivid sketches of women characters move through these "evening stories": charming and gay, wicked and nagging, often clever, and seldom if ever meek. What is admired and what is despised, what is loved and what is feared, what is desired and what is rejected: these things are to be glimpsed as the colourful narratives flow.

One of the most difficult things for people of differing cultures to enjoy is common laughter. If the street tales of Baghdad and Cairo occasionally provide ground for this, they may perform a useful function and open the way to more serious forms of understanding. Many of them take place in the byways of the later "God-guarded city of Cairo", but the presiding figures are the generous and powerful Hārūn al-Rashīd, the forceful and glamorous Zubaidah, and the gay and scandalous Abu Nuwās. The women in "The Thousand and One Nights" are caricatures, too good or too bad to be true, and may be enjoyed as such. There is the good wife. "So it befits a woman to stand by her husband, before the world and in her heart, contenting herself with little when he cannot give her much, and to take example from Aishah the faithful and Fatimah the radiant – Allah the Most High bless them both."[18]

And in contrast there is the cobbler's wife. "A whorish, worthless wretch, scanty of shame and mickle of mischief. She ruled her spouse and used to abuse him and curse him a thousand times a day; and he feared her malice and dreaded her misdoings; for that he was a sensible man and careful of his repute, but poor-conditioned. When he earned much he spent it on her, and when he earned little she revenged herself on his body at night, leaving him no peace and making his night black as her book."[19]

Many of the wives in "The Thousand and One Nights" are well informed, some too well educated along sinister lines. "My wife, the daughter of my uncle, had learned grammar and necromancy and clerkly craft and divination from her childhood: so she bewitched that son of mine . . ."[20]

It is to be noted that Shahrāzād, narrator of the tales, won her victory not by her charms, with which she was well endowed, but by her good education. She was the daughter of the vizier of a certain king, the kind of man who has only one use for women. A string of unwilling girls had been the victims of his sexual tyranny: a night in his bed, and death in the morning. With the help of her sister, she saved the lives of those next in the succession of rape and slaughter, her weapons being her quick wits and powers of endurance, and the knowledge that she had accumulated. Every morning at dawn when she was due to be discarded and executed, she would reach some cliff-hanging point in the latest story, and live another day.

The popularity of these tales and the function of the story-teller have continued to this day. But there is a vivid incident in a modern Egyptian novel, Naguib Mahfouz's *Midaqq Alley*, its venue a back street in Cairo. A radio is installed in the local coffee shop. When the blind old bard arrives as usual with his lyre, the proprietor sends him rudely away. No longer do people want to listen to the old heroic tales and the "One Thousand and One Nights". "Exit the bard – enter the radio," is the comment.[21]

Falling in Love

"The song of love touches men's souls and takes hold of their hearts."

Ibn Qutaybah

"A young man asked a man of learning, 'The sun is so bright and charming and yet no one has ever fallen in love with it. Why not?' 'It is because,' answered the wise man, 'it is seen every day in most places, but where it is not seen often, it is really loved and its appearance is anxiously awaited.'"

Saʿdī Shīrāzī

"I know of a pair of lovers whose messenger was a well-trained dove: the letter would be fastened to its wing. On this topic I have the following verses.

Old Noah chose a dove to be
His faithful messenger, and he
Was not confounded so to choose:
She brought him back the best of news.

So I am trusting to this dove
My messages to thee, my love,
And so I send her forth, to bring
My letters safely in her wing."

Ibn Ḥazm

Chapter Seven

Veil and Wimple

One Umayyad prince escaped the sanguinary coup by which the Abbasid Al-Saffāḥ (Shedder of Blood, as he himself chose to be called) seized the Caliphate. Seventy of the reigning family in Damascus were murdered at a banquet in 132/750. The young ʿAbdul-Raḥmān got away, and after many adventures in North Africa reached Spain, where he established himself in Cordoba. This city had been in Muslim hands for less than forty years, since the Arab armies crossed the Straits from Tangier to Gibraltar and swept towards the Pyrenees.

The Umayyad caliphs in Spain presided over a flowering of culture and learning, a civilisation that lasted for six hundred years. Its immense impact on Europe has yet to be fully recognised. The grim struggle to repel or civilise wave after wave of barbarian invaders from north and east absorbed the energies of northern Europe until well into the eleventh century. Meanwhile not only distant Baghdad but also neighbouring Spain lived in the light of a highly developed civilisation. The tide of Arab conquest swept over the Pyrenees and then receded. Later, much that was formative and enriching crossed the frontier. The gentler arts and graces that developed in the Spanish-Arab cities made their way northward: music and poetry and ideas of chivalry passed into Provence and elsewhere. A chivalrous attitude to women showed itself in the development of love poetry, tender and profound.

While Abbasid society became more and more constrained, Spain maintained the freer ways of the Umayyad period. Women poets sang in Cordoba, princesses had their romances, and a tradition of courtly love grew up which had its influence on the growth of chivalry further north. The streams of scholars that flowed southwards to Spain from France, Germany, and England did not only take home the works of Aristotle and Euclid. They learned the music that accompanied the songs of the troubadours; they bought silks that enriched the wardrobes of Saxon ladies and Norman princesses; and they translated the delightful book on love by Ibn Ḥazm, written in the early eleventh century, the fifth century of Islam, shortly before the Norman conquests in England and Sicily refashioned the map of Europe. Its title was "The Dove's Necklace", or "The Ring round the Dove's Throat", *Ṭawq al-Ḥamāmah*. It was written in 418/1027.

In this delicate and humorous work, "we find fully developed all those themes which later became current in the Occident in the poetry of the Provençal troubadours and the German Minnesingers," says the historian Brockelmann. He adds, "A Spanish influence on their art remains very probable, even though it will no doubt never be possible to trace the channels through which it was transmitted."[1]

In his introduction, Ibn Ḥazm tells us that most of his teachers were women. And like all men, he lived first in the women's world of the harem, and was at home in it until he became a man. The subject of women held his interest more than most. "I have myself observed women, and got to know their secrets to an extent almost unparallelled; for I was reared in their bosoms, and brought up among them, not knowing any other society. I never sat with men until I was already a youth and my beard had begun to sprout. Women taught me the Qur`ān, they recited to me much poetry, they trained me in calligraphy."

A friend asked him to compose "an essay describing love, its causes and accidents, neither adding anything nor embroidering anything." He excuses himself for acceding to such a request since, "considering the brief duration of our lives, it behoves us not to expend them save upon those enterprises which we hope will secure for us a spacious destination and a fair homecoming upon the morrow." Yet men of great authority have recommended some light relief. "Recreate your souls with a little vanity that it may the better aid them to hold fast to the truth." And he quotes the Prophet himself as saying, "Rest your souls from time to time: they are apt to rust, in the same way that steel rusts."[2]

The other work by Ibn Ḥazm that became famous was a study of heresies, hotly refuting their various errors.[3] In contrast, "The Dove's Necklace" is indeed recreational reading. The restrictions of the harem are regarded more as a challenge than a barrier to the lover who wishes to reach his beloved. Messengers can make their way through the closed doors, and "How many an inaccessible maiden has proved approachable by using them . . . How many disagreeable surprises have befallen well-protected veils, thick curtains, close-guarded boudoirs, and stoutly fashioned doors . . ."[4]

The staid and godly pilgrim Ibn Jubair, who travelled from Spain a century later, never failed to note with sympathy the women he encountered: their beauty or their misfortune. He could describe the sight of the chain of forts round the mountain above the "ancient and elegant city" of Palermo as "like pearls encircling a woman's full throat".[5] And he may perhaps have experienced such a "fair homecoming" as his compatriot describes in "The Dove's Necklace".

> I have tested all manner of pleasure, and known every variety of joy; and I have found that neither intimacy with princes, nor wealth acquired, nor finding after lacking, nor returning after long absence, nor security after fear, and repose in a safe refuge – none of these things so powerfully affects the soul as union with the beloved, especially if it comes after long denial and long banishment. For then the flame of passion waxes exceedingly hot, and the furnace of yearning blazes up, and the fire of eager hope rages ever more fiercely.
>
> The fresh springing of herbs after the rains, the glitter of flowers when the night clouds have rolled away in the hushed hour between dawn and sunrise, the splashing of waters as they run through the stalks of golden blossoms, the exquisite beauty of white castles encompassed by verdant meadows – not lovelier is any of these than union with the well-beloved, whose character is virtuous, and laudable her disposition, whose attributes are evenly matched in perfect beauty. Truly that is a miracle of wonder surpassing the tongues of the eloquent and far beyond the range of the most cunning speech to describe: the mind reels before it, and the intellect stands abashed.[6]

Ibn Jubair travelled from Spain to Mecca and back in the years 579/1183–581/1185. His style is lively and terse, and he abounds in vivid sketches of the places he saw and the men and women he encountered. He captured for posterity the living tapestry of the world of the Crusades: at the moment when Ṣalāḥ al-Dīn (Saladin) was gathering his forces to recapture Jerusalem.

This was a period of great importance for the future relationships between Muslim and Christian. It is worth taking a look, through the eyes of Ibn Jubair and of other contemporary writers, at women in the society the Crusaders confronted, a society which was at the same time giving so much to Europe at its other points of encounter: Spain, Sicily and the great Mediterranean ports.

The key figure in the Eastern Mediterranean at the time was the Kurdish Ṣalāḥ al-Dīn, founder of the Ayyūbid dynasty. The courteous exchanges between him and his opponent Richard Coeur de Lion even included proposals for a marriage alliance. The match suggested was between Ṣalāḥ al-Dīn's brother ʿĀdil and Richard's sister Joanna, who had been Queen of Sicily until her husband's death. She would have none of it, but it could be contemplated. There were such alliances, made by princesses both in Spain and in Byzantium. The restrictions on women at this period were not unlike in both cultures, and the establishment maintained by Joanna's husband William II in Palermo, while something of a scandal to Christian eyes, had many of the features of a harem.

In Cairo Ibn Jubair saw gangs of Frankish prisoners toiling on the construction of the massive citadel. In Damascus, he saw Ṣalāḥ al-Dīn's troops returning from a raid on the castle of Kerak. "God in His mercy gave to the Muslims here this Sultan, who never retires to a place of rest, nor long abides at ease, nor ceases to make his saddle his council chamber," says Ibn Jubair.[7] He notes the incongruous mixture of war and commerce between the people of Damascus and the Christian cities on the coast. He spent eleven days in Tyre, and watched a Crusader wedding procession while waiting to embark on a Christian ship, crowded with two thousand pilgrims returning from Jerusalem. "May God in His grace and favour soon relieve us of their company!" he exclaims.[8]

Wrecked upon the coast of Sicily, he observed the Norman Kingdom at the height of its unique experiment in the mingling of Latin, Byzantine, and Arab culture. He saw the Christian women copying Muslim customs, and heard the anxieties of the Muslims about their future.

The reigning queen of Sicily when Ibn Jubair was washed ashore on its coast was the English princess Joanna, daughter of Henry II. She travelled to Sicily when she was fourteen years old, and her wedding in Palermo Cathedral was "a fairy tale of

splendour".[9] She was left a widow in 1189, and the following year her brother Richard arrived to rescue her and if possible her considerable dowry as well. He took her on with him to Palestine, where, as already mentioned, she refused to be a pawn in her brother's negotiations.

The court into which her husband William introduced her was an astonishing and brilliant one. Here not only Latin and Arabic were in use, but Greek as well. The administration of the island followed the lines of the former Arab rulers. The vigour of the Normans employed the skill and craftsmanship of both Arab and Byzantine artists and artisans. For a brief moment there was a meeting of minds and a joint endeavour that has left a precious heritage of beauty and scholarship. Jewish scholars played their part, and this unusual flowering is a joint achievement of co-operation between Muslims and "The People of the Book": Christians and Jews, who share with Muslims the privilege of a revealed scripture.

The position of women at court was very considerably influenced by Muslim customs. Ibn Jubair bears this out. He notes that the Christian women follow the customs of Muslim women: they wear veils and cloaks, and "never stop talking". He made friends with a personal servant of King William, the official who "embroidered in gold the king's clothes". This man told him that the King could read and write Arabic, and that his motto was "Praise be to God: it is proper to praise Him." "The handmaidens and concubines in his palace are all Muslims . . . The Frankish

Christian women who came to his palace became Muslims, converted by these handmaidens. All this they kept secret from their king.''

When a terrifying earthquake shook the island, William in alarm ranged round his palace, and heard nothing but cries to God and His Prophet from his women and pages. At sight of him, they were overcome with confusion, but he said to them: ''Let each invoke the God he worships, and those that have faith shall be comforted.''[10]

In spite of the tolerance at court, and the number of mosques still open, there was much foreboding as to the future, among the Muslim community. They felt the pressures of the Christian majority. Ibn Jubair gives one example of the problems exercising the minds of Muslim families.

> We came upon another striking example of their state, such as breaks the spirit in pity and melts the heart in compassion. One of the notables of the town of Trapani sent his son to one of our pilgrim companions, desiring of him that he would accept from him a daughter, a virgin who was nearing the age of puberty. Should he be pleased with her, he could marry her; if not, he could marry her to any one of his countrymen who liked her. She would go with them, content to leave her father and brothers, desiring only to escape from the temptation of apostasy and to live in the lands of the Muslims. Her father and her brothers were disposed to this proposal, since they themselves might escape to Muslim lands when the embargo that impeded them should be suspended . . .
>
> We ourselves were filled with wonder at a situation which would lead a man to give up so readily this trust tied to his heart, and to surrender her to one strange to her, to bear in patience the want of her, and to suffer longings for her and loneliness without her. We were likewise amazed at the girl – may God protect her – and at her willingness to leave her kin for her love of Islam . . . When her father had consulted her as to the project she had said, ''If you hold me back, the responsibility before God will be yours.'' The girl was motherless, but had two brothers and a little sister from the same father.[11]

Ibn Jubair's visit to Sicily was on his return journey. The central part of his narrative is focussed on Mecca and Medina, and there the women made their presence felt in a number of ways: the memories of Khadījah and ʿĀʾishah, and of the endowments of Khaizurān and Zubaidah; the local residents; the crowds of pilgrims; and the magnificent retinues of royal ladies.

The official dates for the Ḥajj are during the twelfth month of the Muslim year, Dhul-Ḥijjah. Those who are in Mecca at other times can perform the rites of pilgrimage. In Ibn Jubair's time the inhabitants of Mecca held a special celebration of the *'umrah,* the lesser pilgrimage, at the beginning of the seventh month, Rajab. This is described by Ibn Jubair in the year 579/1183. It was his first impression of the women of Mecca.

> At eventide the new moon was expected. We saw the streets and byways of Mecca filled with *hawdaj* [dome-shaped camel howdahs] bound to the camels and covered with silk drapings . . . which sometimes . . . fell so low as to draw their hems along the ground. The most remarkable . . . were those of the aunt of the Emir of Mecca and his harem . . . There was no one of the people of Mecca who did not go forth that night on the *'umrah.* Fires were lit throughout the road on both its sides, and lighted torches preceded the camels carrying the secluded ladies of Mecca.

In the Sacred Enclosure itself,

> the women who walked in the hope of a heavenly reward were many, and they competed with the men on that blessed way. May God, by His favour, hear the prayers of them all. During all this, the men met and shook hands, offering prayers and praying for God's forgiveness each on behalf of the other, while the women did likewise.[12]

At the end of the same month, a special day was reserved for women in the Sacred Enclosure.

> They congregated from all parts. They had assembled for it for some days before . . . and there was no woman in Mecca but that day went to the Sacred Mosque . . . Not a man remained around the blessed House. The women rushed to ascend the steps . . . Some shrieked, some wailed, and some cried. "God is great," and others "There is no god but God." Thus they continued for the first part of the day at their ease performing the *ṭawāf* [circulating round the Ka'bah].

At other times women had difficulty in making their way through the crowds to reach the central structure and kiss the Black Stone.[13]

Some months later came the Ḥajj. Among the pilgrims were three princesses who came with the caravan from Iraq. Ibn Jubair waxes lyrical over the size and organisation of this travelling crowd.

> This assembly of Iraqis, together with the people from Khurasan, Mosul and other lands, formed a multitude whose number only God Most High could count . . . You could see the earth shake giddily because of them, and form waves through their great number.[14]

The state in which these ladies travelled presents a very different picture from that of the saintly Rābi'ah al-'Adawiyyah, trudging on foot through the desert with her one small donkey. Another early pilgrim offers less of a contrast. 'Ā'ishah bint Ṭalḥah was the beautiful niece of 'Ā'ishah, widow of Muḥammad. She arrived at the court of the Caliph 'Abdul-Malik in Damascus, and said she was going to Mecca on pilgrimage. He provided her with "sixty mules of royal quality". Her cousin 'Urwah exclaimed, "Oh 'Ā'ishah of the sixty mules, do you perform the pilgrimage every year in this style?"[15]

One of the three princesses was the daughter of the reigning Saljūq of Rūm, and wife of the ruler of Āmid, capital of Diyarbakr, the province of the upper waters of the Tigris. The second was the mother of the ruler of Mosul, and the third was the daughter of the ruler of Isfahan. "She also is of great consequence and impressive circumstance, and is much given to good work. And in all three," comments Ibn Jubair, "is this most strange mixture of pious work and regal pride."[16]

The most important of these women was the Saljūq princess. A century earlier, the incursions of the Saljūq Turks into the lands of the Byzantine Empire and their capture of Jerusalem had been one of the causes of the First Crusade. Border warfare was constant, and at this period the Rūm Saljūqs were at the height of their power. They were in process of wresting the south coast of Anatolia from Byzantine control, and also taking other territories on the Black Sea.[17] The princess who came on this pilgrimage was named Saljūqah, and she was about twenty-five years old.

> The father of this woman is the Emir Mas'ūd. His realm is large, and wide is his sway. More than one hundred thousand horsemen, so we were assured, ride at his command, and for his son-in-law through this princess, Nūr al-Dīn, Lord of Āmid and of other lands, ride about twelve thousand cavaliers. This princess has provided many good works upon the pilgrim road, furnishing water-bearing beasts for this purpose, and a similar number for provisions. With her she brought around a hundred camels especially to bear clothing, provisions and other things.

Saljūqah held up the whole caravan for a day, by disappearing from her place.

> She returned at nightfall, and the arrows of conjecture flew at random concerning the cause of the departure of this much-indulged princess.[18]
>
> The kingdom of her father extends over four months' journey. The ruler of Constantinople pays him tribute. He rules his subjects with admirable equity, and against the Christians wages holy war unceasingly and in a manner most laudable. One of the pilgrims told us that in this present year of 579 he had conquered about twenty-five Byzantine cities. His by-name is ʿIzz al-Dīn but his father's name was Masʿūd and he himself is more commonly known by that name, which is hereditary in that dynasty.[19]
>
> One of the glories of this princess is that Salāh al-Dīn conquered Āmid, the city of her husband Nūr al-Dīn, but left the city to her in honour of her father and gave her the keys. Because of this, her husband remained king.[20]

The typical charity of such princesses concerned the distribution of water.

> Each year, if these ladies do not themselves perform the pilgrimage, they despatch with trusted men some water-bearing camels that quench the thirst of forlorn travellers upon the pilgrim road. This they do throughout the road, on ʿArafāt, and in the Sacred Mosque, each day and night. For this their reward in heaven shall be great . . . You will hear the crier with the water camels announcing with loud voice the free water, and those whose store has been exhausted will hasten to him with their water-skins and ewers that they might fill them. With all his breath the crier will proclaim: "God preserve the royal Khātūn, daughter of the king of such and such a state and consequence," announcing her name and making known her good deed, and bringing the people to offer prayers for her. God will not fail to reward her good works.

Khātūn, he explains, means princess, "or whatever is a fitting designation for a royal lady".[21]

In Medina, Saljūqah made a spectacular entry into the Prophet's Mosque.

> [She was] riding in her litter, surrounded by the litters of her ladies and her handmaidens and led by Koran-readers, while pages and eunuch-slaves, bearing iron rods, moved round her, driving the people from her path . . . Wrapped in an ample cloak, she descended

> and advanced to salute the Prophet – may God bless and preserve him – her servants going before her and the officials of the mosque raising their voices in prayer for her and extolling her fame. She came to the small enclosure between the venerated tomb and the pulpit, and prayed there, wrapped in her cloak while the people who thronged around her were kept back by the rods.

An emir with a splendid retinue also entered the mosque and a sermon was preached. She sat listening, "while we who regarded her marvelled at her regal mien."[22]

Ibn Jubair travelled on with the Iraq caravan. "A world of its own," he calls it. "The appurtenances of industry, the worldly conveniences, the requisites for animal satisfaction, all were present in this nothing-lacking caravan. Long would it take to describe it."[23] In Baghdad, he was most impressed by the choice of sermons available. One was delivered in the palace square, overlooked by the harem quarters, so that the Caliph's mother and other ladies could listen to it from their closed balconies.[24]

The night of their departure from Baghdad, Saljūqah drove through the streets.

> [She] came suddenly upon us with many youths and much circumstance . . . She was withdrawn inside a domed litter placed on two poles that lay between two beasts, one ahead of the other and decked in gilded caparisons. The animals carried her along like a zephyr, speedily and gently. There was an opening both in the front and rear of the litter, inside which could be seen the princess, veiled and wearing a golden head-band. Before her went a mounted troop of her youths and soldiers . . . while behind her was a party of her handmaidens riding both nags and hackneys, on gold-worked saddles. They also wore gold head-bands whose ends fluttered in the breeze. Like a cloud they moved behind their mistress, with banners and timbals and trumpets which they sounded at the mount and dismount. Indeed we saw such pride of feminine sovereignty, such solemn ceremony of rank, as should shake the earth.[25]

The caravan proceeded to Mosul, and a final glimpse of Saljūqah reveals another splendid scene: "one of the most glittering of worldly spectacles and awesome to behold". It was the arrival of the two princesses, Saljūqah and the mother of the ruler of Mosul.

> All the men without exception went forth on horse and on foot; and the women left too, most of them riding . . . The Emir of the

> country, with the leaders of his state, went out to meet his mother. The Mosul pilgrims entered in the company of their princess with ceremony and display . . . The Mas'ūdī princess entered at the head of her troop of handmaidens. The dome of her litter was wholly adorned with pieces of gold shaped like new moons, with dīnārs the size of the palm of the hand . . . The golden ornaments on the necks of her beasts and the mounts of her maidens formed together a sum of gold beyond estimation. It was indeed a sight that dazzled the eyes and provoked reflection. All sovereignty perishes save that of the One God, the Subduer. Who is without partner. More than one of those persons worthy of belief, who knew the princess's affairs, told us that she is known for her piety and her charity and is celebrated for good deeds. Amongst these is her spending, while on the Hejaz road, a vast sum of money in alms and in generous payment of expenses of the road. She venerates holy men and women, visiting them in disguise from a wish to gain their prayers. Her conduct is remarkable, for all this is with her youthful age and immersion in the pleasures of the realm. But God guides in the right path those He wishes.[26]

Salāh al-Dīn's sister, known as Sitt al-Shām, Lady of Syria, was travelling with the pilgrim caravan from Damascus when it figured in an important incident a year or two after Ibn Jubair's pilgrimage. The immense fortress of Kerak overlooks the ancient route southwards from Damascus to the Ḥijāz, a road traversed since time immemorial by armies and still more by traders. Abraham must have passed this way, perhaps with Hagar and young Ishmael on the way to their banishment in the deserts of Mecca. This was the route of Khadījah's caravans to and from Syria. Since the Muslim conquest of Damascus in the year 15/636 a caravan of pilgrims has left Syria for the Ḥajj year by year.

By terms of truce with the Franks, this caravan was to go its way unmolested. But Reynard de Chatillon broke the treaty, attacked the caravan, and made a sharp thrust southwards in a bold attempt to reach the holy cities themselves. When the crusaders were defeated in the battle of Hattin, Reynard paid with his life for his breach of faith.

It is likely that Sitt al-Shām's retinue would have been less ostentatious than Princess Saljūqah's, already described. Ṣalāh al-Dīn himself was frugal in his personal expenditure, and it was his boast that he amassed no personal wealth. This sister was "a powerful, intelligent woman, with strong opinions, generous, truthful and kind. Her home was a place of refuge for people in difficulty. She built a college and a tomb to the north of Damascus and endowed both. Thirty of her closest relatives [men she could see unveiled] were rulers. She died in 616/1219 and is buried in the school she founded in Damascus."[27]

The best contemporary historian of the Ayyūbids, who knew many of them personally, was Muḥammad ibn Wāṣil. He was born in Hamah, and lived and worked in Damascus, Jerusalem and Cairo. In his history on the "Affairs of the Ayyūbids"[28] he regularly notes their marriages, and often mentions something of the character and influence of their wives. One spirited mother saved the fortress of Kerak for her absent son by defeating and capturing the attackers. Another was regent during her son's minority. One of Ibn Wāṣil's early memories was the funeral of a niece of Ṣalāh al-Dīn, wife of her cousin Al-Manṣūr of Hamah. As a boy of twelve he attended the funeral, conducted by the Qāḍī his father. He remembers Al-Mansūr receiving condolences in the college he had founded, "seated to the right of the *miḥrāb*, mourning, broken and sad", his sons beside him. The Qur'ān was read, and elegies recited, and a prize was given for the best poem composed for the occasion in the metre of one by the famous Syrian poet, the blind Abul-ʿAlā al-Maʿarrī.[29]

It was a woman who played the leading role in the drama of the overthrow of the Ayyūbids in Egypt. Shagrat al-Durr was a slave of Turkoman origin whom Ṣalāḥ al-Dīn's great nephew Ṣāliḥ Ayyūb is said to have bought from the Caliph of Baghdad. He loved her and married her. He was away in Damascus when in November 647/1249 news came that a French army under Louis King of France had landed at Damietta. Already ill, the Sultan hurried back and he and his wife, who had already acted as his regent, went to Mansurah in the Nile Delta, to organise the defence. There he died. His wife took control of a desperate situation. She concealed the fact of his death, with the help of a doctor who called daily, a slave who forged his dead master's signature on orders Shagrat al-Durr devised, and a servant who took food to the "sick" king's tent. The army was able to defeat the Frankish attack and King Louis was captured.

Meanwhile her stepson Tūrān Shah had hastened back and she handed over the reins of power to him and announced her husband's death. But the leaders of the army murdered Tūrān Shah and installed the queen as Sultan. Coins were struck in her name and she was mentioned in the weekly prayers in the mosques. Peace was made with the Franks on favourable terms, and the French king was released.

This arrangement of a woman acting as Sultan did not meet with approval in Baghdad, and when asked to confirm the appointment the caliph wrote, "Since no *man* among you is worthy of being Sultan, I will come in person and bring you one." So the Queen graciously retired and a soldier named Aibak was appointed. He married Shagrat al-Durr, who continued for seven more years to conduct the administration. She was a jealous wife and her jealousy was her undoing. She made Aibak send away his previous wife, and when he proposed to marry another one she planned his assassination, in 655/1257. He was murdered when having a bath after a game of polo.

The last scene in the melodrama finds Shagrat al-Durr trying desperately to conceal the crime, and then faced with the return of Aibak's former wife and his son, seeking revenge. Cornered at last, she seized her jewels, and tried to pound them to dust so that no one else might use them: and then at the behest of Aibak's former wife she was beaten to death by the slaves of the harem with their wooden clogs. The body was thrown on to a rubbish heap. Days later it was rescued and placed in the tomb she had built, which may still be visited. Visible in the prayer niche is a charming mosaic: against a golden background is a tree of pearls, the meaning of her name.[30]

Thus ended the life of one woman who attained sovereignty in a central province of the Muslim world. Others reigned on the outskirts of empire but none played a role so powerful and influential.

Her rival in this respect is an earlier queen who ruled for over thirty years in Yemen during the period of the Fatimids.

Shagrat al-Durr is not forgotten. She played her part at a turning point in history. Her meteoric career links the last episode in the story of the Crusades with the transition to a new period and a new dynasty, that of the Mamluks, under whose leadership Cairo was to become the centre of the stage.

Queen Arwā al-Ṣulaiḥī's long reign in Yemen had a more local significance. But she must not be passed over. It is worth going back a century in time to trace her remarkable story.

Successors of Bilqis

"I found a woman ruling over them, and she has been given abundance of all things, and hers is a mighty throne."

Qur'ān, 27:23 The Ant

"The Princess was adorned with every qualification required in the ablest kings and the strictest scrutineers of her actions could find in her no fault but that she was a woman. In the time of her father, she entered deeply into the affairs of government, which disposition he encouraged, finding she had a remarkable talent in politics. He once appointed her regent in his absence. When the emirs asked him why he appointed his daughter to such an office in preference to so many of his sons, he replied that he saw his sons giving themselves up to wine, women, gaming and the worship of the wind (flattery); that therefore he thought the government too weighty for their shoulders to bear and that Raḍīyah, though a woman, had a man's head and heart and was better than twenty such sons."

Firishta, sixteenth-century historian of Muslim rule in India

Chapter Eight

Women Rulers

In the pageant of world history, the woman ruler is exceptional whatever her era or region. The few to whom a combination of ability and opportunity brings such responsibility often live in the memory of their people with something of glamour and of grace, and some warmth of gratitude for shouldering unwonted burdens. In the story of the Muslim world such women are perhaps no less and no more unusual than elsewhere.

Some earned themselves a sinister reputation; examples are the able and violent Shagrat al-Durr, and more than one Queen Mother, *Valide Sultan*, who won an effective control of events during the one hundred and fifty years of "Women's Rule" in the Ottoman Empire. Others won high praise, as did the Princess Raḍīyah who ruled in Delhi a few years before Shagrat al-Durr, having succeeded her father the Sultan Shams al-Dīn Iltutmish in 634/1236. She wielded full authority, wearing the imperial robes, administering justice, and leading her troops in battle; but after four years one of her less able brothers managed to supplant her.[1] The traveller Ibn Baṭṭūṭah a hundred years later found a woman ruling the Maldive Islands, and further east in the states of the Malay Archipelago the seventeenth century (eleventh of the Hijrah) saw a number of women succeed to the thrones of Patani and Acheh and other sultanates.

In the Arab world, Bilqīs Queen of Sheba provided an honourable precedent, and it was in her own country in South Arabia that two remarkable women appeared as queens in Yemen. They belonged to a dynasty, the Sulaihids, who supported the Fatimid caliphs in Cairo.

The Arabian Peninsula was the scene of many power struggles as the hold of the Abbasid caliphs weakened. In 359/969 the Shīʿī Fatimid leaders took over Egypt from the Abbasid governor, set up a rival caliph, and started to build the city of Cairo. During the Fatimid period the people of the holy city of Mecca acknowledged sometimes one and sometimes the other of the two claimants to the Caliphate in Baghdad and Cairo.

Among the supporters of the Fatimids was a lawyer, ʿAlī al-Ṣulaiḥī, founder of a Yemeni dynasty which for nearly a century was to support the Fatimid cause, and to preach the Shīʿī doctrines it upheld. For more than half this period its power was in the hands of two outstanding women, Queen Asmā and Queen Arwā, known also as Queen Sayyidah.

The period of Sulaihid power began in 429/1038. It continued up to the death of Queen Arwā in 532/1137. In 473/1080 ʿAlī al-Ṣulaiḥī was murdered on his way to Mecca, and his wife Asmā was taken prisoner. It was after her rescue two years later that she, and later her daughter-in-law Arwā, took charge of affairs.[2]

Queen Arwā's memory, a traveller tells us, is still kept green in the Yemen by monuments to her genius for administration. Among these are roads through the mountain passes. "The broad pavement of well-shaped stones was stepped and followed reasonable gradients, with watering places for man and beast at intervals. It ran up and down the green turfed mountain sides and along it bloomed in her memory a riot of wild flowers . . . Perhaps no one rides up and down the passes we followed without remembering, as a beduin told me, that Queen Sayyidah built them eight hundred years ago."[3] One such road climbs to the town of Jiblah, in early chronicles Dhū Jiblah, which the Queen took as her capital. She is buried there. The abundance of flowers on the surrounding hills is matched by that of the birds, including the hoopoe, which, it is said, in Solomon's day flew from this country to give him news of Bilqīs, Queen of Sheba.[4]

Arwā's reign had many attractive features, aspects which champions of women's influence often hope to see result from a greater female participation in the control of affairs. In spite of the tribal rivalries and disputes endemic in her country, she managed to shift the emphasis of government from arms to agriculture, from fighting to food production: a change typified by her removal of the capital from the traditional stronghold of Sanʿā to the new agricultural town of Jiblah. Prices were lowered, taxes were scrutinised so that they were not extortionate. Her governor in the coastal area of Tihāmah recorded, "To my knowledge no man has a grievance against me."[5] This was after fifteen years, during which the Queen saw his accounts annually. Arwā was adept at negotiation, and on several occasions she broke a military deadlock by conciliation, and she faithfully observed the conditions in any treaty she made. Rivals who thought they could outwit a woman often found themselves at a loss.

She could keep unwelcome aspirants to favour at arm's length. The leaders of her troops recognised her authority and she made every effort to maintain law and order. In this light must be seen the exact and terrible retribution meted out to Al-Aḥwāl, the murderer of her father-in-law, ʿAlī al-Ṣulaiḥī.

Arwā was the daughter of a cousin of the founder of the Ṣulaiḥī dynasty, ʿAlī. Her father died, and her mother remarried, so she grew up at ʿAlī al-Ṣulaiḥī's court, in the care of his queen Asmā. Their son Al-Mukarram married her in 458/1065, and she lived until 532/1137, when she died at the age of eighty-eight.

Her history, and that of her mother-in-law Queen Asmā, are told in a contemporary history by a Yemeni poet, Najm al-Dīn ʿUmārah al-Ḥakamī. He was born during the latter years of Arwā's long reign, and he wrote his book in the Cairo of Ṣalāh al-Dīn, overthrower of the last of the Fatimid caliphs. ʿUmārah was executed for disloyalty to the new regime, in the year 569/1173. His book was composed a few years earlier, only thirty years after Arwā's death, and he himself knew and talked with old men who could recall the events he chronicles. His style is simple, vivid and direct, and the following incidents are given in his words, abridged.

The setting of the drama of the Sulaihids is the south west corner of Arabia, Yemen: its steaming coastal plain; its high mountains, green and fertile as nowhere else in the peninsula; its roads running up into the mountains and northwards towards Mecca; its sea routes linking it to Abyssinia and Egypt. Yemen's connections with the Horn of Africa, and its importance in Egyptian policy, were no less in the eleventh century than they are today.

The characters who play leading roles in the action have some of them already been mentioned. For clarity, they may be listed here.

ʿAlī al-Ṣulaiḥī, who established the authority of the Fatimid Caliphs in Yemen, and for a time in Mecca as well. He wielded spiritual as well as temporal power, and was known as the *Dāʿī,* Summoner to religion.

Asmā, his queen.

Al-Mukarram, his son, who succeeded his father but was stricken with paralysis.

Arwā, or Queen Sayyiddah, wife of Al-Mukarram, who ruled for him and succeeded him after his death.

Saʿīd ibn Najāḥ al-Aḥwāl, contemptuously described by his prisoner Queen Asmā as a "squint-eyed slave (Abyssinian)".

Sabā, would-be successor to Al-Mukarram.

ʿImrān and Sulaimān, brothers trained at Arwā's court.

The Story of the Lady Asmā

ʿAlī al-Ṣulaiḥī had a maternal uncle named Shihāb, whose daughter Asmā had few equals in beauty, and was unmatched in literary culture and intelligence. He asked her in marriage, though the demand for dowry exceeded the bounds of moderation. She was the mother of the king Al-Mukarram, who married the Lady Arwā, the Queen Sayyidah, daughter of Aḥmad the Ṣulaiḥite.

Asmā was of a generous and noble disposition, liberal in the rewards she bestowed upon poets, and in the sums she granted in acts of benevolence and other good deeds. The renown of her splendid virtues extended to her children, her brothers and her kindred. Her husband's poet spoke of her in an ode commencing

"She of the white hands hath bestowed gifts. . . .
She hath impressed upon beneficence the stamp of generosity,
Of meanness she allows no trace to appear.
When people magnify the throne of Bilqīs, I say
Asmā hath obscured the name of the loftiest among the stars."[6]

The Amīr, the glorious *Dāʿī* (Summoner to faith), ʿAlī the Ṣulaiḥite determined upon going to Mecca, may God Most High guard it. He resolved to take with him the Lady Asmā, mother of the King Al-Mukarram, whom he appointed governor of Sanʿā and his deputy. He set forth at the head of two thousand horsemen.

Suddenly and without warning the troops were surrounded. The Amīr ʿĀlī and his brother ʿAbdallāh were beheaded, and not a man escaped. Power passed into the hands of Saʿīd, son of Najāḥ al-Aḥwāl. He captured Asmā and started back to the town of Zabīd with the heads of ʿĀlī and ʿAbdullāh borne in front of the Princess's litter.

On his arrival he raised them on high, opposite the casement of a house assigned for her use. And Asmā remained a full year the captive of Sa'īd ibn Najāḥ.

All attempts to transmit a letter from Asmā to Al-Mukarram, or from him to his mother, having failed, the Princess herself hid a letter in a cake of bread, and contrived means by which it was given to a mendicant.

Al-Mukarram, on reading the letter, assembled his friends. They burst into lamentations, but soon became eager to vindicate the honour of the tribe. He marched from San'ā at the head of three thousand horsemen. He was an eloquent speaker and a brave warrior, widely known for his resolute character as well as for his bravery. At each halting place he exhorted the people, saying that whosoever cared only for his own life should not be one of them. Sixteen hundred steadfastly adhered to him, and fourteen hundred drew back.

The Abyssinians had assembled to the number of twenty thousand foot, and they were defeated. The first warrior to reach the spot where the two heads were set up, and to stand below the casement of Asmā, was her son. "Uncover thy face that I may know thee," she said. He raised his helmet, whereupon she exclaimed "Welcome, our lord Al-Mukarram!"

At that moment he was struck by the wind, a shudder passed over him, and his face was contracted by a spasm. He lived many years thereafter, but continued to be subject to involuntary movements of the head and spasms in his face.

Then the army entered by detachments, whilst she stood at the casement with her face uncovered. Such had been her custom in the days of her husband, a sign of her exalted rank over the men from whom other women are secluded. Al-Mukarram ordered the two heads to be taken down, and he erected over them a mausoleum. It is said that when he uncovered his face, Asmā exclaimed, "He whose coming is like unto thy coming hath not tarried, neither hath he erred."

Not long after, Asmā died, at San'ā.[7]

The History of the Honourable Lady Arwā, the Queen Sayyidah.

The Lady Sayyidah was born in the year 444/1052, and Asmā superintended her education, her father having died and her mother re-married.

In her personal appearance Sayyidah was of fair complexion tinged with red, tall, well proportioned, but inclined to stoutness, perfect in beauty, of a clear-sounding voice, well read and a skilful writer, her memory stored with history, with poetry and with the chronology of past times. Nothing could surpass the interlinear glosses, upon verbal construction and interpretation, inserted in her handwriting on the pages of books. Al-Mukarram married her during the lifetime of his father 'Alī the Ṣulaiḥite, and she bore him four children.

I have heard more than one aged man affirm that Al-Ṣulaiḥī treated Sayyidah, in her earliest years, with a degree of deference he showed to no other person. "Show her respect," he used to say to Asmā, "for by Allāh she will be the preserver of our race and our crown."

Upon the death of his mother Asmā, the king Al-Mukarram made over the superintendence of affairs to his wife. He gave himself up to the pleasures of music and wine. The Queen remained alone in charge of the affairs of the kingdom. It is said that she begged to be accorded her liberty, saying that a woman who was desired for the marriage bed could not be fit for the business of the state, but he would not consent.

After a time the Queen went forth to behold Dhū Jiblah. That city stands below a fortress, between two streams flowing with water both in summer and winter. On her return to San'ā she said to Al-Mukarram, "My Lord, send notice to the people to assemble tomorrow." On their assembling, she told him to look at what he should see. Nought met his eyes but the lightning-flashes of drawn swords and of lance-blades. On going to Dhū Jiblah, she desired him to assemble its people and those of the neighbourhood, and his eyes fell upon men leading rams or carrying vessels filled with butter or with honey. "Life among these industrious people," she said, "is to be preferred." The Amīr al-Mukarram removed to Dhū Jiblah.

In that same year the Queen encompassed by a stratagem the death of Sa'īd ibn Najāḥ al-Aḥwāl, murderer of 'Ālī al-Ṣulaiḥī. His head was put up below the window of the apartment assigned to his widow, in Queen Sayyidah's palace. "Oh that thou hadst eyes, Lady Asmā," exclaimed the Queen, "wherewith to see the head of the 'squint-eyed slave' below his wife's window!"

Al- Mukarram died in the year 484/1091, bequeathing the religious office of *Dā'ī* to Sabā the son of Aḥmad. In his external appearance the *Dā'ī* Sabā was ill favoured, and short in stature. But he was of a benevolent and generous disposition, an accomplished poet, well acquainted with the sayings of the wise. He asked the widowed Queen Sayyidah in marriage. She refused, whereupon he marched to attack her in Dhū Jiblah. She likewise assembled a host, more numerous than his, and the fire of war was kindled and raged for several days. Sabā was told, "By Allāh, she will not agree except by command of the Prince of the Faithful." So he desisted from fighting

> and despatched messengers to the Caliph in Cairo, and the Caliph wrote to the lady three lines commanding her to wed the *Dā'ī* Sabā. A marriage contract was drawn up, and she finally gave her consent.
>
> The *Dā'ī* Sabā hastened to Dhū Jiblah. He remained outside it for a month, his large retinue feasting on food provided by the Queen. The contemplation of her lofty aims and of her noble deeds caused the *Dā'ī* Sabā to feel humbled in his own estimation. He perceived that his reputation was dimmed, and that no person could be fitly compared with her. All her people habitually referred to her as sovereign, and not to him.
>
> He secretly sent a message to the Queen, requesting her to receive him in her palace, that it might be believed by the people that the marriage had been consummated, to which she consented. Some say that she sent him one of her female slaves who closely resembled her, and that the girl remained standing throughout the night at the head of the couch, whilst he sat without ever raising his eyes upon her, until when day dawned he performed his morning devotions and ordered the drums to beat for departure. He then said to the slave, "Tell our lady that she is a precious pearl, to be worn only by whoever is worthy of her." He then departed and they did not meet again. It is reported that he never again had intercourse with a slave girl, or tasted intoxicating drink.[8]

The Queen educated many young men and women at her court. One of her advisers sent his two sons, 'Imrān and Sulaimān, to her.

"She received them with kindness. By her command, although they had reached the years of maturity, they were taught to read and write. Afterwards she married them to two of her slaves brought up under her care."[9]

Later these two men intrigued against a powerful minister of the Queen, the Egyptian Ibn Najīb al-Daulah. Sayyidah first arrested him, then tried to save him, but her emissary was murdered by drowning on the way to Egypt.

> The Queen was greatly afflicted when regrets could no longer avail. Sulaimān and 'Imrān went into her presence exulting over the fate of Ibn Najīb al-Daulah. They came forth exclaiming on the truth of the words of Abdallah ibn Abbas, Cousin of the Prophet: "We used," he said, 'to listen to the traditions preserved by 'A'ishah (the Prophet's widow), but never left her presence without having been reminded that she was a woman.[10]
>
> This was their last interview with the Queen.

She died in Dhū Jiblah in the year 532/1137, and was buried in the mosque she had built there.[11]

Her successor sold Dhū Jiblah and twenty-eight other castles and towns to the new ruler of Aden, who married the surviving Ṣulaiḥid princess, a younger Arwā.[12]

A century's attempt at good government was over, and soon the Fatimids, whom the Sulaihids had so faithfully served, would themselves be overthrown. Others would carry Cairo forward to fresh dominance in the affairs of the Muslim world.

Privacy

"We walked through the winding lanes of the inner city . . .

"My friend and guide stopped before a nondescript wooden door in a blank, mud-plastered wall and said:

'Here we are,' knocking with his fist against the door.

"It opened with a squeak, a very old man bade us welcome with a toothlessly mumbled 'ahlan, ahlan wa-sahlan', and through a short corridor with two right-angled turns we entered the courtyard of the house that from the outside had resembled nothing so much as a mud-coloured barn.

"The courtyard was wide and airy, paved like a huge chessboard with white and black marble slabs. In a low octagonal basin in the centre a fountain was playing and splashing. Lemon trees and oleander bushes, set in small openings in the marble pavement, spread their blossom- and fruit-laden branches all over the courtyard and along the inner house walls, which were covered from base to roof with alabaster reliefs of the most delicate workmanship.

"[Wall-mirrors reflected] the entire courtyard, with its trees, its black and white pavement, its alabaster reliefs, marble window embrasures and carved doors which led to the interior of the house, and the many-coloured throng of guests who sat on the divans and strolled around the water basin . . .

"Such a house – bare and unadorned on the street side, rich and delightful within – was altogether new to me . . ."

Muḥammad Asad

Chapter Nine

Women of Cairo

"Cairo today is what Baghdad was in its prime, and I know of no more illustrious city in Islam." The geographer Maqdisī wrote this towards the end of the tenth century, the fourth century of Islam, only fifteen years after the new City of Victory, Al-Qāhirah, was raised by the Fatimid conquerors.[1] In 368/969, Egypt, plague-ridden and near to anarchy, passed from the hands of Abbasid governors to those of more vigorous rulers from the shores of North Africa. These were the self-styled Fatimid caliphs, supposedly descended from the Prophet's daughter and her husband 'Alī.

The City of Victory was from the first designed to rival Al-Manṣūr's City of Peace. Its rise as a centre of wealth and scholarship was as rapid, and its position was maintained for more than five centuries, until with the Ottoman conquests Istanbul replaced it as the focal point of Islamic civilisation.

With the threads of its long history are entwined the lives of many beloved women. The new dynasty itself took its name from a woman, Fāṭimah. Others of the Prophet's near relatives, five women among them, were said to be buried in Old Cairo, or Miṣr, the traditional name which designated both Egypt and its capital. There was also the reputed tomb of Ruqaiyah, eldest daughter of Muḥammad and wife of the third Caliph, 'Uthmān, with whom she took refuge in Abyssinia in the very early days of the Prophet's mission.

Best remembered of all these women of the Prophet's family was his grand-daughter Sayyidah Zainab, sister of Ḥusain. She is still venerated today, and a whole district of Cairo is known by her name. She was five years old when her grandfather died.

Zainab was with her brother when he was murdered at Kerbela. She saved the lives of his daughters, and of one young son, 'Alī

Zain al-ʿĀbidīn, who was ill at the time. One of the daughters, Sukainah, is venerated in Cairo. She was a charming woman, well known in Medinan society. Zainab herself died in 65/684 only four years after the tragedy at Kerbela. The present mosque named after her in Cairo is a modern one, but it is much frequented. "When I am in trouble I go there and find peace of heart," says one among the many women who crowd it.

Longer memories than these haunted old Cairo and the Nile. The Virgin Mary was commemorated in churches already ancient when the Muslims came, marking the places where the Holy Family rested during their sojourn in Egypt. Earlier history told of a line of renowned queens, culminating in Cleopatra. Egypt of the Pharaohs had a tradition of powerful women rulers: also of property-owning, independent wives. Marriage contracts preserved in Pharaonic documents show this.[2]

To these venerable figures were added many locally respected women, whose tombs brought solace to the common people, and whose annual days of remembrance were the occasion of family parties and holidays. One of these was Sayyidah Nafīsah, said to rank third among women saints in Cairo, after Zainab and Sukainah. She was a great-granddaughter of Ḥasan, son of ʿAlī and Fāṭimah and older brother of Ḥusain. She lived in Fustāt, the city that grew on the site where the Muslim conquerors camped outside Miṣr, at the time when the great legist Al-Shāfiʿī was there. This man, a contemporary of Hārūn al-Rashīd, taught in Baghdad and later in Egypt, and became the founder of one of the four great schools of Islamic law. He was born in 150/767. The purchase deed of his house in Fustāt has survived. He often used to visit Sayyidah Nafīsah, to collect traditions from the many stored in her memory. He would pray the special prayers of Ramaḍān with her, and when he died his body was brought to her house on the way to burial, so that she could pray the prayer for the dead over him.

Sayyidah Nafīsah was buried in a tomb which she herself built, in which she used to sit and read the Qurʾān. She is said to have suggested Sunday as the special day for visits to her shrine, and this has continued to this day. Crowds gather at the time of evening prayer. Her husband wished to take her body to Medina, to the cemetery of Baqīʿ where so many of the Prophet's family lie. But the people of Cairo begged to keep her body, and she has been remembered in the life of Cairo ever since.[3]

There are other local saints associated especially with women, at whose shrines the prayers of the barren for children are thought to be efficacious, and children may find healing.[4]

Cairo's most distinctive contribution to the portrait gallery of women through the centuries is, however, in a different category. Her monuments are witnesses to a succession of women of property who gave generously of their wealth for the relief of poverty and the learning of future generations, benefactresses and patrons of the arts and scholarship.

Muslim women have always been allowed to own and administer their own property. While public responsibilities were denied them, the influence of money and possessions was theirs. As the walls of the harem grew ever higher, and its doors more closely guarded, this was one outlet for their abilities.

In the Cairo of the Fatimids and the Mamlūks, one looks in vain for the successors of Al-Khansā' and the early Arab poetesses. There were exceptions: it was not unusual to find a learned *shaikhah* (feminine of *shaikh*) who taught the Qur'ān and the traditions. Here and there a woman's name appears in the illustrious roll of Islamic medicine and science. Where they abound is in the annals of the court, and on the inscriptions which mark the vigorous competition of the time in putting up beautiful buildings.

Arabic literature is rich in books of travel and geography, and we can see these women at work through the eyes of contemporary travellers, eager observers of the beauties and the customs of their times. At two important moments such a window is opened on Cairo. First Ibn Jubair spent some time in the Cairo of Ṣalāḥ al-Dīn, founder of the Ayyūbid Dynasty after the overthrow of the last of the Fatimid caliphs. Two centuries later, another traveller, Ibn Baṭṭūṭah, whose journeys far surpassed those of his older contemporary Marco Polo, stayed in Cairo in 727/1326, during the reign of the Mamlūk Sultan Al-Nāṣir Muḥammad, the greatest period of building in the city's history.

The century that followed the collapse of the Ayyubid dynasty saw a brilliant outburst of architecture. The Mamlūks were slaves of Turkoman and Caucasian stock. They were reinforced by a constant flow of boys brought from the Caucasus and elsewhere to Cairo, and rigorously trained in the arts of war. A succession of

Sultans presided over a period in which brutality and culture, cruelty and a passionate love of beauty and beautiful things, are combined in a bewildering mixture. Few of the sultans succeeded peacefully. Few reigned for long. But between them – and their wives – they sponsored the creation of treasures of art and architecture unsurpassed in excellence of execution and design. They were also patrons of learned men: philosophers, historians, astronomers and mathematicians, and above all doctors. The great hospital built by Ṣalāḥ al-Dīn was surpassed by that of Sultan Qalā'ūn: both had their separate wards, their sections for women as well as for men, and their dispensaries.

Qalā'ūn's son Al-Nāṣir Muḥammad had a long and chequered reign, and after him eight of his sons succeeded. His effective rule lasted for over thirty years – he died in 742/1341 – and more than twenty major buildings are listed during this time, to be followed by many others in the next decades. A terrible earthquake in 703/1303 wrought much damage, and provided the occasion for an active period of rebuilding. Members of his large family – he had twenty sons and daughters – were responsible for many mosques, colleges, and tombs.

Al-Nāṣir was a man of mixed character, harsh and vindictive, yet devoted to his wives and children. One of his wives was the Princess Toghay, a slave renowned for her beauty, whom he bought for a huge sum. She is said to have been happy with him, and bore him his favourite son, Anūk, whose untimely death caused his father great grief. He spent a fortune on her, and when she went on pilgrimage it is said that the provision made for her had never been equalled. She travelled with Khawand Barakah, mother of a future Sultan, Ashraf Sha'bān, and with the splendid cavalcade were camels laden with fresh vegetables, some actually growing in huge bags of Nile mud. Other such parties took milking-cows with them.[5]

Like many others Princess Toghay freed large numbers of her slaves: one thousand female slaves and eighty eunuchs are the numbers given. She built herself a tomb remarkable for its introduction of a style of work of Mongol origin. On its dome white letters in enamelled earthenware stand against a dark-blue ground, while green faience foliage is interspersed between the letters.[6]

Al-Nāṣir's mother was a Mongol princess, Ashlūn. The threat of Mongol invasion that hung over the world of the Ayyūbids had been repulsed by the Sultan Baibars at the beginning of the Mamlūk period, and some at least of the erstwhile enemies were now good Muslims and allies. Another wife of Al-Nāṣir was Princess Tulbiyah, and her tomb is near to that of Princess Toghay. She was a Tatar princess from the Volga region, kinswoman of the Chief of the Golden Horde, Özbeg Khan. Al-Nāṣir is said to have asked for the hand of his daughter, but the dowry demanded was so large that he decided to accept a cousin of the Chief instead.

Princess Tulbiyah arrived in Alexandria in 719/1319, and proceeded in regal state to Cairo. Her escort were sent home laden with gifts.[7] Özbeg Khan gave another princess in marriage to George, Prince of Moscow, one of the many intermarriages with Christian neighbours. Ibn Baṭṭūṭah visited Özbeg Khan, and accepted the protection of one of his wives, a Byzantine princess, who was travelling to Istanbul.[8]

Eight of Al-Nāṣir's sons became sultans in succession, most of them puppets of some Mamlūk leader. The only one remembered by history is Sultan Ḥasan, whose mosque is one of the most magnificent in Cairo. Erected between 757/1356 and 764/1362, it includes the different types of foundation usually endowed in connection with these buildings. There is the tomb of the founder, probably in this case never used. There are schools for all the four schools of law, Shāfi'ī, Ḥanafī, Hanbalī, and Mālikī, each a miniature mosque in itself.

Al-Nāṣir's eleven daughters were all married to powerful supporters of their father. Each was given a wedding party that cost half a million dinars. Several of his sons-in-law built great mosques. One of them, Aqsunqur, gave space in his mosque to the tomb of the youngest of Al-Nāṣir's family, a boy who was put on the throne at the age of five and murdered shortly afterwards. One of the sisters, Princess Tatar al-Higaziyah, also built a mosque.

Nor was it only royal ladies who made such benefactions. Near the mosque of Sayyidah Zainab is one built by the lady Hadaq Miska. She was a slave brought up in the harem of Al-Nāṣir Muḥammad, and later entrusted with the education of some of his large family. This governess went on pilgrimage, as the inscription on her mosque informs us, and as it happened the traveller Ibn Baṭṭūṭah saw her in Mecca in the year 729/1328. She was a woman of great influence, and became the controller of Al-Nāṣir's harem.

She was even referred to by the title "mother", *wālidah*, of the Sultan, and may indeed have been his nurse.[9]

This governess calls to mind the famous "Nurses' Qur'ān", given in the year 410/1020 to the great mosque in Qairawān, first capital of the Fatimids, in Tunisia. The donor was the children's nurse to the Zīrid prince Al-Mu'izz ibn Bādīs. His grandfather had been appointed governor when the Fatimids left for Cairo, and he himself tried unsuccessfully to break away from the rule of the mad Caliph Al-Ḥākim. Some of his family left for Spain, and had lurid adventures in Granada. But none of this history affected the tranquil skill of the calligrapher who carried out the order of the old nurse. He copied the sacred Book on vellum in bold Kufic script, illuminating the verse divisions with gold rosettes outlined in rich brown, and placing here and there medallions, diamond-shaped or round, with floral designs in the same colours.[10]

Such a work of art was made the subject of a *waqf*, a religious foundation formally established by law. This was more usually a building or property endowed for some specific charitable or educational purpose. Islamic law prescribes exactly how property is to be inherited, and leaves little freedom to the testator in making the will. But wealth can be consecrated by *waqf* to some humanitarian end, and thus protected against confiscation or squandering.

It is a mark of the value set on these glorious Qur'āns, many of which were commissioned in the Mamlūk period, that they should be the subject of such legal gifts. All the beautiful buildings – mosques, schools, tombs – had Qur'āns of matching splendour set in them. A number commissioned by Al-Nāṣir Muḥammad himself have survived. In the exhibition of Qur'āns held in the British Museum in London as part of the World of Islam Festival of 1976, a number of examples were shown, as well as two folios of the "Nurse's Qur'ān".

A later Sultan, grandson of Al-Nāṣir, commissioned two magnificent Qur'āns for a college which his mother, Khawand Barakah, founded in the year 769/1368. She herself gave another similar volume. Pages from all three were to be seen in the exhibition.[11] We have already met Khawand Barakah when many years earlier she accompanied Princess Toghay on pilgrimage to Mecca.

The generosity and the good taste of women of property gave much beauty to the world in which they lived, in the Mamlūk society as in many another. This was obvious not only in the buildings they sponsored, but also in the minor arts, such as jewellery and textiles. There was often extravagance and much pointless spending by those who had no other outlet but their own interests: the bath slippers of one of Al-Nāṣir Muḥammad's eleven daughters, for example, cost over two thousand dinars.[12] Such expenditure receives suitable condemnation from the historians. The luxury in which rich women travelled has already been described. But they were also great patrons of arts and crafts, and endowed Cairo with some of its most beautiful monuments.

While it is the mosques and the tombs that have survived, they were not the only forms of art and architecture in which the women of Cairo were interested. Every mediaeval visitor to Cairo comments on the magnificence of many of the houses, and not only of the palaces of the rulers. A traveller during the Fatimid period speaks of dwellings four and five storeys high, and some even of seven storeys, with gardens on the roof.[13] The large numbers of gardens are noted in every description of the city. One of the most detailed is that of a French envoy to the Sultan Ashraf Al-Ghūrī (907/1501–922/1516) the last Mamlūk sultan before the Ottoman conquest. The French party was taken to lodgings near the Nile: splendid rooms, with baths supplied with hot and cold water by a "subtle" system of pipes. "Nearby are many spacious, sumptuous gardens full of all sorts of fruit trees: citrons, lemons, limes, oranges, apricots, cassia, and 'Adam's apples', so called because through them Adam disobeyed God's commandment. These gardens are watered morning and evening by water drawn from the Nile by cattle and horses."[14]

Cairo was also a place of gaiety. Feasts and holidays of the most varied kind then as now brought its people out on to the streets. Ibn Baṭṭūṭah specifically mentions the participation of the women and children in these. He approached the city by river, coming from Alexandria. No provision was needed for this journey, for there was a chain of bazaars on the banks, ready to meet every need. He reckons that there were thirty-six thousand boats plying on the Nile.

In the city itself, "boundless in multitude of buildings, the meeting place of comer and goer, whose throngs can scarce be contained in her for all her size and capacity'', he found twelve thousand water-carriers. He went to ''The Garden'', a beautiful public park on the island of Roda. This is frequently mentioned in accounts of Old Cairo, and in the Arabian Nights. ''It is a pleasure park and promenade, containing many beautiful gardens, for the people of Cairo are given to pleasure and amusements. I witnessed a fête once in Cairo for the Sultan's recovery from a fractured hand; all the merchants decorated their bazaars and had rich stuffs, ornaments and silken fabrics hanging in their shops for several days.''[15] In spite of periodic attempts to restrain them, it would seem that the women entered happily into all these enjoyments.

What life was like for the ordinary women outside the sheltered world of court and palace is a question that awaits research. As regards freedom of movement they would seem to have been better off than their richer sisters. For these, solace was to be found in the private gardens where they were free to take the air. Roof-gardens are mentioned, but most made use of the interior courtyards, large or small, which are the basis of the design of many famous gardens from Spain to Persia. Early treatises on agriculture include instructions on gardening and landscaping.[16] The Persians developed the traditional layout and reproduced it on exquisite carpets. Straight pathways, intersecting at right-angles, separate square patches of green on which fruit trees and decorative plants abound. Canals and fountains supply water, and summerhouses give shelter from the heat.

In the lives of women mainly confined to their homes, gardens humble or palatial played an important part. There were country orchards to visit, too, with scented jasmine and white briar rose as well as fruit trees. ''What charm there is in the old gardens of date palms and orange trees!'' writes one English lover of Egypt. ''Down alleyways of warm dust the citrus fruit hangs peacefully on the trees like Andrew Marvell's 'golden lamps in a green night'. Or, in the spring, the heavy orange blossom scent drenches everything, as the silver moonlight bathes the whole scene. For it is at night that the scent is strongest.''[17]

Beyond present enjoyment, and today's relief from dust and glare, lies the hope of the Garden of Paradise. For the Muslim man or woman, the home of future bliss is foreseen as a garden, green and well watered, beneath which rivers flow.[18]

Gardens Beneath which Rivers Flow...

"A sign for them is the earth that is dead:
We give it life, and produce grain therefrom which ye eat.
And we produce therein orchards and date-palms and vines,
and we cause springs to gush forth therein:
That they may enjoy the fruit thereof:
It was not their hands that made it: Will ye not then give
thanks?"

Qur'ān 36:33–5 Yā Sīn

"If any do deeds of righteousness, be they male or female,
and have faith, they will enter Paradise."

Qur'ān 4:124 Women

"Verily the Companions of the Garden shall that day have
joy in all that they do:
They and their wives, in pleasant shade, on thrones reclining:
Theirs the fruit of their good deeds and theirs all that they
ask:
The word from a Merciful Lord for them is: Peace!"

Qur'ān 36:54–7 Yā Sīn

"Praise be to God, Who hath subdued the earth to His servants that they may tread spacious ways therein . . .

Who hath made the stars to rise for guidance in the darkness of land and sea . . .

Who hath made also the water to descend from the heavens and hath revived the earth after its death, and hath made fruits of every sort to grow thereon . . .

Who hath created its regions with diversities of plants . . .

And who hath made perfect His bounty towards His creatures."

Ibn Baṭṭūṭah's introduction to his travels

Chapter Ten

The Varied World of Islam

Cairo under the Mamlūks was at the height of its influence in the Muslim world, and its rulers maintained relations far afield. The Mediterranean was alive with shipping, passing to and fro between Venice and Alexandria and the other great Mediterranean ports. Eastwards the stream of travellers, diplomatic and mercantile, academic and religious, flowed steadily through Asia. A few were from Europe, such as Marco Polo and his father and uncle, who reached as far as the court of the Mongol Great Khan Qubilay in Peking; and a hundred years later a Spanish ambassador to the court of Tīmūr in Samarkand. Their travels were surpassed by those of Ibn Baṭṭūṭah, who set off from Morocco half a century after the Polos ventured east.

In the fourteenth century AD, the eighth of the Muslim Era, the world of Islam stretched from Spain to China and southwards across the Sahara into Africa. Ibn Baṭṭūṭah visited almost every part of it. Wherever he went he took special note of the women, and if he settled for long enough he married. He found a very wide variety of custom and practice.

Asia in his day had a breathing space between two waves of Mongol conquest. The first was that of Chengiz Khan, whose grandson Hūlāgu destroyed Baghdad in 658/1260. The second was led by Tīmūr, the dreaded Tamerlane, who established his capital in Samarkand in 772/1370. Already the Ottoman Turks were advancing in Anatolia, and Ibn Baṭṭūṭah gives one of the few first-hand accounts of their early days in their first capital of Bursa.

Ibn Baṭṭūṭah set off as a young man from Morocco in the year 726/1325. He was appointed as *qāḍī*, judge, to the pilgrim caravan. His first act was to halt the company for a day to celebrate his marriage with a girl from Fez.[1]

During the next twenty-eight years he logged an estimated seventy-five thousand miles. We have already noted his visit to Cairo. In Alexandria he met an old man who had three brothers: one in India, one in the province of Sind, and one in China. "You must visit them all," the man said. And so he did.[2]

The extraordinary conglomeration of races and languages through which he travelled was held together by common links of faith and law, so that in any part of it his qualifications as *qāḍī* won him respect and hospitality. When he finally returned home to Morocco and dictated his memoirs, he could depict life as he had seen it in the courts of India and China, in Mongol and Byzantine palaces, as well as amid all the hazards of the road and the sea. In many places he observes that the women were very beautiful, a fact he could hardly have noticed if they had been closely veiled. He was often received by leading women, for instance the four wives of the Chief of the Golden Horde, Özbeg Khan.[3] He benefited from the protection of one of them, a Byzantine princess, and travelled with her escort to Istanbul.[4]

In some places the freedom of the women shocked him. When he visited the Maldive Islands, on the way to Ceylon, he found a woman ruler. "It is a strange thing about these islands that their ruler is a woman, Khadījah. The sovereignty belonged to her grandfather, then to her father, and after his death to her brother Shihāb al-Dīn, who was a minor. When he was deposed and put to death some years later, none of the royal house remained but Khadījah and her two younger sisters, so they raised Khadījah to the throne. She was married to their preacher, Jamāl al-Dīn, who became Wazir and the real holder of authority, but orders are issued in her name only."[5]

Ibn Baṭṭūṭah was appointed *qāḍī*, and resided long enough to marry four wives, and to endeavour to make his mark on the customs of the islanders. In this he was not successful. "Their women do not cover their heads, not even their queen does, and they comb their hair and gather it at one side. Most of them wear only an apron from their waists to the ground, the rest of their bodies being uncovered. When I held the office of *qāḍī* there, I tried to put an end to this practice, but I met with no success. No woman was admitted to my presence in a lawsuit unless her body was covered, but apart from that I was unable to effect anything. I had some slave-girls who wore garments like those worn in Delhi, and who covered their heads, but it was more of a disfigurement than an ornament in their case, since they were not accustomed to it."[6]

Women, he says, were accustomed to hiring themselves out at a fixed wage. Ten or twenty of them might be found in a rich man's house, often employed as spinners. "It is easy to get married in these islands on account of the smallness of the dowries and the pleasure of their women's society. When ships arrive, the crew marry wives, and when they are about to sail they divorce them. It is really a sort of temporary marriage. The women do not leave the country."[7]

On the other side of the world, south of the Sahara, he found the women even more scantily clad, in spite of the general enthusiasm for religious practices. In Mali, he visited the local *qāḍī* on a feast day. His children were chained up. "I will not let them loose until they know their Qur'ān lesson by heart," he said. At the same time, his servants were naked. When Ibn Baṭṭūṭah queried the freedom with which men and women conversed, the husband of one of the women concerned rebuked him. "The association of women with men among us is a good custom and is carried on in a suitable manner. It arouses no suspicion and our women are not like those in your country."[8]

In another tribe, possibly the Tuaregs, "their women are of surpassing beauty, and are shown more respect than the men. The state of things amongst these people is indeed extraordinary . . . These people are Muslims, punctilious in observing the hours of prayer, studying the books of law and memorising the Qur'ān. Yet their women show no bashfulness before men and do not veil themselves, though they are assiduous in attending the prayers. Any man who wishes to marry one of them may do so, but they do not travel with their husbands, and even if one desired to do so her family would not allow her to go."[9]

One wonders if this comment reflects the personal experience of the much-married Ibn Baṭṭūṭah himself.

With such a range of liberal interpretation and variety of custom it is not surprising that the centres of Islam should strive to set a stricter standard, to which hopefully the outlying provinces would in the long run conform. During the Mamlūk period in Cairo repeated decrees were issued urging strictness in veiling, and restricting the right of women to take part in activities outside their homes, and even to pay visits to the cemeteries. The frequency with which these orders were given is an indication that obedience on such matters was hard to enforce.[10]

Ibn Baṭṭūṭah sat at the feet of two respected women teachers of religion, in Damascus. One of them gave him his licence to teach there.[11] He also makes mention of many shrines of women saints, places he visited in Cairo, Damascus, Hebron, and Jerusalem, as well as, later, in India. In Delhi he describes the tomb of Raḍīyah Begum Jalālat al-Dīn, daughter of the Sultan Shams al-Dīn Iltutmish. This princess was one of the few Muslim women to rule over a kingdom. Her father established himself in Delhi and ruled with vigour for over thirty years, until his death in 634/1236. He chose his daughter as his heir because of her courage and intelligence. One of her brothers seized the throne, but the populace supported Raḍīyah. She was installed as Sultan, assumed the imperial robes and gave public audiences every day, revising and confirming the laws of her father and distributing even-handed justice. She rode armed on horseback at the head of her troops, and never veiled her face. Ibn Baṭṭūṭah says she ruled with absolute authority for four years, after which she was overthrown by another brother and killed. He found the Muslim girls in India well educated. There were numbers of schools for them, and many knew the Qur'ān by heart.[12]

Ibn Baṭṭūṭah notes especially the respect shown to women by the Turks. "They hold a more dignified position than the men." "The Turkish women do not veil themselves." Not only royal ladies but also "wives of merchants and common people . . . will sit in a waggon drawn by horses, attended by three or four maidens . . . The windows are open and her face is visible . . . Sometimes a woman will be accompanied by her husband, and anyone seeing him would take him for one of her servants."[13]

He travelled through Anatolia and visited the newly-captured city of Bursa. The Sultan Orhan was away, and it was his wife Nilüfer Hatun who received the distinguished visitor, a fact that modern Turkish women writers have not failed to note.[14] This lovely city, capital of the early Ottoman sultans, is overlooked by the snow-capped mountain Uludağ. It surrendered to Orhan in 727/1326, as his father Osman lay dying. He it is from whom the

Ottoman line took its name. The castle church was at once turned into a mosque, and Osman is buried there. "A great city," Ibn Baṭṭūṭah calls it, "with fine bazaars and broad streets, surrounded by orchards and running springs. Outside it are two thermal establishments, one for men and the other for women, to which patients come from the most distant parts. They lodge there for three days at a hospice which was built by one of the Turkmen kings."[15]

These are the only buildings he mentions, but magnificent tombs and mosques were to follow. The tomb of Orhan contains no fewer than twenty-one sarcophagi, including that of his wife Nilüfer Hatun, his daughter Fatma Sultan, and other wives and children. Each of the royal tombs is a family sepulchre, witness to a stable pattern of family life which was not enjoyed by later generations of the dynasty in Istanbul. One such tomb includes the sultan's nurse as well as his children.[16]

One other woman of this period was never forgotten. She was a Serbian princess, Despina, married to Orhan's grandson Bayezid after he had conquered her country. The victorious advance of the Ottomans suffered a severe set-back a few years later, when Tīmūr with his Mongol army swept into Anatolia from the east. They defeated Bayezid and his troops at Ankara in 805/1402.

Bayezid was taken captive, and so was his queen. Later tradition held that this had enduring consequences for the imperial family. Five hundred years later, the last Sultan, after meeting an attractive cousin, daughter of the Khedive Ismail, is said to have expressed regret that the Ottoman tradition did not permit the sovereign to marry a "free girl": one who was neither born a slave nor captured in war. Madame Emine Foat Tugay, in a charming book which gives life to many of the vanished customs of Ottoman Turkey, gives the widely circulated story of Despina.

"This tradition dates back to the very beginning of the fifteenth century. Bayezid I was defeated at the battle of Ankara in 1402 and was constrained to assist at a banquet given in celebration of the victory over his own armies and himself. On that occasion he saw his queen, Despina, a Serbian princess, reduced to a menial position and forced to wait upon the victor. From this time onwards, to prevent a repetition of this humiliation, sultans and princes chose their wives from among slaves."[17]

A Queen's Mosque in Iran

"Turquoise and cobalt and lapis lazuli blue predominate as always. Touches of purple, green and yellow complete the palette, with pink and dark red in the side īvāns [porches]. There is much white, definitive and dancing. A general background is discovered in the paths of plain brick that surround each jewelled meadow. The life is in the texts, of blazing white and gentian-blue along the parapet, of the same blue mixed with yellow, and interlaced with steel-blue Kufic, around the big īvān where Baysunghur proclaims his mother as the author of so much munificence.

"Colour of this quality dispenses a light of its own. It brings the sun out of the clouds, or, if it is out, makes it brighter. To enter the court of the Mosque of Gauhar is to give the eye a new holiday. It needs no partisanship of the Persian style, but rather an acquaintanceship with other styles, to acclaim this court, among buildings that now exist, as the most beautiful example of colour in architecture ever devised by man to the glory of his God and of himself."

The Mosque of Gauhar Shad, adjoining the pilgrim shrine of Imam ʿAlī al-Riḍā in Mashhad

"Her Highness, the Noble in Greatness, the Sun of the Heaven of Chastity and Continence, Famous for Nobility and Honour and Piety, Gauhar Shad, may her Greatness be eternal, and may her Chastity endure and may her Charity increase with true Thought and high, and with Pious Intent of Heart and Lofty Ideal for fulfilling and accomplishing her hopes in Allah, may He accept it; from her private property for the benefit of her future state and for the Day on which the works of everyone will be judged, with Zeal for Allah and with Desire to please Allah and with Thankfulness for the Benefits of Allah and for the Praise of the Benefits granted by Allah, built this Great Masjid-i-Jami, the Holy House, in the era of the reign of the Great Sultan, and the more Just

Khakan, the more Generous, the Lord of Rulers of the Arabs and of Ajam, the Sultan, son of a Sultan, the Father of Victory, Shah Rukh, son of Timur Gurkani, Bahadur Khan. May Allah make eternal his Kingdom and Empire! And may he increase on the inhabitants of the world his Goodness, his Justice, and his Generosity! Thus may Allah accept her work with beneficent acceptance and may He bless her with His choice blessings and may He grant her the greater of the boons which He has promised to the good!

"Baysunghur, son of Shah Rukh, son of Timur Gurkani, wrote this inscription with hope in Allah in the year 821 [1418]."

Baysunghur's inscription to his mother

Chapter Eleven

Renaissance in the East

As patrons of the arts, women have often influenced the use of more than their own money. Love for them has inspired some of the greatest works of art of all time. Such were the mosque of Bībī Khānum in Samarkand, and the Tāj Maḥall in Agra. Between the construction of these two masterpieces, there came about a renaissance, one of the greatest in the long history of Persian art and civilisation. The Timurid period, contemporary with the Italian Renaissance of the fifteenth century, owed much of its cultural impetus to a woman whose long life was devoted to fostering the arts: Tamerlane's daughter-in-law, Gauhar Shad.

Bībī Khānum was the favourite wife of the redoubtable Tīmūr, known in the West as Tamerlane. He claimed that he was a descendant of Chengiz Khan, and he launched a second tide of Mongol conquest westwards. His story is one of almost unbelievable extremes: brutality and devotion, terror and piety, utter destruction in Baghdad, Aleppo, and Damascus, and glorious buildings in Samarkand. Samarkand, across the River Oxus, lay in country like Paradise, and had a long history going back to the days of Alexander. It lay on the old silk route from China. Chengiz Khan reduced it to ruins, but about 772/1370 Tīmūr chose it as his capital, and an astonishing amount of building took place. The Mongol soldiers camped in their tents while the magnificent mosques and *madrasahs* (colleges) were rising.

In honour of Bībī Khānum, Tīmūr commanded the construction of a fine mosque, and she herself took an interest in the plans and designs. Her husband was spending the plunder from his Indian campaign, and the scale of the operation was immense. A portal thirty to forty metres high was steadied by massive, close-set, round minarets. There were three domes and, in all, eight minarets.[1] But Tīmūr went away while it was building, and when he returned gossip reached him about his wife and the architect. The mosque was completed, but the unfortunate man was hanged from the rafters, and the queen herself was executed. Illustrations to the *Zafarnāmeh*, Book of Victories, which tells the story, show the mosque in process of construction, and then complete, with all its many activities in progress: the *khuṭbah* (Friday sermon) being delivered from the pulpit; ablutions and prayers; reading of the Qur'ān. In a gallery at the top is a row of women, dressed in white and veiled, only the eyes being uncovered; and over all, suspended from the roof, the swaying figure of the man who designed the whole.[2]

Bībī Khānum's mosque is in ruins, though even so it is of outstanding beauty and grandeur. It is being carefully restored by the Soviet authorities.[3]

Tīmūr was a strategist at the ancient game of chess, as well as on the battlefield. News of the birth of his fourth son was brought to him as he played, and he named the most able of his sons Shah Rukh, King's Castle (the "rook" among chessmen). This boy was to succeed him and to rule for more than forty years: 807/1404 to 850/1447. He showed a talent for peace rather than for war, and his reign stands out in the bloody annals of his family as a period of enlightenment and growth: one of those surprises sprung by history, when the forces of civilisation seem suddenly too strong for the violence and destruction that have held sway.

Shah Rukh married a wife, Gauhar Shad, "Joyous Jewel", who helped him greatly. His times are notable for his own encouragement of science and literature, and for his wife's magnificent mosques in Mashhad and Herat, and for the continuance of his work by their two sons, the famous astronomer Ulugh Beg, and the calligrapher Baysunghur, who records his mother's beneficence in the inscription still to be read in her mosque in Mashhad.

Shah Rukh moved his capital south from Samarkand to the strategic city of Herat, now in North-West Afghanistan, where he was already installed as his father's deputy. Ulugh Beg governed on Shah Rukh's behalf in Samarkand, and there he set up an observatory. His mother made a special journey from Herat to see it. He drew up astronomical tables that were a notable advance in the science of the stars, and were long used by European astronomers.[4]

A library was established in Herat, and Baysunghur, the younger son, was in charge of it. Glorious manuscripts written and illuminated in it are extant, some of them in the hand of another son of Shah Rukh, Ibrāhīm Sultan.[5] No fewer than forty calligraphers and illuminators were constantly employed there.[6]

Colleges were established alongside the great mosques of Herat and Mashhad, to teach theology, with endowments for those who studied. At Gauhar Shad's college in Herat each student received clothes, a grant of money, and a bed. They could also marry. The story runs that a visit of inspection to the newly completed college was announced. The Queen set out with two hundred girls of her court, all the students having been chased out. One, however, remained. He awoke from a nap to see one of the girls, to their mutual delight. Gauhar Shad decided to deal with the matter with characteristic thoroughness. The two hundred girls were married to two hundred students, and each was allowed to see his wife once a week – provided that he worked hard in between visits. This she did, says the historian, "to arrest the progress of adultery".[7]

Shah Rukh's ability to govern made all these cultural activities possible. He had a pacific temperament quite unlike that of his father, and did his best to heal the wounds which the latter had inflicted on Western and Central Asia by an uninterrupted sequence of wars and predatory raids conducted with unequalled frightfulness.[8] He married Gauhar Shad in 791/1388, and she lived and worked in Herat for over sixty years. Her life is recorded by the historian of the Mongols, Khondemir, who wrote at the court of the Emperor Bābur. An Indian official, Mohun Lal, gathered local tradition about her when he visited Herat in 1834. Her buildings in Herat were then still standing, and he describes them.[9]

Herat in her day was the capital of an empire which stretched from the Tigris to Sinkiang. Her versatility, and her tragic death, left a lasting impression which the glories of her buildings did not allow to fade. Mohun Lal heard her described as incomparable among women, and popular ballads sang of the love her husband bore for her. Her mosque and her college in Herat were destroyed as late as 1885, when they were demolished, possibly on British advice, to hinder the advance of an expected Russian invasion.[10] Her mausoleum still stands.

The Virgin's Tree in Cairo. Legend holds that the Holy Family rested here.

The college of Madar-i-Shah, built by the mother of Sultan Husain, Isfahan, AH 1126/AD 1714

The mosque Gauhar Shad built in Mashhad, alongside the tomb of Imām ʿAlī al-Riḍā, has been repaired in the last few years, and is in full use. This, her great work, was started in 808/1405, the year after the death of Tīmūr. It was completed in 821/1418, and in the following year her husband Shah Rukh paid an official visit to it, and gave a heavy gold lamp to hang in the sanctuary.[11] She also added to the endowments of the other major centre of Shīʿī pilgrimage in Iran, the sister shrine in Qum, where Fāṭimah al-Maʿsūmah is buried.[12]

In the court of Gauhar Shad's mosque stands a small building known as The Mosque of the Old Woman. The story goes that when Gauhar Shad was buying land one aged woman refused to sell a small plot in the middle of the proposed site. She insisted that a separate mosque should be erected on her piece of ground. The Queen complied with this request.[13]

Family relationships during the last years of her long life were anything but happy. Baysunghur died early, in 847/1443, of drink. His son was her favourite grandchild, but she antagonised another grandson, Ulugh Beg's son. Shah Rukh died suddenly, in 850/1447, when away with her on a campaign in Rayy, near the present Tehran, a journey which she had encouraged. Ulugh Beg's son seized her baggage and all her animals as well, and the seventy-year-old queen had to follow her husband's body on foot back to Herat, "with an ordinary linen scarf thrown over her head and a staff in her hand", says the Mongol historian Khondemir.[14] This same grandson of hers proceeded to murder his father, and then died a violent death himself.

The years of anarchy that followed Shah Rukh's death were brought to an end only by another descendant of Tīmūr, Abū Saʿīd. He attacked Herat, and was so enraged by the support the aged Gauhar Shad gave to his rival, her own great-grandson Ibrāhīm, that he executed her: in 864/1459. She was over eighty, but even then her influence was evidently powerful enough to warrant such action.

She was buried in the mausoleum which she had herself constructed, and had decorated "with a feminine elegance that became its founder".[15] Her favourite grandson and his son Ibrāhīm were laid alongside her. On her tomb was written, "The Bilqīs of her time".

Fifty years later another descendant of the house of Tīmūr came to Herat, on the way to India, where he was to found the empire of the Moguls. The future emperor Bābur was deeply impressed by what he saw there. In 1510, Herat was taken by Shah Ismail, first of the Safavid dynasty of Isfahan; and the days of the Timurid renaissance were at an end. The massive *Survey of Persian Art* comments: "Bābur and the Moguls inherited its humanity, which transformed the face of India: Persia its art, which became the basis of Safavid culture. We, in our museums, have its paintings; in our libraries its literature. In its home, now divided into Persia, Afghanistan, and Turkestan, we have also its buildings."[16]

The architecture of the Mogul emperors also owed much to that of their ancestors. It was a descendant of Tīmūr, Shah Jahān, emperor in India from 1038/1628 to 1069/1658, who built the matchless Tāj Maḥall. His wife Mumtāz died; and her grief-stricken husband started building her tomb in the year after her death. Shah Jahān was the master builder among a dynasty of great builders; the peak of perfection was reached in this act of devotion to his wife. His austere son Aurangzīb, who dethroned him, built no tomb for his father, but laid him like an afterthought by his wife's side; though Aurangzīb too built many fine mosques and a small copy of the Tāj for his own wife.

In the Tāj Maḥall the riot of colour that adorns the mosques and tombs of Iran and Samarkand is exchanged for the purity of white. No higher tribute to womanhood has ever been paid: in its purity, its delicacy, its perfect workmanship, its spacious design and intricate detail. Mumtāz does not rest alone, for round her central tomb are the four small mosque tombs of her maids of honour.

Mumtāz and Shah Jahān had a favourite daughter Fāṭimah, known as Jahān-Ārā. She and her brother Dārā Shukoh had a strong tie of affection. Dārā Shukoh became a disciple of a famous teacher and Ṣūfī, Mullā Shah. His sister corresponded with this master and convinced Mullā Shah of her sincerity in her wish to follow the Ṣūfī way. She travelled with her father to Kashmir, and there Mullā Shah paid a visit to her father. In her own account she tells of the deep impression made on her by her first sight of the master, from her hiding place behind the *purdah*. The following day her brother initiated her into the order of Mullā Shah, on his authority. She went to the chapel of the palace to pray; and, back in her own room, she poured out her soul in thankfulness for the "immeasurable happiness" God had vouchsafed to a "weak and unworthy woman".[17]

Mullā Shah, we are told, had a great affection for all his pupils, but especially for this princess who, he said, had such depth of mystic knowledge that she might have acted as his deputy.

The pattern of womanhood which the Tāj Maḥall commemorates has in it this golden thread of dedication which certain women always sought and followed.

Husbands and Wives

"The perfect husband . . . He walks in with laughter in his eyes and he smiles when he goes out. If I ask him for something he gives it to me and if I refrain he gives it me of his own accord. If I work, he thanks me and if I am remiss, he forgives me."

Umm Abān, sister of Hind bint Sufyān and aunt of the caliph Muʿawiyah

"Nasreddin Hoça wanted to taste the blessed state of polygamy, and took to himself a young second wife. Before many months were out his friends found the Hoça completely bald and asked the reason. 'My old wife pulls out all my black hairs so that I may look as old as she; my young wife pulls out my white hairs so that I may look as young as she. Between them I am bald.'"

"After Nasreddin Hoça's first wife died, he married again. The woman he married had also been married previously. One night as they lay in bed, Hoça's second wife started to talk about her first husband, telling Hoça what a wonderful man he was. Hoça then started to talk about his first wife, saying she was the most wonderful woman he had ever known. But his second wife could talk faster than Hoça, and so she was winning the discussion. Hoça finally became so angry that he kicked her out of bed, and she fell on the floor.

"The next day the woman went to a *qāḍī* and made a complaint against Hoça. When the trial started, she told the court that he had kicked her out of bed on to the floor.

'Did you really do that, Hoça?' asked the *qāḍī*.

'No, I didn't,' said Hoça. 'It was this way. We were in bed together when a friend of hers came along and got into bed with us. Then a friend of mine came along and got into bed too. With four of us in the bed together it became very crowded, and she fell out.'"

Chapter Twelve

The Years of Seclusion

The Ottoman period brought the segregation of women to its height. Gradually the curtain that ensured privacy in the Prophet's home hardened into what for many were prison walls. The covering pulled across the face to ensure respect became an impenetrable veil. The process by which this came about is a matter of controversy and surmise. The veil, however widely adopted, was certainly not a Muslim invention. Persian custom in pre-Islamic days protected women to a far greater degree than was prevalent in Arabia. A Greek house had its *gynaeceum*, the part specially reserved for women, and this was a feature of Byzantine life. In the early church there was a tradition of separate accommodation for men and women.[1] Insecurity must have played its part in making seclusion seem desirable. Only where law and order prevail can women safely assume freedom of movement: and this was too often lacking.

The increasing segregation of women had a stifling effect. Between the time of the early Abbasid caliphs, when Abu Nuwās could learn and recite the dīwāns of fifty women poets, and the twentieth century, it would be hard to name as many women writers in the first class, across the whole field of the Muslim world. Talent there must have been, and some found expression – but not circulation.

The imposition of the veil was never universal. It was an urban custom, and peasants and bedouin did not adopt it. Women worked, as they still do, in the fields alongside their men.

The capture of Istanbul by Mehmed the Conqueror in 1453 and the conquests that followed set the pattern of government in the Middle East for almost five hundred years, and inaugurated an era of brilliant culture. Yet under the Ottoman regime the restrictions on women greatly increased. In her book *Women in Turkey*[2]

Doctor Tezer Taşkıran describes this process and the reforms which followed before and after the revolution led by Atatürk. Doctor Taşkıran herself took part in many of the recent developments she describes, as student and later as teacher of philosophy in the Universities of Istanbul and Ankara, and as a member from 1943 to 1954 of the Turkish Grand National Assembly.

The strict confinement of women was, she says, in contrast with their freedom in earlier Turkish society.

> Women were not veiled at the time of Mehmed the Conqueror. They wore a scarf over their heads but their faces were uncovered. The early sultans did not segregate their wives, nor did they employ eunuchs to guard their women, and there were no elaborate pompous palace ceremonies. It was from the Byzantines that these customs were passed on to the Turks.
>
> In modest homes there were no separate quarters for men and women. The majority of the Turks were monogamous. But the influence of the upper classes spread to the rest of society, and with it women were reduced to a secluded and confined life.
>
> The peasant women, however, were not affected by this trend. The women who worked in the fields with the men were never as tightly veiled as their sisters in the cities. Even today, their headwear is used more for protection from unknown men than for concealment from their own community. As far as the nomadic tribes are concerned, they have retained many of the old Turkish traditions up to today.

Doctor Taşkıran goes on to list the indications of women's contribution to society right through what has been called "the Secluded Period", from the sixteenth century to the Tanzimat era, 1255/1839 to 1293/1876, when many reforms were attempted. She gives many examples of women participating in the practice of medicine, in commerce, and in social welfare through generous endowments given for the poor. But in spite of these exceptions, she says, it remains true that in general women were ignored. They were given no education, and often were unable to obtain their legal rights in marriage questions.[3]

This retrogression was not only in the secretive harem quarters of the Sultan's Saray,[4] the palace with its dark passages and splendid halls, its maze of cubicles and its secluded gardens, where hundreds of women spent their lives. It was also the case in the cities of the earlier Arab empire, which sank to the status of provincial towns, garrisoned and governed by a Turkish ruling class.

To the Turks it seemed that through their conquests in Europe they were bringing the blessings of civilisation to peoples benighted and backward. If the subject populations of Arab lands saw Ottoman rule differently it is not surprising. The orthodox Arab view of the period is voiced by the historian Philip Hitti. "Throughout the four centuries of Ottoman domination . . . the whole Arab east was in eclipse . . . The subjugated peoples shared a common fate of excessive taxation and oppressive rule. No wonder if under such conditions no creative work of art, science, or literature was produced by Arabic-speaking peoples."[5] The whole population was affected, not least the women. At the end of the Mamlūk period in Cairo there were numbers of educated women, some of them holding certificates permitting them to teach the Qur'ān, and even jurisprudence. By the nineteenth century, after three hundred years of Ottoman rule, women had been deprived of their right to learn.[6]

Recent historians have revised such sweeping condemnations, and in Turkey itself the women were in comparison less restricted. But even so, among the causes of the decline of the empire must be reckoned the crushing confinement of women, not merely to physically limited quarters, but to narrow channels of thought.

In the civilisation which had its centre in Istanbul there was much that was lovely, much that was gracious. Poetry flowed in melodious rhyme, modelled on the Persian. One great architect, and many lesser ones, drew the magnificent curves of domes and the slim uprights of minarets on the skylines of the capital and other cities. Calligraphers delicately traced illuminations on paper made of silk, or boldly embossed the words of the Qur'ān on tiles in shades of colour none can now repeat. Silk and leather, gold and jewellery, inlaid furniture and metal work; every luxury trade was brought to a decorative perfection. Much of this exquisite output was made for women, and used by them. The Europe of the sixteenth century trembled at the military prowess of the Ottoman armies; in the seventeenth century it began to delight in the things of beauty which made their way into the drawing rooms of London and Paris.

One unexpected aspect of Ottoman rule was the astonishing power wielded by a series of women at the heart of the Empire. The so-called Reign of Women began with the wife of Süleyman the Magnificent, the Russian Roxelana, and continued for about one hundred and fifty years, until the death of Turhan, mother of the Sultan Mehmed IV.[7] The hundreds of girl-slaves and the further hundreds of eunuchs who looked after them, together with the whole establishment of the Sultan's family, his sisters, his children and their mothers, were under the control of the *Valide Sultan*, Mother of the Sultan. Powerful personalities, confined in too narrow limits, found ways to control and direct the lives of their supposedly free menfolk. The tales of intrigue, romance and sudden death that leaked out from behind the closed doors tell one of the darkest chapters in the history of women anywhere.

The women in the Sultan's harem were not solely occupied with the intrigues and struggles for the succession. They played an active part in affairs of state, and some of the Mothers of Sultans corresponded with foreign rulers. An interchange of letters and presents took place between Queen Elizabeth and Valide Safiye, mother of Mehmed III. In 1599 a ship called *The Hector* docked in Istanbul, with an organ on board as a gift for the Sultan, and a coach for his mother. The organ had been damaged, and the coach was nearly bestowed on the Sultan himself, but, as the ambassador explained to Sir Robert Cecil, the lady was already expecting it.

In a warm letter of thanks she assures the Queen that she was using her influence with her son, in connection with the capitulations which had recently been negotiated. "Your letter has arrived . . . God willing, action will be taken in this respect! We do not cease from admonishing our son His Majesty . . . and from telling him: 'Do act according to the treaty!' . . . May you too always be firm in friendship! . . . And you sent us a coach; it has arrived and been delivered. It had our gracious acceptance. We too have sent you a robe, a girdle, a sleeve, two gold-embroidered handkerchiefs, three towels, one crown studded with pearls and rubies."[8]

Other leading women took a great interest in the development of architecture. The architect Sinan designed several of his buildings for women of the Sultan's family. His main patron was Süleyman (926/1520 to 973/1566), known to Europe as The Magnificent and to his own people as The Lawgiver.

Sinan's transformation of Istanbul was contemporary with

Michelangelo's work on St Peter's in Rome. His output was extraordinary by any standards. He tells us himself that he erected three hundred and twelve buildings: mosques, schools, tombs, palaces, caravanserais, bridges, aqueducts, bath-houses.[9] Some of these were as far afield as Mecca, where one princess of Süleyman's family was engaged in repairing and extending the water-works associated with the Abbasid Queen Zubaidah. A woman began them, and a woman should restore them, this later benefactress said.[10]

Süleyman had a daughter, Princess Mihrimah. She had a passion for building, and in co-operation with Sinan an unusual opportunity for fulfilling it. For her he built three mosques. The first, the Jetty Mosque, is in Üsküdar (Scutari), close by the shore, where it looks as if it is moored to the quay. The next was in honour of the Princess's husband, Rüstem Pasha, probably a memorial commissioned by his widow after his death. It is small, an oratory rather than a place for congregational prayer, and its interior is like a garden, beautified by tiles depicting tulips and white blossoms. The factories of Iznik were evolving such tiles, "never to be equalled in range and depth of tone, richness and variety of pattern".[11] The third was a larger mosque, named after her, on the edge of the city.

Sinan's greatest work the Süleymaniye complex, dominates the whole city, crowning the summit of the highest hill and overlooking the Golden Horn. In it is the tomb of Süleyman, and at his side that of his wife Roxelana.

Some of her successors in wielding power from behind the walls of the Harem were also enthusiastic builders. Notable among them was Hadice Turhan, favourite of the Sultan Ibrahim and mother of Mehmed IV. She lived from 1037/1627 to 1094/1682. Her mosque, the Yeni (new) Valide mosque, is the fourth largest in the city. (The "old" Valide mosque honours a previous Valide Sultan, on the Asian side of the Bosphorous.) The colossal Yeni mosque was still new when in 1716 Lady Mary Wortley Montagu was at the British Embassy and explored Istanbul, often finding the anonymity of the veil a help in doing so.

Lady Mary was the wife of a diplomat, briefly and rather unsuccessfully British Ambassador in Istanbul in 1716–18. Turkey and Austria were at war, and in his attempts to mediate he took too pro-Turkish a line to please those who had sent him. But his wife, a lively and inquisitive lady with an enquiring mind and a vivid pen, left a valuable record of their adventurous journey through Vienna, Sophia, and Adrianople, as well as of her explorations of the capital.

In the London from which she came, Sir Christopher Wren's great dome of St Paul's was as recent as those of the architects employed by Hadice Turhan. The ladies used to watch their work from a special building, the Queen Mother's Pavilion, built alongside the new foundations. Lady Mary was greatly impressed by the completed structure. She writes exuberantly, using her own spelling. "The mosques differ only in Largeness and richness of Materials. That of the Valide is the largest of all, built entirely of marble, the most prodigious and I think the most beautiful Structure I ever saw, be it spoke in honour of our sex, for it was founded by the mother of Mahomet the 4th. Between friends, St Paul's church would make a pitifull figure near it."[12]

A contemporary poet was Sidkî, daughter of Kamr Mehmed, one of the learned men in Istanbul during the reign of Mehmed IV. She was a Ṣūfī, lived a celibate life, and died in 1703. She sang of divine rather than human love, and perhaps her poems *The Treasury of Lights* and others were an inspiration to the Queen Mother and her ladies as they pored over the architect's plans of the new mosque.[13]

The best accounts of life in the harems of the Ottoman period come from a few visitors, women who were invited into homes and succeeded in building a bridge of friendship. It was not until the days of Halide Edib, at the beginning of this century, that we have descriptions from the Muslim women themselves. Some insight into the life and scope and attitudes of women, especially of the ruling class in their gracious houses in Istanbul, Cairo, or Jerusalem, can be gleaned from the letters of European women, first of whom is Lady Mary.

Lady Mary's further encounters convinced her that the Turkish women, restricted though they were, were on the whole at least as free as their counterparts in Europe.

> 'Tis very easy to see that they have more liberty than we have, no woman of what rank so ever being permitted to go in the street without two muslins, one that covers her face all but her eyes and another that hides the whole dress of her head and hangs half way down her back: and their shapes are wholly concealed . . . You may

> guess how effectively this disguises them . . . This perpetual masquerade [masked ball] gives them the entire liberty of following their inclinations without danger of discovery.
>
> Upon the whole I look upon the Turkish women as the only free people in the Empire . . . 'Tis true that their law permits them 4 wives, but there is no instance of a Man of Quality that makes use of this Liberty, or of a Woman of Rank that would suffer it . . . Amongst all the great men here I only know the Teftedar [the Treasurer] that keeps a number of slaves for his own use . . . and he is spoken of as a Libertine or what we would call a rake, and his wife won't see him tho she continues to live in his house.
>
> Thus you see, dear sister, the manners of Mankind do not differ so widely as our voyage writers would make us believe.[14]

Lady Mary has vignettes of incidents in women's lives, such as the marriage of a daughter of the Grand Signor (Sultan), already a widow at thirteen, to a fifty-year-old favourite of her father's. The child burst into tears on seeing this second elderly husband.[15]

She describes the gardens in the harems, with their high trees.

> In the midst of the garden is the Khiosk, that is a large room, commonly beautified with a fine fountain in the midst of it . . . the scene of their greatest pleasures, where the Ladys spend most of their hours, employ'd by their Music or Embroidery. In the public gardens there are public khiosks where people go that are not so well accommodated at home, and drink their Coffee, sherbet etc.[16]

A dinner with the Grand Vizier's lady was somewhat disappointing.

Lady Mary notes:

> the little magnificence of her house, the furniture being all very moderate, and except the Habits and Number of her slaves nothing about her that appear'd expensive. She guess'd at my thoughts and told me that she was no longer of an age to spend either her time or Money in Superfluitys, that her whole expense was in charity and her Employment praying to God. There was no affectation in this speech, both she and her husband are entirely given up to Devotion. He never looks upon any other woman, and what is more extraordinary touches no bribes, notwithstanding the example of all his Predecessors.[17]

The next call, however, made up for this lack of display. The wife of another high official, Fatma, was a young beauty, and her house a paradise. Black eunuchs and ranks of beautiful young girls, damasks embroidered with silver, gold-brocaded kaftans, children almost covered in jewels: the description flows ecstatically on.[18] Fatma became a good friend, and was delighted to see Lady Mary again on a later visit. "You Christian ladies have the reputation of inconstancy," she said, "and I did not expect that I should ever see you again." In a further conversation, Fatma refused to believe Lady Mary's assurances that Christian ladies were normally faithful to their husbands. "Your eyes, your hands, your conversation is for the public. What do you pretend to keep for your husbands? Forgive me, I would like to believe you, but you want me to do the impossible."[19]

Less beautiful than Fatma, but with "a fine face more decay'd by sorrow than by time", was the widowed Hafisa, favourite wife of the Sultan Mustafa II, deposed in 1703. On her husband's death, she was told to leave the Saray and find another husband. She had borne five sons for the Ottoman family. All, however, had died, and only a daughter remained. So she had to go. She chose to marry the old man who, years before, had made a present of her to the Sultan when she was ten years old. "But she never permitted him to pay her one visit, tho it is now 15 year she has been in his house, where she passes her time in uninterrupted mourning with a constancy very little known in Christendom, especially in a widow of 21, for she is now but 36."[20] In her sorrow, she kept up the richness of the life to which she had been accustomed; her dress and her person were loaded with jewels: a chain made of two thousand emeralds, another emerald the size of a turkey's egg, earrings of pearl-shaped diamonds the size of hazel-nuts. The fifty-course dinner was "extremely tedious, but the magnificence of her table answer'd very well to that of her dress."[21]

Another feature of life in the harems of Istanbul was through Lady Mary to reach England and be accepted in English society. This was the practice of inoculation against smallpox. This terrible scourge killed thousands in frequent epidemics, and Lady Mary herself had narrowly escaped from death two years before she went to Turkey. In Adrianople she found that a form of inoculation was a general and successful habit.

> The Smallpox so fatal and so general amongst us here is entirely harmless by the invention of engrafting (which is the term they give it). There is a set of old women who make it their business to perform

> the Operations. Every Autumn in the month of September, when the great Heat is abated, people send to one another to know if any of their family has a mind to have the smallpox. They make partys for this purpose.
>
> There is no example of any one that has dy'd in it, and you may believe I am very well satisfy'd of the safety of the Experiment enough to take pains to bring this useful invention into fashion in England.[22]

Her son was "engrafted" in the following year, and back in England in 1721 her daughter had the same treatment. An epidemic raged, and the success of the operation on Lady Mary's children was used to bring the possibility to the notice of the public. Princess Caroline led the way, and the doctor who had been in the Embassy in Istanbul with the Wortley Montagus inoculated the Royal children and a number of others. Controversy raged, but Lady Mary's courage and example prepared the way for the work of Dr Jenner on vaccination later in the century, and for its acceptance. So Lady Mary's friendships in Turkey were the means of saving countless lives as the simple practices of those old women in Turkey set an example for England.[23]

There can have been few sights more beautiful than a tulip festival in Topkapı Palace. Each April a fête was held in the gardens, in bright moonlight. On miles of shelves vases of tulips were ranged, with coloured lights and glass globes of coloured water which reflected the lanterns and fountains. From the trees hung innumerable cages of canaries. Music, the song of birds and the splashing of fountains filled the air, while showers of fireworks illuminated the sky. One night was specially reserved for the ladies of the Harem.[24]

Many strange stories are told of the succession of Queen Mothers. One of them, Nakşidil Valide, is said to have been a French girl from Martinique, captured by pirates on her way home from a convent school in Nantes. The Bey of Algiers sent her, so the story goes, as a present to the Sultan Abdül Hamid, and for thirty years she lived in the Saray. Her son was born in 1785, and grew up to be the vigorous Sultan Mahmud II, who opened the way to the first reforms in the Ottoman Empire.

The story is only a little more difficult to credit than that of the Venetian Baffo, who wielded considerable power as wife and mother of earlier sultans. Whether or no he had a French mother, Mahmud II (1223/1808 to 1255/1839) was one of the strongest of the Ottoman line. His policy helped to turn the tide against Napoleon, and at the same time allowed much that was European into Turkish society. It was the first grey dawn of a new day for Turkey.

From the first, those who dreamed of revolution in Turkey thought that a change in the status of women must be an integral part of it. Ziya Gökalp, one of the greatest thinkers of the Turkish revolution, stressed the equality and the influence that Turkish women had enjoyed in early times.

The bridge between the old Turkey and the new, between Ottoman society and modern times, is spanned by the life of Halide Edib Adivar. Born in 1884, she grew up in the household of a palace official, and she was the first Muslim Turkish graduate of the American College for Girls in Üsküdar. From 1903 until 1916 she worked in lycées as teacher and as inspector, and in 1916 she was sent on an educational mission to Syria. On her return, she married Dr Adnan Adivar. Both played prominent parts in the events following the defeat of Turkey by the Allies, and the War of Independence.

Teacher, journalist, author and soldier, she was the heroine of the New Turkey, and she had the gift of expressing what millions of others also experienced. She was active as a writer as early as 1908–9, at the time of the revolution of the Young Turks. In 1911 she wrote a novel, *New Turan*, a love story incorporating the ideals of a reborn pre-Ottoman tradition. "The book is a political and national Utopia," she says, "where women have the vote, and where they work with the qualities of head and heart which characterise the best Turkish women. The simplicity and austerity of their lives have become different since the magnificent days of the Ottomans, with the unhealthy luxury and parasitic tendencies of a class of women which only a high but degenerate civilisation like the Ottoman creates."[25]

The same ideals lived with her throughout her long life. She was alongside Kemal Atatürk during the War of Independence, but after the founding of the Republic in 1923 she broke with him, and felt it wiser to go abroad. Her husband started a short-lived independent party, but when in 1924 it collapsed he too left Turkey. They lived in England and France and did not return until after Atatürk's death in 1938. From then until her death in 1964 she once again played a part in the affairs of her country, as Professor of English Language and Literature in the University of Istanbul, and as a member of the Grand National Assembly from 1950 to 1954.[26]

Her feeling for the new Turkey was not inconsistent with a deep and lasting pride in the greatness of the Ottoman tradition, the best of which she thought must not be lost. Looking back to the old days, she describes a visit as a child to the Süleymaniye Mosque one night in Ramaḍān.

> I was on the shoulders of the tallest man in the crowd. Below me the lights of the lanterns swung in the dark depths of the long winding mysterious streets. Above me light circles and gigantic lettering, also in light, hung in the blue void, while the illusive tracery of the minarets, the soft droop of the domes, appeared dimly or disappeared in the thickness of the blue distance as we walked on. And so we reached Süleymaniye and plunged into the great crowd gathered inside.
>
> The gray space was now a golden haze. Around the hundreds of tremulous oil lights a vast golden atmosphere thickened, and under it thousands of men sat on their knees in orderly rows; not one single space was empty, and this compact mass, this human carpet, presented a design made up of all costumes, ages, and ranks. The women prayed in the gallery above . . .
>
> I have often prayed in most of the mosques in Istanboul, but I have never entered the Süleymaniye again, although I have walked many times round it and visited the museum which used to be its soup-kitchen in earlier times. I did not want to alter the memory of the divine and aesthetic emotion which I had had in the days of my early childhood, and I knew it was not possible to repeat it without destroying the integrity of that first impression.
>
> Whatever my feelings are towards some parts of the Ottoman past, I am grateful to its conception of beauty as expressed by Sinan in that wonderful dome. The gorgeous colouring of the Byzantines, the magic tracery, and the delicate lace-like ornament of the Arab influenced him in many ways, but he surely brought that flawless beauty of line and that sober majesty in his Turkish heart from its original home in the wild steppes. There is a manliness and lack of self-consciousness here which I have never seen in any other temple, yet the work is far from being primitive or elemental. It combines genius and science as well as the personal sense of holy beauty which is characteristic of the Ottoman, and it can hold its own with the architectural triumphs of any age.[27]

The Old Order Changes

"Sirs, if there is ignorance in our country, it is general ignorance. It does not only affect women but also men.

"We have been educated by our mothers and they have done the best they could. But our present standards are not adequate for present-day needs. We need men with different attitudes and a deeper understanding, and the mothers of the future shall educate these men."

Atatürk

"A spark is what begets fire.
A river begins with a stream.
A drop and a drop are what swell into seas and lakes."

Robert Shaaban: *A Testament to my Daughter*

Istanbul, an Eighteenth Century impression

The Shalimar Gardens in Lahore

Chapter Thirteen

Turning Point

In the 1850s, on the shores of the Bosphorus, a struggle took place fraught with the greatest consequences for the future of women.

The Crimean War was an inglorious affair, fought largely between British and Russian troops. The sufferings of all involved, including the Turkish army, were indescribable. But fortunately there were on the spot those who made it their business to describe them. Public opinion in Britain was aroused. The unprecedented step was taken of sending out a group of women nurses.

Their arrival did not pass unnoticed. The newspaper *Ceride-i Havadis* followed the course of events, from the problems of the British wounded during the early stages of the war, the appointment of Miss Nightingale, and the arrival of the first and second parties of nurses in Istanbul, to the end of hostilities and the evacuation of the hospital. Documents preserved in the Prime Minister's Archives in Istanbul refer to gifts made by the Sultan: a sum of money to be divided between the nurses, and for Miss Nightingale herself a valuable diamond bracelet, now in the National Army Museum, Chelsea.

Today Turkey is proud of Florence Nightingale and of her association with the country. Her personal quarters in the Selimiye Barracks are kept as they were when she used them, and in 1961 the Florence Nightingale School of Nursing was founded in Şişli, Istanbul. In a monograph on Miss Nightingale, published in 1975, an eminent Turkish authority on surgery, Dr Nimet Taşkıran, remarks that the Sultan's gifts were the only act of international recognition of her work at this time. The value of the bracelet, he says, was such that one of the best villas on the Bosphorus could have been bought with the price of it; but Miss Nightingale was not one to relax, by the Bosphorus or anywhere else. Dr Taşkıran quotes the verse inscribed in the bracelet, which he interprets as a reference to her capacity for enhancing the value of the most menial service: "The radiance of the diamond makes even the humble agate take on the glow of rubies."[1]

Things were not at all like that, however, when Miss Nightingale reached Istanbul. The barracks in Üsküdar (Scutari) allotted to the wounded were windswept and dirty. To the British Ambassador in his beautiful home in Pera, the incursion of the nurses was unwelcome. To the military authorities it was an intrusion into a male world where death could be regarded as inevitable rather than preventable. To Turkish society, it could be shocking that women's faces should be seen, even though the rest of them was encased in a heavy uniform as decorous as any costume their Muslim sisters wore, a dress which offered no comfort in the heavy work they undertook.

But these women in the barracks of Üsküdar, who fought their way through every obstacle to perform the most menial tasks of service to the wounded, cholera-stricken victims of the Crimean War, won a victory that was the key to advance for the women not only of Britain but of the world.

Across the blue waters of the Bosphorus, life in the Sultan's entourage continued. The ruling Sultan, Abdül Mecid (1839–61) was moving his harem from the Topkapı Saray to the marble splendour of the new Dolmabahçe Palace at the water's edge. The rooms in the old Saray, which had seen so much intrigue, so much boredom, so much drama, were occupied by discarded concubines whose old age, after a lifetime in the harem, had to be provided for.

There could be no greater contrast than that between the ideals of woman's role represented by those buildings within sight of each other, in Istanbul and in Üsküdar. The one gave a rigorous training in all the arts of sex. The other represented the struggle to use the whole range of women's gifts, their courage, their ability and skill. Florence Nightingale and her companions focussed this in a dramatic fight to serve: to give, in terrible conditions, the best of which they were capable.

Life in the Sultan's palaces could hardly have travelled further from the ideals of the days of the Prophet. It had reached a concentration on the sexual role of women to the exclusion of

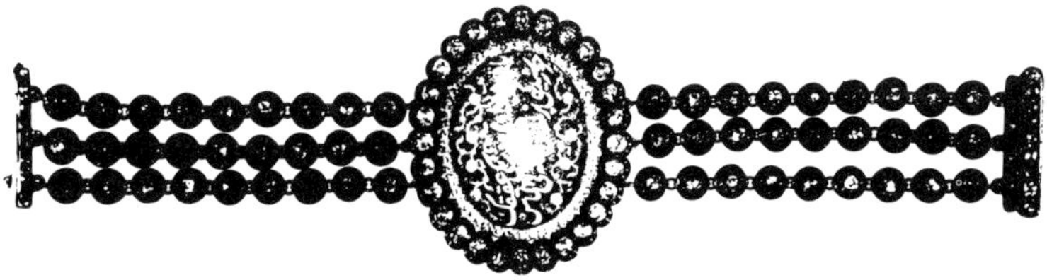

almost everything else. The nurses in Üsküdar were closer to the spirit of dedication of the first women of Islam. The names are recorded of many who in the time of the Prophet nursed the wounded and tended the sick. They would have understood the burning faith that carried Florence Nightingale through days and nights of horror. She never could forget the thousands who died, whose sacrifice, as she later said, cried out not for revenge but for reform.

A choice lay ahead for the gathering forces of women's emancipation. Many voices in Europe and the United States had by now been raised in favour of this. Already two contrasting notes were sounding: two conceptions of freedom, complementary but different. Freedom *from* restrictions and oppression: and freedom *for* every kind of service, and the opportunity to gain the skill for it.

There is a very modern note in Florence Nightingale's struggle. It was highly professional. The care of the sick was to be an affair of governments, not just a woman's individual act of mercy. She fought to establish a profession, with status and standards. It was a battle against prejudice, against corruption, against entrenched attitudes of male superiority. And it was a fight to serve, a struggle for the freedom of women to give their distinctive best to what needed to be done: to be allowed out of the isolation in which they had been kept and to play a full part in the work of a nation.

Other notes have sounded in the story of the emancipation of women in the century that followed. But this one is a key to understanding women's advance not only in the West but in the East. Many times it has been the challenge of service in a national crisis that has carried women forward. The fact that Florence Nightingale's key victory took place far from Britain and in the midst of an international conflict is symbolic of its importance for humanity, not just for one section of it.

There have been periods in human development when ideas have stirred on a scale wider than one country, one continent, one cultural region. In his study *Civilisation,* Sir Kenneth Clark comments on certain examples of "an extraordinary outpouring of energy, an intensification of existence . . . There have been times in the history of man when the earth seems suddenly to have grown warmer or more radio-active . . . times when man has made a leap forward that would have been unthinkable under ordinary evolutionary conditions."[2]

The advance of women in the last hundred years and more is one example. It has been world-wide, and no part of the globe is without some manifestation of it, even if the progress is uneven.

There are many threads in the pattern of change. Many of the founders of the women's professions in the West, Florence Nightingale among them, acted under the compulsion of a sense of God's calling. They felt they were expressing a fuller concept of Christian womanhood than the restricted role their mothers and grandmothers had filled.

The pattern of emancipation in the Muslim world has also many threads. The work of the pioneers followed closely on that of their sisters in Europe and the United States, and there were links of friendship throughout. But it must not therefore be assumed that the one development was solely derived from the example of the other.

The strong sense of independence voiced by leading women in the Arab World and further afield emphasises the importance of recognising their advance as no mere copy of Western "progress". This is the last thing that most of them want. "Your civilisation may look bright to you: it does not look so bright to us," said one student. They seek to foster new growths of freedom without jeopardising their roots or losing their identity.

Their fight has been one for participation in the life of their nations – for responsibility and choice. To gauge it, as some Western writers have done, merely in terms of greater sexual freedom, is to undervalue their aims and the abilities they seek to express.

The story of the advance of women in Muslim countries in this century is an important part of the wider story of a new phase of women's participation in the work and the running of the world. They have their own distinctive and valuable contribution to make to this whole development.

In the latter years of the nineteenth century voices were raised in many parts of the Muslim world calling for reform in the conditions of women. There is no reason to look to outside critics for evidence of the stifling restrictions then in force. Every one of the thinkers who were seeking a renewal of Islam united in condemning the limitations imposed, and in endeavouring to persuade public opinion that to keep women in seclusion and ignorance was no part of a true Islam. However much the foreign, non-Islamic origin of restrictive customs such as the veil is stressed, it cannot be denied that they were for long observed – and prized – by millions of Muslims. There was a crying need for a renewed dignity and status for women, and by the turn of the century this was widely expressed.

"It is fortunate that the emancipation of women was the result of an all-party programme rather than a sex struggle," writes Halide Edib in her book, *Turkey Faces West*.[3] One notable feature of women's advance in the Muslim world has been the number of far-sighted men who have worked for a greater freedom for women. Many examples could be given, from Qāsim Amīn, whose book *The Emancipation of Women* shocked the salons of Cairo in the year 1899, to King Faiṣal, who set in train the present rapid escalation of women's education in Saudi Arabia.

Opposition there has been, and plenty of it, but the struggle has never so far been conducted on a basis of antagonism between men and women. It has been in terms of enlightenment against backwardness, progress against reaction, not one sex against another. In Western countries there have been two contrasting tendencies in the women's movements. "Women's Liberation" has come to be associated with an antagonistic attitude, in contrast with "Emancipation", which has aimed at progressively removing the restrictions on women and giving them fresh opportunities of expression. A woman writer clarifies the distinction as she sees it: "Emancipation insists on equal status for distinctively female roles. Liberation demands the abolition of any such distinctive roles." "Emancipation means the removal of all barriers to female opportunities. Liberation would compel women into male roles by devaluing female ones."[4] In these terms, the story sketched in the following chapters is one of emancipation.

In the Arab World a partnership has developed between men and women, in personal terms as well as general. One of the women who broke into the sphere of university teaching in Egypt in the 1940s and 1950s speaks of the steady support she and others had from their husbands. "It was a struggle with circumstances," she says, "but not a fight against anyone who was trying to keep us out. We had to find the way to seize the opportunities that offered, and to carry out the work involved." Professor Fatmah Moussa Mahmoud has been head of the Department of English Literature in the University of Cairo. Her husband, also a professor, is a leading psychologist. This pattern of man and wife, both carrying heavy responsibilities, is common in the professional life of Egypt. "The choice between marriage and career which faced women in Britain has not been our problem," Professor Fatmah Moussa continues. "We have had very few who followed the example of the single women who advanced the professions in the West. With the help of our families we have combined marriage and career."[5]

In the course of the present century hundreds and thousands of such women have by their individual initiative and enterprise created a new climate of opportunity across the breadth of the Muslim world. The following chapters cannot attempt to cover the whole ground. A selection is given of some of the places and events where women have contributed most to the historic development of their people.

Cairo 1919

"The ladies came out in protest: I watched their rally.
They assumed their black garments as their banner,
Looking like stars shining bright in the midst of darkness.
They marched down the road, making for Sa'ad's house,
Making clear their feelings, in a dignified procession.
When lo, an army approached, with galloping horses,
And soldiers pointed their swords at the women's necks,
Guns and rifles, swords and points, horses and horsemen
formed a circle round them,
While roses and sweet basil were the women's arms that day.
The two armies clashed for hours . . .
Then the women faltered, for women have not much stamina.
Defeated, they scattered in disarray towards their homes.
So let the proud army rejoice in its victory and gloat
over their defeat,"

Ḥāfiẓ Ibrāhīm (1871–1932), the People's Poet,
on the Women's Demonstration of 1919 in protest
against the banishment of Sa'ad Zaghlūl

"Woman must be regarded as equal to man and must shed the remaining shackles that impede her from taking a constructive part in life."

Egypt's National Charter, 1962

Chapter Fourteen

The Egyptian Story

Like oil, women's movements in the Middle East and Asia are a phenomenon of the twentieth century. The first oil in the area was discovered in the early 1900s. Just before this, in 1899, a Cairo lawyer published a book entitled *The Emancipation of Women* (*Taḥrīr al-mar'ah*). Both events marked the beginning of historic changes.

Later, the development of oil would accelerate the pace of social change and vitally affect the future of women in large parts of the Arab World. But the tide of change was already rising long before the oil came on flow. In the longer perspectives of history the era of oil may prove to be a transitory phase. The development of a new role for women is assuredly a permanent growth.

At the turn of the century there was a ferment of change in the Muslim world. Two great reformers had been at work. Jamāl al-dīn al-Afghānī became the leader of reformist movements in Turkey and Iran, and also in Egypt. One of his followers was Shaikh Muḥammad 'Abduh, child of the Delta, educated in the stronghold of Islamic conservatism, the University of Al-Azhar. Both faced the challenge posed to the Muslim world by the upheavals in the West: the French Revolution, the Industrial Revolution, the rapid developments and expansion caused by scientific discoveries and their application. But however great was the stimulus from Western progressive thought to these men, the foundations of their teaching were wholly Muslim. Al-Afghānī saw Islam as essentially "a world religion, thoroughly capable by reason of its inner spiritual force of adaptation to the changing conditions of any age".[1] Both saw the future in terms of the renewal of a true Islam, with the flexibility it originally possessed, a self-assurance and certainty that enabled it to absorb the gifts of other civilisations without loss of identity.

Among the many social reforms advocated by Muḥammad 'Abduh was the emancipation of women, and the restoration to them of rights given in the Qur'ān but concealed by the restrictions of Ottoman society. A brilliant young lawyer, Qāsim Amīn, made this aspect of reform his own.

The issues of reform were much discussed in Cairo society. One outstanding woman of culture was Princess Nazlī Fāḍil, daughter of Mustafā Fāḍil, whose private library later formed the nucleus of Egypt's present National Library. In the 1880s she organised a "salon intellectuel" where she received scholars and political leaders like Al-Afghānī, 'Abduh, Sa'ad Zaghlūl, and Qāsim Amīn. Amīn was at first strongly against women's emancipation.

> He became converted to the cause when Darcourt, a French judge in the mixed tribunal in Cairo, published a book in which he said that the main cause of the retarded state of development in Egypt was the Harem system and the veiling of women. Qāsim Amīn opposed him. Princess Nazlī Fāḍil invited him to her house, and from the very first meeting she managed to sway him towards the cause of women. Later he became the champion of women's emancipation.

His first book, "as expected, was received with general disapprobation."[2]

Many of Muḥammad 'Abduh's proposed changes were strongly opposed in Cairo. He was ridiculed and lampooned, and it was not surprising that Qāsim Amīn's writings on behalf of women received the same treatment. This was not, however, the only response to the new ideas. Muḥammad 'Abduh was criticised – but in 1899 he was appointed Rector of Al-Azhar. The changes he initiated took that ancient stronghold of faith into a new phase of its history. Little more than half a century later, as part of its further expansion and modernisation, the first women were accepted, and the Principal of its Women's College now sits in council with the heads of faculties, in the buildings dedicated to the memory of Muḥammad 'Abduh alongside the thousand-year-old mosque which is still the heart of the university.

Born in 1863, Qāsim Amīn qualified as a lawyer in Cairo in 1881, and made his way to France for further study. After the traumatic events of 1882, when British forces occupied Egypt and put down the uprising of 'Urābī Pasha, the young lawyer co-operated with the two reformers, Afghāni and 'Abduh, both of whom took refuge in Paris.

It was more than the legal position of women that he wished to improve. A renaissance was stirring in the Arab World, not least in Egypt. Women had the right and the capacity to participate in this, he felt, and to this end he devoted his legal skill, his writing talent, and his considerable emotional powers.

In Cairo, a statue of great beauty commemorates this "Awakening", (*al-nahḍah*). It stands between the Nile and the imposing buildings of the University of Cairo, the founding of which in 1909 was a major step in progress. The sculptor, Maḥmūd Muktār (1891–1934), was an artist who sought his inspiration in Egyptian themes. His representation of the resurrection of his country shows an Egyptian peasant woman standing with her right arm on the head of a sphinx. Her left holds back from her face the lifted veil, and her eyes are fixed on the future. It is a powerful representation of Egypt in transition.[3]

Qāsim Amīn's first book, *The Emancipation of Women*, provoked an angry response from more than one of Egypt's leaders. Many of Muḥammad 'Abduh's reforms they embraced, but this was too much for them. Qāsim Amīn followed up the argument with a second book in 1901, *The New Woman (al-mar'at al-jadīdah)*. His approach was, and has remained, highly controversial. He is still criticised as an influential apostle of westernisation, who misled rather than enlightened his people. In his first book he attacked the current treatment of women as a violation of Islam itself. But, as Dr Zakī Badawī points out in his study *The Reformers of Egypt*, Qāsim Amīn himself shows the intensity of the conflict between Islam and Western concepts. "His first book sought to prove that the freedom of the woman was the intention of the Sharī'a: his second ignored the Sharī'a altogether and drew its concepts from the West."[4] Many were apprehensive of such a development. The debate continued, and when Amīn died, in his early forties, there was little to show for his life's work.

Yet in that same year, 1908, the first of many initiatives in the field of social welfare was taken by a group of Cairo women. And in the homes of Cairo those who would give substance to his concept of "the new woman" were growing to maturity.

One woman already working with him was Malak Ḥifnī Nāṣif, a gifted teacher and writer, who grew up in the midst of the controversies aroused by the growing clamour for reform. Her father was a distinguished member of the group round

Muḥammad 'Abduh, and he gave his daughter a liberal education. She went to the training college for teachers associated with the Ṣaniyyah School, which was founded as early as 1873 and played a pioneer role in the training of Egyptian women. She wrote under the pen-name *Bāḥithat al-Bādiyah,* "Searcher from the desert". In 1911 she presented to the Legislative Assembly a ten-point programme on women's rights, the first formulation of its kind in Egypt.

When she died in 1918, another woman from the same circle of leading families was ready to take up the task. Madame Hoda Sha'arāwy's father was Speaker of the Legislative Assembly, and her husband was one of its members prominent in the struggle for Egypt's independence. In her was found a leader round whom others could unite and make themselves a force in the life of their country at a crucial stage in its development. Already the ideas had been expressed, and the ideological foundation laid, on which the freedom of women could be built. In the 1920s Egypt's women charted a course which many others followed: a path which, in contrast to that of Atatürk's Turkey, sought to cleanse and expand tradition rather than to break completely with it.

There were many other notable pioneers. Madame Ṣafīyah Zaghlūl gathered round her in 1919 a number of women, Hoda Sha'arāwy among them, to act in support of her husband's party, the Wafd. She took an active part in the nationalist movement and twice followed her husband into exile. But after his death in 1928 she kept in the background, though she later took part in the founding of the Federation of Arab Women's Unions in 1944.[5] In the life of Egypt, Copt and Muslim suffered the same disabilities and worked together to remove them. The members of the Wafd Women's Organisation, like the founders of the Egyptian Feminist Union, came from both communities. A host of women, by their individual and corporate actions, created a new climate of opinion in which changes could be carried out.

Cairo in 1919 was in a state of uproar. It was becoming clear that the enlightened ideas of self-determination with which the post-war world was ringing were not to be applied by the Allies to Egypt, nor yet to its Arab neighbours. The fires of patriotism had been kindled, and it was opposition to the British Occupation that occasioned the first public appcarance of Egypt's women. The national spirit focussed in Sa'ad Zaghlūl, leader of the Wafd party, and when he was refused permission to go to England to plead Egypt's case, there were demonstrations. Four of the party leaders, including Madame Shaʿarāwy's husband, were exiled, and an uprising took place. There followed an extraordinary scene in which hundreds of veiled women marched through the streets of Cairo. There were two such demonstrations, on March 16 and April 10, and Hoda Shaʿarāwy was at their head.

These dates appear and reappear in modern Egyptian literature, much as does the Easter Rising of 1916 in that of modern Ireland. As well as the memories of the participants, novels and short stories include descriptions of the events from many differing points of view.[6] The central facts are that British troops found themselves faced by a crowd of women – no less formidable for being heavily veiled. Among them were the wives and daughters of many of Cairo's leading families. To be in the streets unescorted was a bold procedure, let alone the unprecedented initiative of open opposition to authority. The soldiers were nonplussed. Tragically, on April 10 a stray bullet killed one woman in the crowd.

Some actions carry an importance beyond the immediate picture, and add a new dimension to the scene. Hoda Shaʿarāwy's bold act of patriotism was one of these. Further steps on the path of participation in national life were soon to be taken.

The symbol of women's inferior status was the veil. The sign of their stepping into public life must be its removal. This decisive step was taken by Madame Shaʿarāwy in 1923. In 1922, she and her friends formed the Egyptian Feminist Union, *al-ittiḥād al-nisāʾī*, and in the following year three of them went as its representatives to a conference of the International Alliance of Women in Rome. They already had friends in Britain, where the Women's Suffrage Movement had rejoiced in the granting of the vote to women at the end of the First World War. Among those at the conference was Margery Corbett, later Dame Margery Corbett Ashby, who stood for parliament at the first opportunity, in December 1918, and was already a veteran of many campaigns in the field of women's advance. She was to become a life-long friend of the Egyptian women, and one of the constant links between the growing women's movements in the Middle East and Asia, and their friends in Europe.

Madame Shaʿarāwy and her companions, Nabawiyah Mūsā

and Sēza Nabarāwī, returned from Rome. What followed is assessed by one of the most eminent among the women who were to follow them. Madame 'Azīzah Ḥusain has for many years represented her country on the United Nations Status of Women Commission. She is also Chairman of the Cairo Family Planning Association. In 1953 she was in Washington with her husband, Egypt's ambassador to the United States. Speaking at Princeton, she said:

> Thirty years have passed since the first Egyptian woman who dared to defy Egyptian conservatism dramatically cast her veil into the Mediterranean, as she stepped out of the ship that brought her back from a women's conference in Rome. For a long time Egyptian public opinion was outraged by Madame Hoda Sha'arāwy's shocking act: for a long time Sha'arāwy Pasha could not forgive his wife for the embarrassment she had caused him by her scandalous behaviour before the important government officials who had gathered to meet her.
>
> One by one, however, other Egyptian women followed her footsteps, and gradually the women of Egypt pulled down the silken curtain that separated them from the free world – the world of men. The voluntary removal of the veil by Egyptian women marked the beginning of a process of gradual emancipation.[7]

For Hoda Sha'arāwy herself, the price of her action was divorce. But some years later her husband asked her to re-marry him, which she did for the sake of their children.[8]

The newly-formed Egyptian Feminist Union set to work. Its objectives are summarised as follows, in a booklet published for their Golden Jubilee celebrations in 1973.

1. To secure for women equal rights in education at all levels.
2. To obtain for women equal political and civil rights.
3. To abolish licensed prostitution.
4. To raise the marriageable age to sixteen for girls and eighteen for men.
5. To secure on behalf of women favourable reforms in certain aspects of Family Law, such as restrictions of divorce in accordance with the Muslim Law, custody of the children, alimony and such problems.[9]

1923 saw the election of the first parliament in Egypt, replacing the earlier Legislative Assembly. Two of the objectives of the Feminist Union were raised in this parliament: equal educational opportunity, and a minimum marriage age. Within a few months, a law was enacted fixing the legal age for marriage as suggested. In the following year, 1924, a phrase was included in the new constitution, giving an equal chance of education to girls and boys. The members of the new society could take courage from these immediate successes, and address themselves to the long task of making them and the other points on their programme a reality in the life of their nation.[10]

There were many notable pioneers in these early years. Among them three examples may be given, each in her different way typical of others in her generation: Iḥsān al-Qūsī, Nabawiyyah Mūsā, and Bahiah Karām.

Mrs Iḥsān Shākir al-Qūsī was among those who took part in the demonstrations of 1919. In the late twenties she went with her husband to study at the American University of Beirut, and was the first Muslim woman to graduate there, in 1929. This was three years ahead of the first women graduates of Cairo University. She took an active part in the life of the University, and she won a prize in an oratorical contest, choosing as her subject the veil, and claiming that the Qur'ān does not prescribe it as an essential for the Muslim woman. She thus justified her own unusual presence unveiled in a large mixed university.[11]

Her life's work lay in the field of social service. She established a school for social workers, and the women she trained played a large part in developing the welfare services now available in Egypt.

Nabawiyyah Mūsā concentrated her efforts on the intellectual emancipation of women, and especially on their opportunities to work. Unlike most of her generation, she never married. She accompanied Hoda Sha'arāwy to Rome in 1923. Her book *Al-mar'ah wal-'amal* (Women and Work) had already been published in Alexandria in 1920. It was the first to deal with the subject, and was a plea for equality of opportunity in both education and employment. Such a claim aroused strong opposition, but Nabawiyyah Mūsā took to task her own sex, as well as her critics. Women, she says, have themselves contributed to the restrictions placed on their capabilities.

She gives a vivid picture of the contrast between life in the country and life in the city as she saw it, and of the comparative freedom and responsibility of the country wife. Hard though their lot might be, the peasant working force, she thought, gave greater respect and equality to their women.

> Consider the poor Egyptian peasant, *fallāḥ*, and his wife. Both have gained a similar and equal share of experience and knowledge. Often the man recognises the wife's superiority in making decisions. [The peasant] prides himself on the fact that he never embarks on any important project without asking his wife's opinion; she shares his work; she knows all about his daily problems – the obvious ones and the secret ones. If the husband happens to die and leaves behind orphans and as little as an acre of land as sole means of support, the widow, through sheer hard work and dedication, often manages not only to survive but even to make her assets grow . . .
>
> The poor of both the rural and the urban sectors, even sometimes those of middle income, are helped out by their wives. Our religion does not forbid such a condition. Are we to consider them as unbelievers? These families are the backbone of Egypt and the real source of its wealth. Upon them the progress of the country relies. No, religion is not to be blamed in these matters, but, rather, customary rules which have evolved from ignorance.

In comparison, the secluded life of the city woman is seen as cutting her off from reality. "So let us do our utmost to educate women equally with men," is the conclusion.[12]

Educational opportunity did indeed come in the following years. An army of dedicated teachers arose. Among the first of the inspectors of the new schools was Bahiah Karām. She recalls especially the spread of schools in the country areas, and the welcome she and her colleagues received in the villages. In the 1950s she was asked to advise on setting up educational systems in some of the newly independent African countries, and she is thus an example of the contribution made by Egyptian educators not only in their own country but also in many others in the Arab and African world, which have relied on graduates from the Egyptian universities for many of their teachers.

The developments in women's education may be followed through the fortunes of one family, the four daughters of a physician, practising in Cairo in the first quarter of the century. Dr Kāmil al-Sa'īd, at a time when education for girls was a rare commodity, determined that his daughters should have the best. In the early 1920s he sent the two elder girls to school in England. From Cheltenham Ladies' College they went to London University. The first, Karīmah, went to Westfield College to study education. She returned to spend many years in secondary schools as teacher and principal. Through the problems of the girls she taught, and of their families, she developed a great interest in social problems. She was transferred to work in the Ministry of Education, and in 1965 was appointed Under Secretary, the first woman to hold that position. On her retirement, she was asked to take on the responsibility for the women's side of the Arab Socialist Union, which was the only political party in Egypt during a period of over fifteen years, from 1962 to 1978. One of its aims was to develop new forms of social initiative, in the villages as well as in the towns, and to cover the whole nation by forming committees of women who would tackle local needs and problems. This aim she greatly furthered. She moved round the country, and narrowed the gulf between city and village. "We give suggestions, not directives," she said. "In whole areas there may be only one woman graduate, and such places ask for suggestions what to do. It is essential to keep in touch with what is actually happening, so that the work in headquarters is relevant."[13]

For their education her two youngest sisters stayed in Cairo. In 1925 a government secondary school for girls was established, with the same curriculum as that for boys, leading to a baccalaureate and university entrance. Amīnah, born in 1914, was thus able to have her schooling from home. In 1929, the first girls in this school qualified for entrance to Cairo University. The Rector was Aḥmad Luṭfī al-Sayyid, a liberal thinker and a great supporter of women's education. The Dean of the Faculty of Arts was Dr Ṭāhā Ḥusain, blind writer and scholar, one of a number of prominent Egyptians who had offered to advise the women on legal and other matters.[14] He decided to admit the girls. Amīnah al-Sa'īd, in a programme broadcast by the BBC on "The New Egyptians" (August 1977) described what happened.

> The Director of Cairo University was a very progressive man and he decided to allow girls to come. When we went to talk to him before the school year opened, he took a promise from us never to mention it to anybody. He said: "You will sneak into the university. The day of the opening you will be there, five or ten girls, and it will be too late for anybody to dismiss you." So we kept the promise, we never mentioned it to anybody, and the first day we were there, the first girls to come into the university.[15]

There is a photograph of the first graduates, gathered by Hoda Sha'arāwy at a party in their honour in 1933. Behind the huge bunches of flowers the faces are gay and determined. Among them was Sohair Qalamāwy, who was to be the first to win her way on to the staff of Cairo University, and then to become professor and head of the Department of Arabic Literature.

Amīnah al-Sa'īd decided on journalism. She worked closely with Hoda Sha'arāwy until her death in 1947. In 1954 Amīnah started the woman's magazine *Ḥawā* (Eve), which has the largest foreign circulation of any Arabic paper. It is to be found on the bookstalls wherever Arab journals are sought. It is produced by Dār al-Hilāl, a publishing house that has grown out of one of the first Egyptian periodicals, *Al-Hilāl* (*The Crescent*). This first appeared in 1892 and still continues. The company now publishes large numbers of books and magazines for the whole of the Arab World, and Amīnah al-Sa'īd is its President. She is one of the most respected and forceful voices in modern Egypt, and has often been one of President Sadat's entourage during important journeys. She was in Jerusalem with him in November 1977.

Both President Nasser and President Sadat have supported the advance of women. The laws now governing their working conditions are as advanced as anywhere in the world, said Mrs Amīnah in the same BBC programme quoted above. She added:

> But it was not quite like that when I started in the Thirties. I earned £2 a month, and then £4 a month. I remember when they gave me a rise to £6. I thought myself a capitalist and above reproach, and started to be lazy in my work, so they fired me. It was a very good help for me, because this firing me pushed me into rethinking myself. I had to read and read and read to improve my knowledge in everything, so only two years later they came and begged me to come back with £60! They fired me with £6, and they got me back after two years with £60. As it is, a working woman even now has to have a lot of courage to prove herself.[16]

The last male preserve in the University of Cairo was the Faculty of Engineering, which for long resisted admitting women. One of those who entered it when the doors finally opened was Mrs Amīnah's daughter-in-law, who is now chief engineer in her own stone factory, situated in the desert outside Cairo, where marble is cut up to make slabs and tiles. These are in great demand in Cairo's building boom. She herself designed some of the machines, trained her work-force, and went into production. Even with the respectable precedents for women owning and running a business, such work is far from easy. She says:

> I think I am the first woman to work in the stone industry, so of course at the very beginning I faced some discontent. My workers think that a woman is inferior to a man, and because they respect me very much, they talk to me as ''Mr Engineer''. When I was at a secondary school I discovered that I liked mathematics very much, and also mechanics and the scientific branch in general. So I decided to join the faculty of engineering. My father wanted me to be a physician or something more feminine, but I decided what I wanted to do.[17]

The women of this family are not isolated instances. They dramatically represent the activities of two generations of Egyptian women who pioneered their way into different professions earlier regarded as the preserves of men, thus making it possible for hundreds and thousands of women to work side by side with men on an equal footing in almost every occupation and profession.

Political advance came more slowly than professional. After the death of Hoda Shaʿarāwy the outstanding figure in the women's movement was Durriyah Shafīk. Her style of leadership was very different, militantly feminist and somewhat flamboyant. With her is associated the gaining of political rights. Even before 1952 she led a demonstration demanding these.

1952, the year of Egypt's Revolution, was a landmark for women as for the nation as a whole. Free secondary education had been granted in 1950; after the Revolution university education was made free, and therefore became available on a far wider scale. In 1954 a body was set up to revise the constitution, and no woman was included in it. Durriyah Shafīk and others boldly challenged Nasser by starting a hunger strike – on the premises of the Journalists' Syndicate, to ensure maximum publicity. In the 1956 constitution Nasser in fact granted political equality to women: they were given the vote, and in the following elections two women were returned to the People's Assembly.

The National Charter, issued in 1962, summed up a process already far advanced. ''Woman must be regarded as equal to man and must shed the remaining shackles that impede her from taking a constructive part in national life.''[18]

The 1970s have been the jubilee years of the advances begun by the pioneers of the 1920s. One by one, the events that followed the revolution of 1919 have been recalled and celebrated. In March 1973, the Hoda Sha'arāwy Association (as the Egyptian Feminist Union had come to be called) held Golden Jubilee celebrations in Cairo.

The hall was crowded with hundreds of women, many of whom had been the first to venture into some chosen field of work, and thus play their part in building a modern nation. Presiding was Mrs Bahīgah Rashīd Sidqy, who joined the Feminist Union in 1925, only two years after it was founded. Her husband, Ḥasan Rashīd, was a leading composer, and part of his opera *Anthony and Cleopatra* enriched a musical evening given to the guests. She herself has gathered and published many of the folk songs of the villages in the Delta and Upper Egypt: an example of a piece of work begun by one woman and later taken up at government level.

The President's wife, Mrs Jihān Sadāt, spoke at the opening ceremony. Her own efforts have been channelled in two directions: care for war victims and their families through the organisation known as *Al-Nūr wal-'Amal* (Light and Hope), and a steady campaign for a better legal position for women. This was to some extent achieved by a presidential decree amending the Personal Status Law, ratified by the People's Assembly on 3 July 1979.

Delegates from Arab countries came to the 1973 Jubilee celebrations, together with others from the United States, the Soviet Union, Rumania and Hungary. A great ovation greeted ninety-three-year-old Dame Margery Corbett Ashby from Britain. She spoke of fifty years past and fifty more ahead: of women's character and women's programme. "The moral courage that can face up to ridicule – that is the rarest of virtues," she said. "We work with men to bring about peace and justice."

Madame Seza Nabarāwy, who was with Hoda Sha'arāwy in Rome in 1923, was present: also Iḥsān al-Qūsī, veteran of 1919, who was later responsible for the development of the training of social workers, a large profession now honourably established. Among many educators and writers were the sisters Karīmah and Amīnah al-Sa'īd. There were numbers of pioneer doctors: Dr Ḍuḥā Ghunaim for instance, widow of a much-loved Minister of

Health, who bravely took on her husband's work in the field of child medicine after his untimely death; and Dr Zahīrah 'Ābidīn, whose work on rheumatism and tuberculosis among children centres in her own hospital, built in the clear air near the Pyramids.

The daughters of these pioneers are many of them eminent in their own lines. In the succession of grandmother, mother and daughter, there are many instances where the grandmother could not read, the mother is a professor, and the daughter has stepped into a different professional field.

Tribute should be paid to the part played by unknown mothers in the women's movement: numbers of great-hearted women, generously determined to aid their daughters' progress. One professor acknowledges her gratitude to such a mother, bringing up her family in the Cairo of the thirties. Unable herself to read, she was determined that her three daughters should be educated. The establishment of Government Secondary Schools for girls opened the possibility of further education to a new class, the traders and shopkeepers of Cairo. But it cost money. In this family, payment of fees was out of the question. The eldest girl was sent to the one available free school for "women's education", teaching embroidery. It was hard and it was dull and the girl came home in tears, refusing to go again. She got a beating for her pains. "No daughter of mine is going to sit at home untaught, and then be entirely dependent on her husband." The two younger girls won coveted scholarships to secondary schools, and then to university: they are both professors, and their sister holds a post in the Ministry of Social Affairs.[19]

Not all mothers were so helpful. Professor 'Ā'ishah Murād is the pioneer of both physical education and physiotherapy in her country. When in the early 1930s she had the opportunity to go to England, her mother determinedly stood in her way. It was some years before another scholarship came her way: to Bedford College of Physical Education. By hard work, she managed to qualify in both Physical Training and Physiotherapy. Back home, her inexhaustible energies were divided between her teaching, her clinic and her family. She also nurtured the Girl Guide Movement, which grew to several thousand strong under her leadership, and she maintained her own and Egypt's links with the world at many international conferences. Her daughter, Magdah Fahmy 'Izz, went to Cairo's School of Ballet. She then spent eight years in Moscow. Her thesis for her Doctorate of Philosophy was based on the study of Pharaonic dances as depicted in early Egyptian murals. A brilliant dancer, her passion is teaching, especially children. Examples of her choreography have been taken abroad by prize-winning Egyptian teams.

Of the original aims of the Egyptian Feminist Union, most have been achieved. Regulated prostitution was abolished in 1949.[20] In 1950, secondary education was made free for girls as well as boys, and free university education followed after the Revolution of 1952. In that year only 3,490 girls were at university. By 1970, the figure had risen to 43,255: an increase in the percentage of girls to boys from 8 per cent to 28 per cent.[21]

In 1956, the right to vote was given to the women of Egypt, and shortly afterwards the first women stood for election to the National Assembly. In 1962, Dr Ḥikmat Abū Zaid was appointed Minister for Social Affairs, a post in which she was followed by Dr ʿĀʾishah Rāṭib, Professor of International Law in Cairo University, and in 1977 by Dr Amāl ʿUthmān. Also in 1962, the University of Al-Azhar opened its doors to women, and Dr Zainab Rāshid set up the Al-Azhar Women's College, now housed in new buildings with over three thousand students drawn from all over the Muslim world. Women graduates of this and other Egyptian universities have contributed greatly to the development of educational and medical services in other parts of the Arab World and of Africa. As diplomats and lawyers they hold responsible positions in the United Nations and other international bodies.

"There has been a very great change in the public status of women," says Professor Sohair Qalamāwy. "What is needed now is an equivalent change in her personal standing within the family itself."[22] "The amendment of the Family Laws is the only one of the original objectives unrealised," stated a report on the Hoda Shaʿarāwy Association, at the time of the 1973 Golden Jubilee Celebrations.[23]

Mrs Amīnah al-Saʿīd and others have been campaigning for years to bring about such changes, and Madame Jihān Sadāt has steadily exerted her influence in this direction. There have been many set-backs, but in July 1979 a Presidential decree introduced a new law of Personal Status, which was ratified by the People's Assembly. It introduced a number of reforms, though by no means all that had been sought.

More important even than a change in the laws is the need for a profound alteration in attitudes. Mrs Amīnah al-Saʿīd stresses this, in a lecture on "The Arab Woman and the Challenge of Society".

> As the world has changed so radically, so has the status of woman changed from that of a follower or marginal person to one who has the status of a full and equal person and citizen. In the Western countries, this movement proceeded gradually . . . [taking] perhaps long enough for people to digest the changes. But as for us, in the Arab countries, the change when it did come, came very late and very suddenly . . .
>
> One of the most important challenges facing the Arab woman today is trying to equate her inner self, her thoughts and attitudes and feelings, with the contemporary social reality about her . . . Society may move at an astonishing speed, but the mind is not able to keep up the pace . . . We have yet to achieve a balance between the development of the *form* of our new societies, and the development of the *content*, personal and general, of those societies . . .
>
> We cannot simply design a new person, a new society, by building an outer model. What we must do is change the person, the society, from the inside. For it is difficult for an individual to work to change the life around him until he has been successful in changing himself into a person with a new style of ideas, a new set of *mores* which he can apply in the fields of work, as well as in personal relations. Such change must come to the whole community before new goals can be achieved. Thus it must be clear by now that not only should woman be changed and elevated, from inside as well as from outside, but we must work with the same force to change the essence of the man as well. For the man must work together with the woman to be able to co-ordinate these new values, to be able to face the obvious difficulties, the inevitable clashes which will occur in both the spiritual and the material spheres of life.
>
> Even in the most progressive parts of the Arab world we have scarcely begun this mammoth task.[24]

Co-operation for Progress

"The State is a carriage with two wheels – its men and its women – working together for progress."

Muḥammad ʿAlī Jinnah

"Social welfare is an enabling process – a catalyst to help people realise their own needs. Each effort is unique. In some cases there are resources available. In others, innovation and hard work are all there is to rely on, and even though the result may seem less impressive it is far more important. To start schools and hospitals is not enough. We must build *people,* who are the fabric of community development."

Begum Tazeen Faridi, Secretary General of the All Pakistan Women's Association, 1974

"A bird cannot fly with one wing,
And it is known that one hand cannot clap."

Jamīl Ṣidqī al-Zahawī, Iraqi poet

Chapter Fifteen

The Birth of Pakistan

Islam reached the Indian sub-continent almost as soon as it penetrated along the north coast of Africa. Within a few years of the Prophet's death traders from Arabia were practising their faith in Sind (now part of Pakistan), and Bengal (now part of Bangladesh). A military expedition invaded Sind as Arab armies were sweeping across Spain, in the year 94/712. Some illustrious names of women in India's history have already been mentioned. The rule of the Mogul emperors united the peninsula for the first time, and only came to an end with the coming of the British. It was finally abolished after the tragic events of the Revolt of 1857, (known to the British as the Indian Mutiny and to Indians as the first War of Independence). The fortunes of the Muslim communities, and the status of their women, were at their lowest ebb.

It is worth quoting an assessment of this period by a woman historian. Dr Parveen Shaukat Ali writes:

> The status of women during the Muslim rule over the sub-continent, and later under British rule, was based mostly on custom and environment produced by the interaction of various cultural and religious groups. It was not, however, strictly according to religious principles. Islam had given woman a very respectable niche, had conferred upon her certain fundamental rights in matters relating to marriage, divorce and inheritance. Her social dignity and the contributions she could make towards the betterment of life in society were recognised in unequivocal terms. In practice, however, over the Indo-Pakistan sub-continent like the rest of the Muslim world, women were degraded in social prestige and economic equality. They were mostly confined to domestic drudgery and, draped in *purdah*, they were completely debarred from public life. Ideals of chastity and virtue were formulated in a manner that always favoured men.[1]

Conditions, she continues, further deteriorated after 1857, when the Mogul rule came to an end. Muslims felt a deep sense of humiliation and despondency. But towards the end of the century there were signs of regeneration. One of these was the Aligarh movement, led by Sir Syed Ahmad Khan. He and those who worked with him opened new vistas of progress.

> They dispelled the false notion that Islam was hostile to change, and that it locked the Muslim community within the impenetrable fortress of conservatism. Many of them were great scholars of the Quranic doctrine, and their interpretation of Islamic principles of social organisation compelled the Muslims to take a fresh look at the orthodoxies and customs which had retarded their progress for such a long time. The imperceptible infiltration of the ideals of Western liberalism also helped a great deal in creating an awareness which was needed to revise the dead hopes and aspirations of the Muslims.
>
> It was in these circumstances that the Muslim women over the sub-continent for the first time felt the pulse of liberation.[2]

Syed Ahmad himself said, "There is no doubt that for the development of national culture and civilisation the education of women is essential."[3] Alongside the famous university he founded in Aligarh, a college for women played an important role in opening new possibilities for them, and his daughter Mrs Mumtāz J. Haidar was Principal of this college for over thirty years, from 1935 onwards. Muḥammad Iqbāl, spiritual father of the revival of Islam in India, also emphasised that the place accorded to woman in Muslim society was derogatory both to human dignity and to Islam itself. These ideas were formulated and carried forward by Amīr 'Alī, whose classic work *The Spirit of Islam* first appeared in 1891. It was dedicated to his wife, and it contained a chapter devoted to the position of women.

Amīr 'Alī did much of his life's work in England. His writing aimed at stimulating fresh thought in the minds of his own people, and also at educating English public opinion about India. For fifty years he was a contributor to *The Nineteenth Century*, one of the periodicals which did so much to form opinion and spread liberal ideas at the turn of the century. In reply to attacks on the spiritual and ethical standards of Islam, he wrote two articles in this journal: "The Real Status of Women in Islam" (1891) and "The Influence of Women in Islam" (1899).[4]

"Taken as a whole, the legal status of the Mohammedan woman

is not more unfavourable than that of a European woman, whilst in many respects she occupies a decidedly better position," he said. "If they do not in another hundred years attain to the social position of European women, there will be time enough to declaim against Islam as a system and dispensation."[5]

His writings were parallel to those of Muḥammad ʿAbduh and Qāsim Amīn in Egypt, and carried to a wide and influential audience the same liberalising ideas, rooted in the same Muslim traditions.

The growing desire throughout all India for freedom was reflected in the founding of the National Congress in 1885, and of the Muslim League in 1906. Though finally unable to reconcile their different ambitions, they worked together in opposing British rule. Syed Ahmad and others who succeeded him strongly emphasised the common loyalties of all Indians. The struggle for freedom was carried forward together, and women played a conspicuous part in it.

In Muslim India, women were already coming to play an influential role. The State of Bhopal, in Central India, was ruled by a succession of princesses from 1844 until 1926. In 1901 the third of these, Sulṭān Jahān Begum, followed her mother and her grandmother as Nawāb of this important territory, with its seven thousand square miles of fertile land and forest. She encouraged agricultural and industrial development, and paid special attention to providing medical care and education for women. She started schools with all these aspects of her people's life in view. In her book, *An Account of My Life*, she describes the founding of the first school for girls in 1903. The provision of mistresses was the greatest obstacle, she says. European ladies would not suit, principally because of the language difficulty. Muslim teachers were most difficult to find. And there was no suitable curriculum ready to be adopted. True, there were a few schools for girls in British India, but the British could not fully understand the requirements, and this was a responsibility that should be borne by the Muslims themselves. So, she continues, "I made the best of my resources and made a start with a few classes in which the Holy Quran with its translation, Urdu, Arithmetic, Geography and Domestic Economy were taught. For the opening ceremony the school rooms and the adjoining grounds were tastefully decorated with flags and bunting of all colours."[6]

One hundred and forty girls under ten were enrolled. Closed carriages decorously carried them to and from their homes. In 1907, a similar school was opened for Hindu girls "whose claims on my attention were quite as insistent as those of their Mussalman sisters."[7] It was a small beginning, but one that would rapidly expand, until a few years later numbers of schools and colleges all over the Indian sub-continent would be opening their doors to the successors of those first one hundred and forty little girls.

An American writer recounts an unforgettable visit to the Begum twenty years later, shortly before her death. "She told me of her interest in building schools and hospitals, not splendid palaces and public edifices as her mother had done." She had the satisfaction of seeing a change in public attitude, especially to women's education. "In the beginning I had to pay the parents. Now they ask to have their daughters admitted and pay for the privilege." She measured her achievement not by bricks and mortar but by the awakening of her people through her efforts.[8]

In 1915 the Begum of Bhopal and others founded the All India Muslim Ladies Conference, which aimed at creating a general awakening among Muslim women. One of her colleagues was Begum Habibullah of Lucknow. She was a woman of wide influence, coming of a family which traced its descent from the Prophet, and which had long been associated with one of the great Ṣūfī orders. She took an interest in the founding of the first mosque in England, at Woking in Surrey. She was one of those who followed the example of Bhopal in starting schools for girls in different parts of India. Later, at Jinnah's request, she was to move the resolution which fully enlisted women in the Pakistan movement, at Patna in 1938. After the 1947 partition, she herself stayed on in Lucknow, until she died in 1975 at the age of ninety. Her daughter Begum Tazeen Faridi, however, went to Karachi, was a founding member of the All Pakistan Women's Association, and for many years its Secretary General.

The first steps taken by the ladies who met together in 1915 were directed towards setting up more schools for girls. Soon, however, women in a number of leading families began to take part in political activities. In the 1920s women still in *purdah* demonstrated that they could participate effectively in national affairs. Others, in increasing numbers, laid aside the veil. In 1930

Begum Shah Nawaz was one of the delegates sent to the Round Table Conference in London. Fāṭimah Jinnah, younger sister of Muḥammad 'Alī Jinnah, accompanied her brother to this conference.

This forward movement among Muslim women was still limited to a handful of families which had taken a lead in accepting Western education. "The majority of Muslim women," says Dr Shaukat Ali, "were still illiterate, and their participation in national life was almost non-existent. Most of them were still the mute spectators of the changes taking place around them. In the name of custom and religion their life was still confined to the four walls of the house. Co-education, mixing with men outside the limited circle of one's own family, was still an unpardonable social sin. The tempo of political changes on the sub-continent was however so fast that these conditions could not last."[9] From 1938 onwards the enrolment of women in the League became an important feature, and they were actively associated with every move towards the new state. The Quaid-i-Azam, Muḥammad 'Alī Jinnah himself, compared the state to "a carriage with two wheels, its men and its women, working together for progress".[10] In a speech at Lahore in 1942, delivered at the Jinnah Islamia College for Girls, he appealed for the co-operation of women. "I am glad to see that not only Muslim men but Muslim women and children also have understood the Pakistan scheme. If Muslim women support their men, as they did in the days of the Prophet of Islam, we should soon realise our goal."[11]

1938 was notable for a decisive advance in women's political and social standing, assuring them of a prominent place in the struggle for Pakistan and in the future state. In December, at a conference in Patna, the All India Muslim League adopted a resolution outlining the role of women and forming an All India Muslim Women's Sub-committee. This was the period of Fāṭimah Jinnah's active leadership. A dentist by training, she devoted her time and energies not to her own career but to the support of her brother, acting as his hostess. Following the Patna Resolution, she made a rapid tour of India, establishing women's committees. Her enthusiasm and example won the hearts of many younger women. Those who joined her "symbolised the new generation of female leadership. They were brave, unveiled and progressive in outlook and ambitions. They infused new dynamism in the feminist movement and, uninhibited by custom and tradition, they taught Muslim women to agitate and protest against injustice."[12]

Among them was Begum Shaista Ikramullah. She belonged to the Suhrawardy family, prominent in Bengal, where her cousin was prime minister. She lived in *purdah* until 1933 and she had an unusual education. Qur'ān learning and kindergarten started for her at the same time, and the colourful, busy life of a large traditional household was combined with the education of a convent school. In 1940, when she first met the Jinnahs, she was living in Delhi, and her husband was a leading civil servant, which made political activity difficult for his wife. He and many others still did not take seriously the proposition of the formation of Pakistan, and indeed it was only in 1940 that the policy of a separate state was officially adopted by the Muslim League.

Fāṭimah Jinnah asked her to sponsor the formation of the Muslim Women Students' Federation. Thus began many years of outstanding service to the cause of Pakistan, at a point when many in leading circles in Delhi did not have the courage to give open support. When Pakistan was established in August 1947 Begum Ikramullah went to Karachi, and she took her seat in the first session of the Constituent Assembly of Pakistan in February 1948.

Later she described her career in a book, *From Purdah to Parliament*. In it she talks of her friend Fāṭimah Jinnah, and what her leadership gave to the cause of Pakistan.

"So many people now doing very important work for Pakistan were given their first job by Miss Jinnah. She is an extremely good judge of character and capabilities and she has a quality rare in prominent people, that she does not get taken in by flattery. She can assess a person pretty shrewdly almost on the first meeting but no amount of trying would get you on much further with her unless she herself wished it." "Not everyone has the knack of finding the right person for the right place, or giving the right person an opportunity." Her skill lay in "finding and setting other women to do useful jobs", and wherever she went she started some useful work, as well as setting up a political framework: Women's Industrial Homes, for example, and Relief Committees, which foreshadowed the later work of the All Pakistan Women's Association.[13] She was also the founder of the

Fatimah Jinnah Women's Medical College, Lahore.

After her brother's death only a year after the establishment of Pakistan, she stayed in the background, though in 1965 she was persuaded to stand for President. This "Mother of the Country", *Madar-i-Millat*, as she was known, came second in the poll which elected President Ayyub.[14]

August 1947, and the achievement of freedom, was only the beginning of Pakistan's struggles. The years that followed were to be full of physical and material anguish. Ill-prepared for partition, vast numbers of people moved across improvised boundaries, driven by fear from homes in which they no longer felt secure. Those moving west met others moving east for the same reasons, and many were killed. Muslims, Sikhs, Hindus, all clashed and all suffered. When the human tides subsided some twenty million had been uprooted and an estimated two million men, women, and children were dead.

The two halves of the new nation, separated by a thousand miles from each other, both had crowds of helpless refugees. It was in this emergency that the women of Pakistan came out of the shelter of their homes. "In the relief and rehabilitation of the homeless millions, women and girl students from schools and colleges made tremendous contributions. They cooked, distributed medicines, worked in mobile dispensaries, established homes for the weak and the destitute . . . and demonstrated their immeasurable ability for social work."[15]

The wife of the first Prime Minister, Liaqat Ali Khan, played a leading part in this phase of the nation's history. Begum Ra'ana was a dynamo of energy, and inspired by her example women who had never before left home came by the hundred to help in the hospitals and transit camps. At night they drove in trucks to take blankets, clothing and food to those by the roadside who had not yet been able to reach a camp. The Prime Minister made his headquarters in Lahore, where refugees were pouring in over the border, ragged, penniless, diseased. Cholera broke out, hospitals were hopelessly overcrowded and understaffed. The immediate organisations set up were merged in 1949 in the All Pakistan Women's Association (APWA), which has since then for thirty years been a force for social change and educational development throughout the country.

Twenty-five years later, at the Silver Jubilee Conference of

APWA, Begum Tazeen Faridi recalled the days of the founding of the association.

> Some of us were old, others young, some revolutionary, some conservative, but all fired with one dream: Pakistan. In February 1949 APWA was founded by Begum Liaqat Ali Khan, the far-sighted partner of a wise husband. This was no individual effort but the result of getting together a band of highly motivated women from all walks of life, including highly qualified professional women and housewives. In the Prime Minister's house was APWA's first office. Here women from many environments, social and political, would meet and chalk out plans. Artisans would bring their wares, women and child refugees would bring their complaints. It was through the co-operation of many interests and many local leaders that APWA gained its roots through all the districts of East and West Pakistan.[16]

Three years later, she adds, at a conference attended by women from many Muslim countries, "the organisation decided to deal with the whole spectrum of women's problems and changed from an emergency rehabilitation body to a full-fledged women's movement."[17]

APWA is voluntary and non-governmental, and has provincial and local branches all through Pakistan. Though non-political, it has a powerful voice in government circles, and it maintains links with many women's organisations abroad. It has taken the initiative in tackling social needs of all sorts: in starting schools, clinics, cottage industries, and in family planning. Other organisations have picked up different threads in the needed reforms: the Federation of University Women, the Business and Professional Women's Association, Girl Guides, and many others. Between them they have been responsible "for creating a tremendous wave of social consciousness among the hitherto secluded and conservative women of Pakistan. This is, in its achievements and potentialities, a social revolution of far-reaching import . . . The fact that it has taken place, and continues to gather momentum, without violence and undue bitterness, noisy demonstration or unseemly wrangling, is a tribute, among other things, to the wisdom and common sense of APWA's Founder President."[18]

Begum Ra'ana's husband died at the hands of an assassin in 1951. "God gives and God takes, but God's work of service to humanity must go on, and must rise above all personal grief, however great," she said, carrying out an engagement to open a hospital two days later.[19] Her work for her country has taken her far afield: as ambassador to Holland, Italy, and Tunisia; on committees and commissions of the United Nations and the International Labour Organisation; as governor of the province of Sind, and chancellor of the University of Karachi. As early as 1950 she paid a visit to Cairo, to the successors of Hoda Shaʿarāwy in the Egyptian Feminist Union.[20] In 1979 she received the Human Rights Award of the United Nations.

To establish and continue clinics, workshops and schools with voluntary workers is no easy task. Ten points are given in the same Silver Jubilee Report, "ten commandments" for leaders, evidence of a practical approach and a wide humanity. They call for a genuine love of people; an openness to learn; an intense faith; a desire for co-operation; the courage to experiment; personal initiative; infectious enthusiasm; willingness to revise and re-think; a simple approach; and finally, tenacity: "Hang on, in spite of setbacks, and win through."[21]

Some women in the new nation also stepped into prominence in the political arena. The transformation of a divided and ineffective Muslim League into the successful instrument for the birth of a nation had surprised many observers. Begum Ikramullah describes it as "one of the greatest miracles of modern times".[22] It was due at least in part to the mobilising of the women, with their unexplored potential of initiative and ability. She herself was one of the first members of the Constituent Assembly. She describes the occasion of its opening. One by one, each member came up to the dais to offer allegiance to the new state. In the debate that followed, it was suggested that the Assembly should meet alternately in Karachi and Dacca. Begum Ikramullah, herself from Bengal, took courage to speak up in support of this. The Prime Minister, Liaqat Ali Khan, remarked in mock horror, "Women never understand the practical difficulties." "If they had," was the retort, "we would not have got Pakistan today." "And so my parliamentary career began," she says.[23] She was a member for seven years.

She was to take part in a long struggle. It was recognised that without the active help of the women freedom would not have been achieved. But however great their contribution, they were disappointed by the lack of recognition they received. The Constituent Assembly had a dual function: day-to-day legislation, and the drafting of a constitution. Dr Shaukat Ali describes what took place.

> Pakistani women faced an uphill task for the recognition of their rights. Since religion played a very decisive role in the creation of Pakistan, immediately after its inception religious circles became very active in their demand to mould the character of Pakistan society strictly according to the notions they had traditionally accepted as part of the religion. One of such notions was that women had to be saved from Western education, and the hue and cry for female rights was considered a political stunt of vested interests. The result was that in the Constituent Assembly which met to draft the constitution of Pakistan, the conservative elements put up a stubborn resistance to every issue that was raised in defence of women's rights. Begum Shah Nawaz and Begum Shaista Ikramullah, the leading women representatives in the Assembly, had to fight bitter battles against entrenched male prejudices in the Fundamental Rights Committee, the Franchise Committee, and the Nationality Committee.
>
> In September 1954, at the last meeting of the Constituent Assembly, the charter of women's rights was put forward for discussion and adoption. The charter asked for a 3 per cent reservation of seats for women in the Central and Provincial Assemblies, and also sought equality of status, equality of opportunity, equal pay for equal work, and demanded female rights for Muslim women under the Islamic Personal Law of the Shariat. The charter of rights became a subject of prolonged and acrimonious debate. Its critics pointed out that many of the demands envisaged in the charter had not been legally accepted even in the advanced countries of the West, and for the new state of Pakistan, caught up in the troubles of nation building, it was not possible to adopt such a radical measure. Its supporters, however, pointed out that to deny women their fundamental rights was preposterous because they constituted almost half the electorate in the country.[24]

Each of the various attempts to draw up a constitution in Pakistan has contained an impressive list of equal rights for women, including the vote at twenty-one, and the reservation of a number of seats in the national and provincial assemblies in view of the difficulties involved for women in entering public life. The constitution of 1973 laid down:

1. All citizens are equal under the law.
2. There shall be no discrimination on the basis of sex.
3. Nothing in this shall prevent the making of any special provision for the protection of women and children.[25]

Women made good use of the opportunities the constitution afforded them in the provincial assemblies, as well as at the centre. The massive immigration of 1947 added to a complex mixture of indigenous peoples. The four provinces that make up the present Pakistan differ in language, culture and history. The majority, Punjabis and Sindis, have more resources and education than do their brothers and sisters in the border provinces of Baluchistan and the North West Frontier. Each of these has its links of tribe and language across the borders into Afghanistan and Iran, and in the 1970s they have been restless members of the national whole. Similar factors to those which in 1971 detached East from West Pakistan are elsewhere present. There is a delicate balance between the unifying ideology of Islam and the strong regional loyalties. APWA itself, with its network of social and educational work throughout the nation, has been one of the bridges between the different elements in the population.

Nearly four million of the women of Pakistan live in the hills and valleys of the North West Frontier Province, where the regional language is Pushto and mountain tribes guard the historic Khyber Pass between Afghanistan and the Indus Valley. Only 10 per cent of the population is urban. The level of literacy, of education and of health care is lower than in the rest of the country, and most of the women are still in *purdah*. They have nevertheless found opportunities to play an active and varied part in the development of their people. Some stepped forward at the time of the referendum held in 1947 to decide whether or no the province would join Pakistan. One woman became provincial Minister of Education. Others have made their mark in social work, journalism and broadcasting. More than a hundred community centres have been established, with the aim of fostering self-help, qualities of leadership, and skills that can improve the individual's economic position.

"Our Frontier women have contributed something to the whole nation," says one of them. "Islam is its one binding force. Our living has fallen short of its ideals. That is why we are divided. We need an aim and an incentive big enough to keep us together: building a nation rather than merely adding to a population."

The pioneers of the days of Independence are still a force to reckon with. They have served Pakistan in many capacities, in public and in private life, and have been prominent in government and diplomacy as well as in education and health. Among many doctors one may be mentioned. Dr Fatimah Shah, who used her medical skill in the work of APWA from its beginning, later lost her sight. Undeterred, she went abroad for special training, and took on the needs of the blind. In 1976 she was elected President of the International Association of the Blind. She was APWA's choice as Woman of the Year in International Women's Year, 1975. Following the pioneers are the growing numbers of women in all the professions: teachers, lawyers, doctors, nurses and social workers.

There is a long way to go. To bridge the gap between theory and practice, legal equality and actual status, is a slow process. But the pioneers can see a long distance covered. Begum Ikramullah, writing after her seven years in parliament, speaks of the demands of those days of new and heavy responsibility, not only in parliament but also outside the country, when she was sent as a delegate to the Third Session of the United Nations in Paris in 1948, and later to study educational methods in the United States in 1951. With all this work went the constant care of home and children. "I tried very hard not to fail," she says.

"In the dust and strife of life in Parliament, I often longed for the peace and leisure of the days in *purdah*. But there could be no turning back, no return to the secluded and sheltered existence of the past . . . I had to continue on this new road on which the women of my country had set out, in which one could taste the joys of achievement as well as the bitterness of failure, and know both hope and fear, disillusionment and attainment.

"And who can deny that this is a richer, fuller and a more rewarding existence?"[26]

The next generation looks ahead. Dr Shaukat Ali, reviewing the situation in 1975, says:

> Like the rest of the world, the feminist movement in Pakistan has been growing in strength and popularity, but it still has a long and hard road ahead of it.
>
> Acceptance of the charter by the legislature and a favourable review of women's legal status are not sufficient to ameliorate the lot of Pakistani women. They still suffer from basic inabilities. The humdrum domestic world consumes most of their time and energies, and their destiny continues to be at the mercy of the male members of society. In education and professions, their path is still strewn with

insurmountable barriers of custom and religious prejudices. The women of Pakistan, however, have not been disheartened by the social and economic disadvantages which still hinder their progress. They have powerful organisations which act as pressure groups and articulate women's interests, and work for the protection of their rights . . .

Compared to riot-ridden suffragette movements in the Western countries, the feminist movement in Pakistan has been comparatively uneventful. Public demonstration and protest for the defence of women's rights have been only brief interludes in the otherwise smooth and peaceful reformative crusade for the uplift of the down-trodden better half of Pakistan. The objectives of most of the feminist organisations are education, vocational training and economic independence. Many of them get generous subsidies from the government to meet the ever-increasing expenses of their educational work. In spite of difficulties, through publicity and propaganda they keep the decision-making chambers of the country under constant pressure, and through their perseverance have been able to win many silent battles against conservative and reactionary forces.

It would be wrong and misleading to say that their final victory is round the corner. The path is still long and uncertain and some quarters continüe to be hostile. But the general atmosphere in society is encouraging and one can hope that in the years ahead the women of Pakistan will be able to acquire a respectable position which would be supported by law and religion.[27]

Women in the Algerian Revolution

"Me? A hero? Who told you that? The hero is Algeria. As for me, well, I was only one person in a large group . . .

"There were thousands of Jamilahs, just like me. They all moved, like me, from the Qasbah to the French quarter. Carrying bombs in their handbags and throwing them into cafés. I'm not really sure why all the publicity ended up centring on me. For there were many women in the prison with me, subjected to the worst kinds of torture, and they didn't betray their comrades either . . . All of us were parts in the whole . . . Our aim was revolution, our aim was independence. We won both.

"Down with legends, my friend! . . . The Algerian woman lives, her existence was proved by her performance in battle, and she continues to prove her existence in working for her country. You can find her everywhere, as a member of parliament, a teacher, an office worker. It's true we don't find as many women in politics as men, but women have always imposed their views in a quieter way without public fuss. I believe the role the Algerian women play today, rebuilding what has been demolished, regaining what has been lost, is as important as the role they played in battle."

Jamīlah Buḥrayd, heroine of the Algerian Revolution

Chapter Sixteen

Independence and After

The immense upheaval in the Muslim world in the years following the Second World War represents a change as great as any other in its history. One of the major outcomes of the First World War was the final disintegration of the Ottoman Empire, and with it the structure that had held together the central Muslim lands for four centuries. Many then supposed that Islam as a political influence was in decline.

Sixty years later, in the late seventies, the picture was very different. In 1975, no fewer than forty-six sovereign independent states had a Muslim majority, and a number of these were by constitution Islamic.

It was in the years following the end of hostilities in 1945 that most of these states came into being. And it was in the independence movements of these nascent nations that their women found a new voice and new functions.

If the collapse of the Turkish empire marked the end of one chapter in the history of the Muslim world, the retreat of the Western imperialist powers in the late forties and fifties marked the close of another. For four hundred years the Western powers had been increasing their area of control in Africa and Asia. Almost all the millions of Muslims outside the Ottoman Empire came under foreign control: on the Indian sub-continent, in the Malay peninsula and in the scattered islands of Indonesia and the Philippines. The Dutch and the Portuguese were followed by the French and the British. Islam was on the defensive, and the walls it built to defend its inner life against the infiltration of foreign ideas and customs gained it the reputation of a reactionary, unchanging system very different from its earlier days of expansion and greatness.

In the second half of the nineteenth century the tide turned.

This was the work of thinkers and writers over a wide field: in India as well as in Turkey and Egypt. All of them spoke of the current harsh restrictions on woman as an evil to be combated, a state of affairs unworthy of Islam itself.

After the thinkers came the nationalists. Military groups and political organisations were in varying degrees of readiness to take over in the wake of the retreating empires. The colonial powers in some cases removed themselves with speed, and the traumas of independence were in the event internal rather than in the struggle against the foreign power. The story differed in each country. The first major arena in the drama of post-war independence was the Indian sub-continent, where in 1947 the people were divided into two (later to become three) states. The bloodless revolution of 1952 in Egypt, which expelled King Farouq and the British, led the way in the Arab World. Syria and Iraq were both involved in revolutionary changes. In Tunis and Morocco, agreements were negotiated with the French which saved much bloodshed. In neighbouring Algeria there was a long and terrible war before independence was achieved.

In the Sudan, the problem was different again. After independence there were seventeen years of war between north and south, Arab and African, before in 1972 a settlement and a constitution could be reached which promised a unity vital for the future. In Libya, the overthrow of King Idris by Colonel Mu'ammar Gaddafi and the Revolutionary Command Council, in 1969, was an even bigger landmark than the earlier departure of the Italians.

In every case the birth pangs of the new state were the occasion for new action by its women, and carried them into fresh spheres of responsibility.

There was a prelude to all these post-war events, in Lebanon and Syria. While the Second World War was still in progress both countries succeeded in wresting from the French an acknowledgement of independence, even though the last French troops were not withdrawn until 1946, after the end of hostilities.

Lebanon reckons its independence from 22 November 1943. In that year the French authorities found the members of the government not sufficiently co-operative, and decided to replace them with others who would not insist on the immediate granting of the promised independence. On 10 November the President, the Prime Minister and other notables were arrested and taken to the remote village of Rashaya in the south of the Beqaa Valley. Ten days later they were released and returned to power. The day of their return, 22 November, is celebrated as Lebanon's Independence Day.

There is no doubt in the minds of the women who were active at that time who it was who forced the French to change their policy. Every day the leading women gathered in the home of the President, Shaikh Bechara el-Khoury, or that of the Prime Minister, Riad el-Solh. They made their plans, which included ensuring that no shop in Beirut opened. The wife of the British minister to Syria and Lebanon, Lady Spears (the novelist Mary Borden), encouraged them. She writes:

> The women of Beirut were too much for them. They started off from Madame Chamoun's house, a small group, away on the other side of town and as they passed down the streets, other groups joined them; and then the women who saw them from the windows came running down, and there were many Moslems among them; Moslems, Druzes, Christians, Maronites, Greek Orthodox, Roman Catholics, even Presbyterians . . . They were all out that day and they numbered hundreds when they reached the Place des Canons . . .
>
> They went three times on three different days through the town . . . and the gendarmes hustled them and tried to bar the way, but when the French ordered the gendarmes to turn the water hoses on them they refused.[1]

She adds a comment, poignant to read amid the tragic strife of some thirty years later. "They brought to birth a united spirit, and I do not think it will be easy to snuff it out." After 1943, the women of Lebanon worked together in many ventures: in valuable social and educational reforms, and in cultural achievements such as the brilliant Baalbek International Festivals. Politically they were less effective, but they may yet prove to be agents of reconstruction in a shattered Lebanon, when this becomes possible.

One outstanding leader in the Lebanese independence movement was Miss Ibtihāj Qaddūrah, a close friend of Madame Hoda Shaʿarāwy. In many Arab countries women were taking up the causes Hoda Shaʿarāwy and her friends had espoused. In 1944, Miss Qaddūrah wrote to her proposing a closer link between their activities. Her letter crossed with one making a similar suggestion. A conference was called in Cairo, and delegates from a number of

Arab countries took part in forming the All-Arab Federation of Women. As always, for Hoda Sha'arāwy world issues loomed larger than women's rights. She had already summoned one conference to Cairo, in 1939, to consider the Palestine question. These conferences, and the united action of the women, played their part in the creation of the League of Arab States in 1945.

Hoda Sha'arāwy died in 1947. Ibtihāj Qaddūrah succeeded her as President of the All-Arab Federation. From her base in Beirut she organised annual gatherings in a number of Arab countries, including Iraq. In 1948, Iraq sent two women delegates to the opening conference of the United Nations, the first of many Arab women to take part in its activities.

Among the many nations in Africa and the Arab world which gained their freedom during the 1950s, Algeria alone won it through force of arms. The process of the birth of nationhood was everywhere important for women. Not least was this so in Algeria, where the seven bitter years of war made a deep mark on social structures and attitudes.

"In those days heroism was a national duty, assigned to all Algerians," said Jamīlah Buḥrayd, the woman who above all others typified the spirit of the struggle for independence.[2]

"It is true what she said: there were thousands of Jamīlahs," comments an observer. "One example is an old housekeeper who today takes care of a woman doctor and her family. She was one of the messengers working for liberation in Algiers. What an intelligent, purposeful woman she is even now! Four of her sons died in the struggle. When news of death came to a family during the revolution, the women went up to the roof and began their shrill and joyful ululation, calling 'God is great! He has given us a martyr'."[3]

One articulate observer and participant in the Algerian struggle was a doctor from Martinique. Frantz Fanon was black of skin and French by language and education. When hostilities began, in 1954, he was head of the Psychiatric Department in the Blida-Joinville Hospital, south of Algiers. He resigned two years later to work with the Algerian revolution. In 1961, while the war was still in progress, he published his book *The Wretched of the Earth*.[4] In it he notes two sides of the active participation of women in the war. On the one hand, there were new roles for a hitherto sheltered section of the community. On the other, there were advantages in maintaining the traditional customs, in order to frustrate the enemy. Attempts by the French to modernise the Algerian family and to break the veiled, home-bound imprisonment of the Algerian woman, had to be resisted, he says. The woman who sees without being seen frustrates the coloniser. There is no reciprocity.

At the same time a new Algerian woman was born. Arab women who carried weapons, grenades and messages for the FLN broke free from their traditional confinement and subjugation. For the first time women began to travel unaccompanied from Oran to Constantine or Algiers; to stay with unknown families; to give refuge in their houses to militants while their own husbands were away; to wear either European clothes or, alternatively, the traditional protective *haik*, as the tactics of the struggle demanded; to act on their own initiative, to develop their own personalities, to state their own opinions in the presence of male relatives, to make their own choices in marriage. "The couple became the basic cell of the commonwealth, the fertile nucleus of the nation," writes Fanon. There is a simultaneous emergence of the citizen, the patriot, and the modern spouse.[5]

In this last statement, Fanon misread the temper of the Algerian people. What they were fighting for was closely bound up with a Muslim identity, and this he failed to appreciate. The constitution drawn up after the departure of the French immediately declared Islam as the state religion and Arabic as the national language. It gave women full citizenship and the right to vote, but did not alter the dominance of men in family life.

If Fanon romanticised the Algerian woman, it is nevertheless true that her heroism inspired her sisters elsewhere in the Arab World. When independence had been won a group of Algerian women visited the Arab capitals and were everywhere fêted. Their courage and loyalty had become a legend. In Kuwait, their arrival was the occasion for the educated women to abandon the veil. At the airport, the ladies of the reception committee were veiled. When a few days later they bade farewell to their guests, they were not.[6]

Militancy on the part of women in a national struggle has a long and honoured tradition behind it, from the days of the Prophet onwards. In societies under threat, the women always play an important part. They may indeed form a robust core of resistance, since they are less open to outside influence: they do not have to meet and negotiate with alien rulers, nor use a foreign language. Also they form the hopes and aspirations of the next generation. The songs they croon can be those to which warriors march, and they kindle the imagination and ambition of boys as well as girls.

Examples can be quoted from recent times. President Anwār Sadāt, in his autobiography *In Search of Identity*,[7] describes his childhood in a village by the Nile. It was the ballads sung and sung again by his mother and his grandmother, celebrating events in the struggle against the occupying power, that first sparked in him a love for his country and a desire to serve it.

A generation earlier, King ʿAbdul-ʿAzīz Ibn Saʿūd used to speak of a sister of his father who played a great part in his youth. "'You must revive the glory of the house of Ibn Saud,' she would tell me again and again."[8]

A similar spirit was shown by women in the Sudan, at the time of the rising led by Al-Mahdī in the 1880s. Only the victorious could return home. Wounded or on the run, men took to the hills to fight again, for their women would not receive them.

Such attitudes throw light on the dichotomy between militancy and obedience: a conflict between the advance of women to new responsibilities and the deeply felt need to enhance the national identity, the fight for which plays so great a part in any freedom struggle. The position of women, and the customs connected with them, are so closely bound up with Islamic law and social structure that there are many setbacks and much heart-searching in the development of a wider role for the women. They themselves may seem to turn their back on hard-won freedoms and responsibilities, even where these have been seen as fully allowable in Quranic terms. The veil, which the majority of Muslims today do not regard as essentially Islamic, may find unexpected supporters. These reactions are occasioned and encouraged by what is seen as the very real threat to Islamic standards posed by the militant materialism of both East and West, and especially by the signs of laxity and decadence observed in Western society.

In Algeria, time is needed to resolve such questions. One of the institutions that emerged from the freedom struggle was the Union Nationale des Femmes Algériennes (UNFA). In the National Charter of 1975 its role is described in the following terms: "In regard to the amelioration of the condition of women, action should be taken above all to change the mental and legal environment which is negative in regard to them and often prejudicial to the exercise of their recognised rights as wives and mothers, and to their material and moral security." And again: "The UNFA should be aware that the emancipation of women does not imply abandoning the ethic so deeply held by the people."[9] The Union is in the forefront of programmes in the rural areas to promote literacy and hygiene, and it encourages women's representation in local government and in the General Union of Algerian Workers.

The growing point for Algerian women is their place in the steadily expanding educational programme: one of the great achievements of the new state, since schooling collapsed almost completely with the departure of the French. Many girls are still taken out of primary schools at the age of ten or eleven, and the figure given for illiteracy among adult women in 1970 was 91 per cent. In contrast to this, increasing numbers of girls are to be found in secondary schools, and in higher education, where in 1975 they formed 20 per cent of the student population.[10] In the medical schools women are over 35 per cent of the total. Doctors, lawyers and teachers give increasing service, and if they enjoy little personal liberty their younger sisters and their daughters may find greater scope.

In 1975, following the referendum on the National Charter, elections were held for the new National Assembly. Out of 261 candidates, 39 were women, and nine of these were elected, four of them in Algiers.

In general terms, the emancipation of women is accepted as a national goal. In practice, decision making is in the hands of the men, and the participation of women in national life is still minimal. There is a long way to go: but to the growing body of trained and experienced women, the direction in which they are travelling is clear.

Every government in the Arab world today regards the status and role of its women as of great importance, however widely the policies may vary. Three aspects of the question demand consideration: the legal position of women, their role in the work-force of the nation, and their right to education.

The most sensitive of these questions is that of legal status.

While new constitutions readily accord equal citizenship – the right to vote, for instance – matters of family law and inheritance are in almost all Arab countries governed by the Muslim law, the *Sharī'ah*. Whatever its original intent, its application has been the cause of much complaint. A wife might not even know whether she had been divorced or not; and she could be repudiated after many years of marriage, without redress. Women reformers, especially in Egypt, have sought for years to attain equality for women in matters of divorce, and to have marital cases brought before Common Law courts rather than religious ones.

In 1956, the year of its independence, Tunisia promulgated a Personal Status Code, bringing family affairs under the jurisdiction of the Common Law courts. Polygamy was forbidden, and women were given equal rights with men in seeking divorce. They could also choose whom they would marry, rather than be bound by the father's choice.

President Bourguiba, a steady champion of women's rights, set out to open new doors to them. He was aided in this by his able French wife, who came to Tunis with him in 1928 and was a faithful companion through all the ups and downs of his career; and also by his second wife, Madame Wassila Bourguiba, who played a militant part in the Independence movement and later gave a lead to the women of the country in their emancipation.

The battle for national freedom had first to be won. Other questions were subordinate to this first essential. "We can discuss the veil on the day when its disappearance no longer represents a threat to the integrity of our national personality," said Bourguiba in 1928. "But today, when the threat of absorption, obliteration and annihilation is hanging over our country, to agree to give up one feature of our personality would be suicide."[11] One of his first acts when national freedom had become a reality was to sweep away not only the veil but also many other restrictions on women.

In Tunis there are wide discrepancies between city and country: between the sophisticated writers and artists in the capital and illiterate peasants' wives in the countryside; between the girls graduating from the University of Tunis and those whose way of life and customs are described by Dr Nādiah Abū Zahrah in her studies of the village of Sidi Ameur in the Tunisian Sahel.[12] The Union Nationale Des Femmes Tunisiennes, founded in 1956, seeks to bridge the gaps and helps to make modern facilities available in the country areas. This organisation has concentrated much of its efforts on a massive programme of family planning.

Across the Arab World, in public or in private, the debate continues about the status of women. The example of Tunisia in changing the law of Personal Status was not followed elsewhere. Attempts at introducing similar changes failed more than once in Egypt owing to the opposition of the religious authorities, and especially of those in charge of the University of Al-Azhar, to anything which seemed to tamper with the precepts of the Qur'ān. However, on 3 July 1979 President Sadāt used his presidential privilege to introduce an amended Personal Status Law. This was ratified by the People's Assembly, which has the right to accept or reject – though not to amend – such decrees. There were many protests, but this time the Shaikh al-Azhar, His Eminence ʿAbdul-Raḥmān Biṣār, sought to reassure the nation through radio and television interviews that the Sharīʿah had not been contravened.

The terms of the new law fall short of those of the Tunisian code, and of the hopes of the reformers in Egypt. It has been criticised by the orthodox for going too far, and by the reformers for not going far enough. It did nevertheless introduce changes which would alleviate much hardship. It dealt with polygamy, divorce, maintenance, custody and residence.

The 1979 law maintains the man's right to divorce and polygamy, but curbs both. The consent of the first wife must be obtained before a second marriage. A divorce cannot simply be pronounced by the husband but must be formally registered with the *ma'zūn*, the official who deals with matters of marriage, and who now plays a role in divorce as well. The divorce is not valid until the wife has been informed. The divorced wife is entitled to the house in which she lives, and to its furniture, and the husband must move elsewhere. If it is rented, he must pay the rent. He must give the woman the equivalent of 40 per cent of his salary for three years, and if the marriage has lasted for more than fifteen years she is entitled to this maintenance for life, or until she remarries. In regard to custody of the children, girls may stay with the mother until they marry, and boys till the age of fifteen. Before this, maintenance was negligible and children were handed back to the father at the age of eleven for a girl and nine for a boy.[13]

The decree was intended to be followed by a more comprehensive law. The argument is far from over. In all these matters, alterations in social custom are at least as important as changes in law. Polygamy, for example, is legally allowable, but it has become very rare in modern Arab society.

Constitutions drawn up in the newly independent states gave legal expression in most cases to equality of citizenship for men and women. Women received the right to vote in Algeria, Egypt, Iraq, Lebanon, Libya, Morocco, Sudan, Syria, Tunisia and South Yemen.[14] Where a constitution did not include this right, it was later added: in Egypt in 1956, in Jordan in 1966. The involvement of women in the democratic process in the Sudan was ensured by a law which requires a minimum proportion of women on every representative body: the proportion is 25 per cent on village councils.

With the right to vote went the right to stand for election to the national assemblies. Egypt's first members were elected soon after the vote was granted. In 1979, thirty seats in the People's Assembly were reserved for women, who can also stand as candidates for any of the others.[15] In Syria in 1975 there were five women among the one hundred and eighty-six members of the People's Assembly. Under Algeria's new constitution, in 1975, nine women were elected. In the Sudan there were at that time women members for each of the eighteen provinces. In Libya women were given the right to run for office as members of the People's Regime, the organisation which then encompassed all citizens and which played an important role in the social and political affairs of the country.[16]

The first Arab woman cabinet minister was appointed in Iraq in 1959. In Egypt a succession of women held the post of Minister of Social Affairs, after Dr Ḥikmat Abū Zaid was first appointed in 1962. In Damascus, Dr Najāh al-ʿAttār was appointed Minister of Culture and National Guidance in 1976, and in the same year Dr Faṭma ʿAbdul Rahmān took charge of the Ministry of Social Affairs in Khartoum, as did Mrs Inʿām Mufti in Amman in 1980.

The rights to equal education and equal pay were acknowledged alongside the right to vote. But equality on paper often represents more of hope than reality. The value of a vote depends on the quality of the elections in which it is exercised. The right to equal education can be exercised only where there are adequate schools and scholarships. Equal pay implies comparable opportunities of employment. Implementing the theory in realistic terms of opportunity is a slow process, at different stages of advance in different countries.

The 1960s brought economic pressures to bear that in their turn opened new doors to women. Their potentialities and abilities had been amply demonstrated by the pioneers. The moment came when these assets could no longer be neglected. There were factors of need, and of opportunity, as each country faced the challenge of earning its living and making its contribution in a disturbed and changing world.

For some, varied factors such as war, inflation and rising population made it more difficult for a large section of the population, especially the urban women, to be maintained by the earnings of the men. New ideas and new educational opportunities coincided with national need. New roles were opened to women, in industry and in the professions.

In other countries, there was the unexpected affluence of oil, bringing new powers and responsibilities. This in itself set in train inevitable social changes. It also meant that resources were available to maintain traditional ways of life. Changes could be accepted or refused, by choice and not by compulsion of either circumstances or need.

Iraq has gone furthest in the enlistment of women in its work-force. ''The employment of women has become an inevitable necessity considering the urgent need for manpower in a country with no more than twelve million people and a giant development plan,'' said a report on *Progress of Women in Iraq*, issued in 1978. The proportion of women in the total work-force more than doubled between 1968 and 1977: from 7 per cent to 15 per cent, while in the professions it was much higher.[17]

In both Iraq and Syria, one of the main instruments for implementing government policy has been a well-organised chain of women's unions. The General Federation of Iraqi Women has committees covering the eighteen governorates of Iraq. Each area is subdivided into hundreds of cells reporting to one of eighty-seven centres through the country. Programmes of hygiene and literacy, child health and vocational training, social research and literature for the newly literate, offer scope for much initiative and talent. The General Federation of Syrian Women is organised along the same lines. The Union Nationale des Femmes Algériennes and the Sudan Women's Union play similar roles.

Jordan, a small country with few resources, launched an ambitious development plan in 1976, calling for improvements in agricultural methods, in irrigation and in industry. Its trained personnel, both men and women, were much in demand in the skill-hungry countries of the Gulf, with a resulting shortage at home, and strenuous efforts were made to attract more women into employment. A symposium on The Role of Women held in Amman in 1977 called for women to acquire no less than forty-two new skills. At the same time, the first Director of the Department of Women's Affairs, Mrs In'ām Muftī, stressed the importance of values as well as skills. The qualities women bring with them into public life should make them pace-setters for standards of excellence and integrity, she said. Mrs Muftī, formerly Principal of the UNWRA Vocational Training Centre at Ramallah, in the West Bank, became Jordan's first woman cabinet minister in January 1980, as Minister for Social Affairs.

All the Arab countries, however conservative in their view of family tradition, have formulated an active policy of women's education. There has been an escalation of education at all levels, and in some of the new systems in the Gulf states there are almost as many girls as boys in school at the primary level. The universally acknowledged target is compulsory education for all, and the actual provision of facilities is advancing with varied success. In Tunisia, approximately one in three pupils in school are girls, in Saudi Arabia one in two. Kuwait can boast that education is available for all its children. The lowest percentage of girls is in North Yemen, where in 1979 only 9 per cent of the total number of pupils were girls and it has been estimated that fewer than two out of every hundred girls of school age attend school.[18]

At the grass-roots level, vigorous literacy campaigns have reached large numbers of women. But the results recorded are very hard to evaluate, and the retreat of illiteracy depends in the long run on the spread of primary education.

Colleges and universities proliferated in the years following independence. In almost every case the new opportunities were opened to women as soon as they were created. In the 1970s at least forty universities in the Arab world were sending out women graduates every year. Examples of the percentages of women students given in 1975 were: Egypt 28 per cent; Syria 19 per cent; Iraq 24 per cent; Tunisia 23 per cent; Algeria 20 per cent; Saudi Arabia 7 per cent; Kuwait 60 per cent (owing to the numbers of men studying abroad).[19] In Libya, where few women appear in public, men and women mix in the universities of Tripoli and Ben Ghazi. The number of women students in 1972 was 948: four times greater than it had been before the revolution of 1969.[20]

Education – and education for women – has in the past decades been given a high priority everywhere in the Muslim world. What is its aim? Not only to enlist the services of half the population in the tasks of nation building; nor solely to give expression to talents otherwise wasted. To the thoughtful Muslim, man or woman, it is a question of quality: the quality of life that grows round a woman in her own sphere of influence. The emphasis on motherhood, and on its basic importance in home and society, is very strong. According to a frequently quoted tradition, the Prophet was asked, "Who shall I honour most?" "Your mother, your mother, your mother," was the reply. It is not just a question of nurturing young children, but of adult relationships of a kind which can bring to maturity men and women of integrity, people in whose hands the future of family and state will be secure.

If the accent in the past pages has been on the growing numbers of professional women in the Arab World, it is fitting for the latest episode in a long history to focus on a woman who has used her position as wife and mother to the full. The story which forms the subject of the next chapter takes us back to where we began, to the heart of Arabia and the home of the Prophet; and to the people who are the guardians of the Holy Places of Islam, and therefore in a special way the guardians also of its traditions.

In Modern Arabia

"It is not permitted to the Sun to overtake the Moon, nor can the Night outstrip the Day: each swims along in its own orbit."

Qur'ān, Surah 36:40 Yā Sīn

"When Abd al-Aziz Ibn Saud was a child, his dynasty had lost the last remnants of its power . . . Among all the members of the family there was only one who had any inkling of what was happening in this passionate heart: a younger sister of his father. I do not know much about her; I only know that whenever he dwells on the days of his youth, the King always mentions her with great reverence.

"'She loved me, I think, even more than her own children. When we were alone, she would take me on her lap and tell me of the great things which I was to do when I grew up: "Thou must revive the glory of the House of Ibn Saud," she would tell me again and again, and her words were like a caress. "But what I want thee to know, O Azayyiz," she would say, "is that even the glory of the House of Ibn Saud must not be the end of thy endeavours. Thou must strive for the glory of Islam. Thy people sorely need a leader who will guide them on to the path of the Holy Prophet – and thou shalt be that leader." These words have always remained alive in my heart.'"

Muḥammad Asad

Chapter Seventeen

Equal and Different

Some lives span an epoch. They overarch the currents of history and form a bridge that opens the way from one world to another.

Such a life is that of Her Majesty Queen 'Īffat, widow of King Faiṣal of Saudi Arabia and for over thirty years his consort and close companion.

Hers is a story in character with others pictured earlier in this book. Here and there the searchlight of history has caught some woman at work. To stand out in this way from millions of others these women had to have the courage to be themselves, and to take on the role that destiny assigned to them. Whatever their limitations, many of them succeeded in some degree in turning the current of an age, and in epitomising the best in it. To remember them is to renew faith in the individual: that a man's or a woman's life can set their people on a new road.

Queen 'Īffat herself grew up in Istanbul. When she was born, the last of the Ottoman Sultans still held court. During her childhood the traumatic defeats of the First World War brought about the loss of an empire and the birth of a new nation.

It was the Turkey of Atatürk and Halide Edib; of humiliations and victories, of upheavals and hopes. A new era was beginning for the women. After the establishment of the new republic in 1923 the veil was abandoned. In 1923 also the first woman doctor, trained in Germany, started to practise. Six women doctors graduated from the University of Istanbul in 1927.[1] Many other women were in training as teachers, lawyers, nurses. The world was opening up for the intelligent, progressive young women of 'Īffat's generation, as it was for their contemporaries in Egypt.

It was a visit from a cousin that changed the course of her life. She came of the family of Sa'ūd, rulers of Nejd, central province of Arabia. Her grandfather was taken as a prisoner from Riyadh to

Istanbul. Like other potentially dangerous opponents of the Ottoman regime, he lived there in comfort but was not allowed to leave. His son, 'Īffat's father, Aḥmad al-Thunaiyān, married a Turkish wife, but he returned to Riyadh where his experience of outside affairs was of great aid to King 'Abdul-'Azīz. He was his adviser through the years of the First World War. In 1919, he accompanied the young prince Faiṣal, aged fourteen, on a visit to England and Europe. Shortly afterwards he died. In 1931 Faiṣal, then Crown Prince, passed through Istanbul on his way home from another European visit. He visited the widow of his kinsman Aḥmad al-Thunaiyān. Mother and daughter were invited to Riyadh, and Faiṣal and 'Īffat were married soon afterwards.

"It was a complete change in my whole life," says the Queen, recalling her arrival in the Riyadh of the early thirties. To move from Istanbul – cosmopolitan, rich in history, electric with change – to this mediaeval fortress deep in the desert was indeed a contrast. The word "Riyadh" means garden, and the city owes its existence to one of the oases scattered through the wide deserts of Nejd. The small walled town was growing but it was not so very different from what it had been when the youthful 'Abdul-'Azīz ibn Sa'ūd wrested it from usurpers by a spectacular feat of arms in the year 1902.

The women of Nejd had the reputation of speaking their minds, and those of the family of Ibn Sa'ūd have exercised considerable influence. The first episode recorded in the life of King 'Abdul-'Azīz pictures him and his elder sister Nūrah slung in saddle-bags on the same camel, fleeing through the night, when his father was expelled from Riyadh. The next picture is of an aunt who kindled in the boy the fighting spirit which would regain his heritage. Most of his many marriages were literally alliances, and served their purpose in binding tribe after tribe to his leadership in loyalty and friendship. His son Faiṣal had very different ideas of wedlock for, while he early contracted more than one marriage, his union with 'Īffat was the enduring centre of his family life.

In 1926 King 'Abdul-'Azīz extended his rule to the province of Hijaz, bordering the Red Sea, and from then on he divided his time between Nejd and Hijaz, and the two capitals of Riyadh and Mecca. Crown Prince Faiṣal was his deputy in Mecca, and it was there and in the Red Sea port of Jiddah that his wife spent much of her life.

Queen 'Īffat was never one to be deterred by difficulties. She set out to get to know her people, their character, their customs, their needs. She identified herself with them, and came to understand their isolation.

> It is not easy for a people who have been cut off from the rest of the world for so long to accept ideas imposed by a new civilisation. We have so many Bedouin – we *are* Bedouin. And we have been asleep. Now we have wakened up and resumed the march of civilisation – a march we once led. What is seen today in Europe and America owes a great debt to Islamic civilisation but, sadly, the Arab and Muslim peoples did not continue their march forward. Now we are trying to catch up with the rest of the world.[2]

The first shocks of change were administered by King ʿAbdul-ʿAzīz himself. Motor cars appeared in Riyadh, and radios brought him valuable news of the outside world. "It is the voice of Shaiṭān," said his Bedouin subjects, as the sounds came out of the air. The King took his radio with him on a tribal visit. As the chiefs gathered round him he switched it on: to a reading from the Qur'ān. There was a hush as they listened. "Can this be the voice of Shaiṭān?" asked the King. Radios were accepted.

"You cannot change the mentality of people by royal decree, nor by money," says the Queen. The changes set in train by King Faiṣal and Queen ʿĪffat were for the most part started before he came to the throne and while money was still short. Change had to begin with respect for Islam itself: true Islam, purified from accretions and illusions, from ideas which people attributed to it and which held them back. "Any state, or any individual, whose life is not based on faith, is lifeless. But to be life-giving, the faith must be rightly taught. This was the King's first concern."

The second phase, that of social development, called for great sensitivity and a correct sense of timing. "We have always taken into consideration the right time for executing any project," whether it might be the introduction of television, or the question of education for girls. There comes a moment when people are ready for the innovation. As King Faiṣal himself said to Mrs Cecile Rushdī, Principal of the college for girls founded in Jiddah by his wife, "We want to go forward on solid ground, not find ourselves in a quick-sand."[3]

Nine children were born to Queen ʿĪffat, and the King and Queen gave much thought to their education. As they grew older, their father made a habit of lunching with them every day, and through them he kept touch with what the younger generation were thinking. "We treated them like friends, and told them not to say 'Yes' out of respect, but to discuss matters with us."

All the children were first taught at home. Then the girls were sent to school in Switzerland, and the boys to school and university abroad: to Princeton and Oxford, Cambridge and Cranwell.

King Faiṣal and Queen ʿĪffat shared the aim that all young Saudis should have the advantage of education, boys and girls alike. As early as 1942, when her eldest son Muḥammad reached school age, the Queen started a school for boys in Taʿif, where generations of Meccans have found refreshment in the hills to the south of their city. The first pupils were the sons of members of the royal family and others connected with it. Here up-to-date methods of education could be introduced in a wholly Saudi setting. It proved to be indeed a "model school", as its name implied (*Al-madrasah al-namūdhajiyyah*), and the experience gained could be used by the many other schools that arose in the following years.

The numbers of government schools for boys rose rapidly in the fifties. But girls were another matter. For years Queen ʿĪffat considered what would be the best way of starting their education.

She chose the occasion of the jubilee of her marriage to start the first girls' school. This was in 1956. "We do not usually mark such anniversaries," she says. "But I felt there was something that could be celebrated: twenty-five years of happy marriage, with never a quarrel or shadow between us."

"My husband knew what I was doing, but I did not embarrass him by asking his permission. I knew there would be opposition. I decided to open the school for orphans, for no one could object to this and people would feel it was justified if it was for so charitable an object." She named it *Dār al-Hanān*, "House of Affection", and worked out all the details of provision and administration with the lady who had taught her own daughters, a Palestinian, Mrs Mufīdah Dabbāgh. She herself worked on the preparations: it was to be a boarding school, and clothes and bed-covers as well as desks and books were needed. A number of people were asked if they would send their girls, and all refused. The school opened with some orphans, and some children of servants in the royal household: fifteen little girls. A doctor and a nurse were available for health care. A year later, the same fathers who had said, "You will corrupt the girls' morals if you teach them," were asking if they might enrol their daughters.

Each year a new class was added. The education was aimed at intelligent girls, and English was thoroughly taught, which was exceptional at the time. The first girl to graduate at the end of her secondary education went to England to be trained as a doctor. The Queen was always concerned with the standard of education given. The school was kept open even during the summer months: the girls would visit their families and then return, so that their education should not be disrupted.

Dār al-Hanān in 1979 had 1200 pupils; 150 of these were studying at the expense of the Queen. She and the Principal, Mrs Cecile Rushdī, are planning a new building, and an extension into adult education, so that young women may be able to take courses in secretarial work, sewing, cooking, languages, computer practice. Young wives who did not go to school will be able to improve their knowledge and gain qualifications which will be helpful to the country. It will be an Institute of Management and Administration for Women, affiliated to Dār al-Hanān.

In 1960, only four years after Queen 'Īffat's pioneer venture in Jiddah, the Government opened a primary school for girls in Riyadh. Once again, the time was right. They had waited till the people were ready. By 1969 there were about forty schools for girls in both Riyadh and Jiddah. A school in Buraidah, a very conservative centre, aroused more opposition. A strong deputation came to see Faiṣal to protest against the project. He received them warmly. "We are all united," he said, "in our loyalty to Islam. Now tell me what the Holy Qur'ān says. Is there anything in it which forbids the education of women?" There was silence. "If there is nothing in the Holy Qur'ān that prevents us from opening a school for girls," said the Crown Prince, "there is no cause for argument between us. As learning is incumbent on every Muslim, we shall open the school. Those parents who wish to send their daughters should not be prevented. Others can keep their girls at home. No one is going to force them." So the school opened – even though for a while armed police had to protect it from attack.

The numbers of schools for girls grew rapidly. Education at every level figured prominently in the Saudi Arabia Five Year Plan, 1975–1980. By 1976 nearly half the girls between the ages of six and twelve in the total population of Saudi Arabia were in school. The achievement of universal elementary education for both boys and girls was envisaged by the end of 1980.[4]

Teachers were enlisted from all over the Arab World, and in the development of higher education the authorities were able to draw on the experience of women who were in charge of large schools and colleges elsewhere. One example was Miss Iḥsān Maḥmassānī, Principal of Bait al-Aṭfāl, the 1400-strong boarding school for girls in Beirut, founded by the Maqassed Society, a charitable organisation set up by Muslim families in Lebanon. Such institutions in many parts of the Muslim world could count on financial aid from Saudi Arabia, and in their turn could contribute their own skills and experience.

Ten years after the starting of the first government school for girls, the Girls College of Education (Kulliyat al-banāt), was founded by Queen 'Īffat in Riyadh. It has a four-year undergraduate curriculum for the training of teachers. In the forward plans for both the University of Riyadh (founded in 1957) and the King 'Abdul-'Azīz University in Jiddah (founded in 1967) separate campuses are envisaged, with equal facilities for men and women. In these universities, as well as in the more recent King Faiṣal University at Dammam (founded in 1975), women students already take courses, and there are affiliated departments for women.

Girl students cannot be taught by, or with, men. Closed-circuit television overcomes this difficulty. The lists of examination successes are published separately, to avoid comparisons. At first, the girls frequently did better than the boys, possibly because they worked harder and had fewer distractions in their leisure time.

Queen 'Īffat has seen widespread results from her pioneering efforts during the forty years since her marriage. Her daughters and other members of the royal family followed her lead by taking initiative in the field of social service. Princess Sārah founded the first women's club in Riyadh, as a channel for the interests of women outside their homes, Al-Nahḍad Philanthropic Society for Women.

Queen Sītā, wife of King Khālid (who succeeded his brother Faiṣal following the latter's tragic death in 1975) shares this interest in social conditions, in the countries she visits as well as in her own. Those who meet her are impressed by the simplicity, even severity, of her dress; her straightforward manner; her knowledge of the Qur'ān, and of proverbs with which she can aptly illustrate points that arise; her desire to be informed on matters put before her. In London, she and her daughter have taken an interest in the many-sided charitable work of the Arab Women's Council, an association chaired by Dr. Esmat El-Said and supported by the wives of Arab ambassadors. Educational and welfare projects all over the world look to the Saudi royal family for support – and receive it. Such giving is not indiscriminate but is accompanied by personal interest and scrutiny, as recipients of such help can testify.

Profound changes are taking place in Saudi society, largely unseen by the outside world. This is in contrast with the sudden alterations by decree which have produced such strong reactions elsewhere, for instance in Iran.

The traditional division into the world of women and the world of men still holds. Candid observers like Madame Nouha Alhegelan, wife of the Saudi ambassador in Washington D.C. and herself a graduate in law of the University of Damascus, note an obsession among western commentators with the question of the veil, an emphasis which tends to trivialise an important debate. The point at issue in the many discussions on the subject of women's role is not the veil itself, but the values which Muslim society treasures and seeks to maintain. High among these are honour and good faith, pre-marital chastity and fidelity in marriage.

"In almost all Arab countries the veil has been abolished, but not by force or by occidental criticism. It has been abolished by the women who decided one day that they did not want it any more. Therefore, if it still exists in other places, it is because those who are wearing it feel that it is part of their tradition and part of their lives. If it seems humiliating to the onlooker it must be realised that the veiled woman would feel humiliated if she were to take it off."[5]

When Queen Elizabeth visited Saudi Arabia in March 1979, she was received in Riyadh by Queen Sītā and the ladies of the royal family. Daughters and granddaughters of King ʿAbdul-ʿAzīz ibn Sa'ud, each knew her place by age in the family hierarchy. The older women present had lived through the whole history of modern Arabia, and had seen their sons and nephews come to wield great power.

Other women had also been invited, representing the growing body of Saudi professional women. There were nine doctors including two obstetricians; there were teachers, two lawyers and a psychologist. Queen Elizabeth asked how many women doctors were practising in Saudi Arabia and was told one hundred.

The women of their generation are now writing the next chapter in the long story of women's contribution to Muslim history. They face many difficult choices, and very great opportunities.

Their vision for the future forms a fitting epilogue to the narrative of the long line of their predecessors.

As she sees it, the Muslim woman's evolution is her own. She has her own identity. She does not have to copy the patterns set by men, nor to escape from them. In this she sees herself as different from Western women.

She looks for a world in which men and women are indeed equal, but in which their different roles are seen to be complementary: where there is co-operation rather than competition, love and understanding rather then the jealousy and hatred which rivalry can bring. Amidst many pressures, she seeks time to develop her relationships in her own society at her own pace, saying to her western sisters, "If we keep the best of our world, and adopt the best of yours, we might – we just *might* – reach the ideal solution."

The questions she faces are not solely, or even primarily, those connected with her own position and role. They are the major uncertainties of the age, problems which concern her whole society and indeed the rest of mankind as well. For it is not only the Muslim world that seeks to stabilise its society in the midst of rapid change. The inheritors of western civilisation feel the need to re-discover the spiritual foundations of their own culture and social structure. In the midst of upheaval, there is a hunger for security: to build a sane society in which human beings can grow and live in harmony.

In such a context, the concept "equal and different" may prove to have a wider significance. It could point to a mutual respect between different cultures, different traditions of faith. It could contribute to a new era in which one does not seek to absorb or dominate another, but each vies with the other to give their distinctive best – the truths with which they feel themselves uniquely entrusted – to the good of the whole; when each seeks the help of the other to set right what is wrong, instead of concentrating on his own virtues and the other's faults. In facing the common tasks of survival in the coming decades, some such basis of co-operation is essential.

The matrix in which such attitudes can develop is the family. To Muslim society it is central: and at the heart of it is still, as ever, the mother. She is the contact point between the treasures of the past and the hopes of the future. If the women in Muslim countries can find their way to fresh responsibilities without eroding the importance of motherhood, the world will have much to thank them for. Others who seek an ideal society may discover that women hold the key to it and, in the words of the Prophet, find Paradise at the feet of mothers.

Postscript

History moves on. Yesterday's bold steps in founding one school have led to today's proliferation of colleges and universities. No longer do young women need to prove their capability to be doctors, teachers and scientists. Their mothers and grandmothers have done that.

Their pioneering needs to be in a different realm: the creation of the things money cannot buy and education cannot ensure.

Research into the life of women in Muslim countries, historical and contemporary, has only just begun. Most of this will be carried out by Muslims, with insights that are eagerly awaited. But the issues raised are of such general interest that others will certainly be drawn to study them.

This calls for an attitude in the non-Muslim which it must be acknowledged has often been lacking: a respect for a way of life which has already lasted for fourteen hundred years, which has nurtured more than one great civilisation, and which is at present in a state of upheaval and expansion. Such respect can be sincere though not uncritical, and can recognise the wide areas of agreement that exist between the traditional values of Islam and Christendom, especially in the honouring of women and the centrality of family life.

If the gigantic tasks of the Twenty-first Century are to be achieved, mutual fear and suspicion must be replaced by a common fight against materialism and corruption. In this battle the millions of women in the Muslim world, with their ideals and their courage, are one of the greatest sources of hope.

Notes

Notes to Introduction (pages 1–7)

Title page:

M. Smith *Rābi'a the Mystic and her Fellow Saints in Islam* (Cambridge 1928) p. 136, from Taqī al-Dīn al-Ḥisnī *Siyār al-ṣāliḥāt*

Aida Tibi "A Study of Al-Ma'āfirī's *Biographies of Famous Women in Early Islam*" unpublished D.Phil. thesis (Oxford 1974) p. xii. Muḥammad ibn 'Alī al-Ma'āfirī was an Andalusian scholar who compiled his book in Damascus in 581/1185, and later became *Khatīb* (official preacher) of the Al-Aqsā Mosque in Jerusalem. MS Chester Beatty 3016

H.H. 'Abdul-Wahāb *Shahīrāt al-Tūnīsiyyāt* (*Les Femmes Tunisiennes Célèbres*) (Tunis 1353/1934) p. 89

1 Ibn Qudāmah al-Maqdisī, *Al-mughnī wal-sharḥ al-kabīr*, Cairo 1345/1926 Vol. XI p. 380. Ibn Qudāmah, a famous jurist, died in Damascus 620/1223. He was teaching there when Al-Ma'āfirī wrote his *Biographies of Famous Women*

2 Muḥammad Ibn Sa'd *Kitāb al-ṭabaqāt al-kabīr* (*Biografen der Frauen*) ed. C. Brockelmann, Brill 1904, Vol viii

3 Aida Tibi, loc. cit.

4 W.N. Arafat, in *Gazelle* No. 4, March 1978, p. 61

5 Bint al-Shāṭi' *The Wives of the Prophet* trans Matti Moosa and D.N. Ranson (Lahore 1971) p. xvii

6 M. Abdul-Rauf *The Islamic View of Women and the Family* (New York 1977) p. 21

7 Karachi, May 12 1979

8 R.F. Woodsmall *Women and the New East* (Washington 1960) p. 373

Notes for Chapter 1 (pages 8–27)

Title page:

Ibn Hishām: quoted by N. Abbott "Women and the State in Early Islam" *Journal of Near East Studies* I, 1942, p. 122

One Thousand and One Nights: H.L. Gerhardt *The Art of Story Telling, a Literary Study of the Thousand and One Nights* Brill 1963, p. 355

1 Ibn Isḥāq *Sīrat rasūl Allāh* trans. A. Guillaume *Life of Muḥammad* OUP 1955, pp. 73–6
2 N. Abbott "Women and the State on the Eve of Islam" *American Journal of Semitic Literatures* 1941, p. 269
3 Ibn Isḥāq, op. cit., p. 72
4 *Qur'ān* 4:3 Women
5 *Qur'ān* 4:129 Women
6 *Qur'ān* 24:30–31 Light
7 *Qur'ān* 33:59 Confederates
8 M.M. Pickthall *The Meaning of the Glorious Koran* Mentor Books (New York n.d.) p. 225; A. Yūsuf 'Alī *The Holy Qur'ān, Text, Translation and Commentary* (Beirut 1965) notes 2983, 3764, 3766, 3768, pp. 904, 1126–7
9 *Qur'ān* 33:33 Confederates
10 Letter from Mrs Taraneh Azima-Kayhan, Geneva, May 1979
11 P. Shaukat Ali *Status of Women in the Muslim World* (Lahore 1975) p. 32
12 M. Smith *Rābi'a the Mystic* (Cambridge 1928) p. 4, from Farīd al-dīn 'Aṭṭār
13 N. Abbott *Aisha the Beloved of Muhammad* (Chicago 1942) p. 48
14 *Qur'ān* 33:28–33 Confederates
15 Bint al-Shāṭi' *The Wives of the Prophet* trans. M. Moosa and D.N. Ranson (Lahore 1971) p. 156
16 ibid., p. 54
17 Maulana Muhammad Ali *A Manual of Hadith* Curzon Press (London) and Humanities Press (USA) 1944, 2nd edn. 1978, p. 326
18 Bint al-Shāṭi', op. cit., p. 195; *Qur'ān* 60:7 She Who Is Examined
19 Bint al-Shāṭi', op. cit., p. 198
20 ibid., pp. 165–6
21 N. Abbott, op. cit., p. 493
22 M.M. Ali, op. cit., p. 352
23 ibid., p. 368
24 ibid., p. 377
25 ibid., p. 328
26 *Encyclopaedia of Islam* New Edn., ed. J.H. Kramer et al. (Leiden 1954) Vol. I, p. 109

27 M.M. Ali, op. cit., p. 392
28 N. Abbott, "Women and the State in Early Islam" *JNES* 1942, p. 365.
29 *Encyclopaedia of Islam* ed. M.T. Houtsma et al. (Leiden 1913–38) Vol. IV, p. 1047
30 Ibn Ishaq op. cit., p. xv
31 N. Abbott *Aisha the Beloved of Muhammad* pp. 212–3
32 ibid., p. 89; *Encyclopaedia of Islam* New Edn., Vol. I, p. 738
33 *Encyclopaedia of Islam* New Edn. Vol. I, p. 455
34 M.M. Ali, op. cit., p. 264
35 Allama Syed Sulaiman Nadvi *Heroic Deeds of Muslim Women* (Lahore 1961) p. 7
36 N. Abbott *JNES* 1942, p. 365
37 *Journal of the Royal Asiatic Society* January 1897, pp. 88–101; M. Smith, op. cit., p. 137ff. A curious sidelight on the panic caused by the early Arab raids on Cyprus may be found in an archaeological discovery in Lambousa, a town on the northern coast, which fell to the Arabs in another attack four years later: 33/653–4. Treasure hidden at this period has been unearthed, and in particular a set of outstandingly beautiful dishes worked in silver, carefully walled up by fugitives before the Arab advance. Known as the David Plates, they represent the victory of David over Goliath and other incidents in his life. They may have been made to celebrate the victories of Heraclius over the Sassanids, so soon before the Arab armies overtook him. *Wealth of the Roman World, Gold and Silver, AD300–700*, Catalogue, ed. J.P.C. Kent and K.S. Painter, British Museum Publications, 1977, pp. 102–112
38 Afzal Iqbal *The Prophet's Diplomacy* Claud Stark (Cape Cod 1975) pp. 63–4, from Ibn Ishaq, op. cit., pp. 638–9

Notes for Chapter 2 (pages 28–38)

Title page:
The first and second quotations are taken from M. Abdul-Rauf *The Islamic View of Women and the Family* Robert Speller (New York 1977) pp. 121–2
1 *Qur'ān* 33:35 Confederates
2 *Qur'ān* 4:124 Women
3 *Qur'ān* 36:54–57 Yā Sīn
4 *Qur'ān* 3:195 'Imrān
5 M.M. Pickthall *The Meaning of the Glorious Koran* Mentor Books (New York n.d.) p. 78

6 *Qur'ān* 33:73 Confederates
7 *Qur'ān* 60:12 She who is Examined
8 *Qur'ān* 4:34 Women
9 *Qur'ān* 7:19–25 The Heights; and cf. 2:35–9 The Cow, 20:117–123 Ṭā Hā
10 A. Yusuf Ali *The Holy Qur'ān, Text Translation and Commentary* (Beirut 1965) note 1006, p. 344
11 *Qur'ān* 12 Joseph
12 *Qur'ān* 66:10 Banning
13 *Qur'ān* 28:9 The Story
14 Yusuf Ali, op. cit., note 5349 on 66:11–12, p. 1573
15 *Qur'ān* 11:69–73 Hūd; 15:51–6 Al-Hijr; 51:24–30 Winnowing Winds
16 Madame Nouha Alhegelan "Women in the Arab World" *Irish Arab World* Summer 1978, p. 13
17 *Qur'ān* 27:16–44 The Ant
18 Yusuf Ali, op. cit., note 3264, p. 983
19 N. Abbott "Women and the State in Early Islam" *Journal of Near East Studies* I, 1942, p. 120
20 *Qur'ān* 3:42 'Imrān
21 *Qur'ān* 23:50 Believers
22 *Qur'ān* 21:91 Prophets
23 *Qur'ān* 3:37 'Imrān
24 F. Schuon *Dimensions of Islam* Allen and Unwin 1970, p. 90
25 *Qur'ān* 24:35, 38 Light
26 Luke 1:46–55
27 *Qur'ān* 3:26–7 'Imrān; from F. Schuon, op. cit., pp. 88–101
28 *Qur'ān* 3:45–9 'Imrān
29 *L'Orient* (Beirut) 24.12.65
30 J. Nasrallah "Le Culte de Marie en Orient" *Bulletin de la Paroisse Grecque Catholique Saint Julien-le-Pauvre* (Paris). Pâques 1971, passim
31 Al Ghazālī *Iḥyā 'ulūm al-dīn* (Cairo) Al-maktaba al-tijāriya al-kubra, n.d., Vol. II p. 50, quoted by F. Mernissi *Beyond the Veil* Schenkman (Cambridge, Mass. 1975) p. 11
32 *Qur'ān* 17:23–4 Israelites; 4:5, 8 Women; 65:6 Divorce; 2:229 The Cow

Notes for Chapter 3 (pages 39–47)

Title page:

Aida Tibi: D.Phil thesis on Al-Ma'āfirī *Biographies of Famous Women*; (unpublished) Oxford 1974, p. 164

1 N. Abbott "Women and the State in Early Islam" *Journal of Near East Studies* I, 1942, pp. 341–2. See also this article for the women of the Umayyad period.
2 P.K. Hitti *The Arabs, A Short History* Macmillan 1948, p. 83
3 N. Abbott *Two Queens of Baghdad* (Chicago 1946) p. 226
4 ibid., pp. 29ff.
5 Maleeha Rahmatallah *Women of Baghdad in the Ninth and Tenth Centuries* MA Thesis (Baghdad 1952) pp. 27–31
6 N. Abbott, op. cit., p. 54
7 ibid., Chapter 1 passim
8 ibid., p. 196
9 D.M. Dunlop *Arab Civilisation to AD1500* Longman 1971, p. 259
10 N. Abbott, op. cit., pp. 228–9 and Chapter 7 passim
11 P.K. Hitti, op. cit., p. 87
12 N. Abbott, op. cit., p. 251
13 N. Abbott, op. cit., p. 235

Notes for Chapter 4 (pages 48–55)

Title page:

Sa'dī, born 571/1194 in Shiraz, wrote the famous *Bustān* (Garden) and *Gulistān* (Rose Garden). For 700 years his poems and epigrams have entertained and educated. A. Abu Turab and Z. Sardar *A Time to Speak* (Leicester 1976) p. 23

Īraj: from A.J. Arberry *Aspects of Islamic Civilisation* Allen and Unwin 1964, p. 397. Īraj Mirzā, 1875–1925, poet at the Qajar Court, travelled in Europe and wrote especially on the themes of motherhood and motherly love, and also wrote poems for children. *Dictionary of Oriental Literatures* General Editor J. Prusek, Allen and Unwin 1974, Vol. III p. 88

1 *Encyclopaedia of Islam* New Edn., Vol. II, p. 844, s.v. Fāṭimah
2 Bint al-Shāṭi' *Banāt al-nabī*, Cairo 1956, pp. 160ff; Muḥammad ibn Sa'd *Kitāb al-ṭabaqāt al-Kabīr* ed. C. Brockelmann, Brill 1904, Vol. viii, pp. 11–20
3 A. Yūsuf 'Alī *The Holy Qur'ān, Text, Translation and Commentary* (Beirut 1965) note 5349, p. 1573, on Qur'ān 66:11–12
4 *Encyclopaedia of Islam* loc. cit.

5 Muḥammad ibn Sa'd, op. cit., p. 205
6 Aida Tibi: thesis on Al-Ma'āfirī *Biographies of Famous Women in Early Islam* (unpublished) Oxford 1974, p. 265
7 G. Le Strange *Lands of the Eastern Caliphate* (Cambridge 1905) p. 209
8 ed. M. de Slane *Ibn Khallikān's Biographical Dictionary, Wafayāt al-a'yān,* (Paris 1842–71) Vol. iii, pp. 463–6
9 G. Le Strange *Baghdad under the Abbasid Caliphate* (Oxford 1924) p. 161
10 *Encylopaedia of Islam* Vol II, p. 1117, s.v. Qum
11 A.U. Pope *Survey of Persian Art* (Oxford 1939) Vol. ii, p. 1202
12 Ibn Baṭṭūṭa *Travels in Asia and Africa, 1325–1354* AD, translated and selected by H.A.R. Gibb, Broadway Travellers (London 1929), p. 177
13 *Encyclopaedia of Islam* s.v. Qum
14 Freya Stark *The Valleys of the Assassins* 1934, Penguin ed. 1952, pp. 207–8

Notes for Chapter 5 (pages 56–67)

Title page:
The first, second and third quotations are from M. Smith *Rābi'a the Mystic* (Cambridge 1928) pp. 27, 28, 60
1 ibid., p. 25
2 ed. J. Schacht and C.E. Bosworth *Legacy of Islam* OUP 1974 p. 122
3 M. Smith, op. cit., p. 97
4 Farīd al-Dīn 'Aṭṭār *Muslim Saints and Mystics, Episodes from Tadhkirat al-Auliyā, Memorial of the Saints* trans. A.J. Arberry (London 1966)
5 ibid., pp. 49–51
6 M. Smith, op. cit., p. 137, from M. Al-Ghazālī *Iḥyā 'ulūm al-dī*n (Cairo 1272) IV 353
7 M. Smith, op. cit., pp. 134, 136
8 'Aṭṭār, op. cit., p. 40
9 'Aṭṭār, op. cit., pp. 40–3; M. Smith, op. cit. pp. 5–6
10 'Aṭṭār, op. cit., p. 19
11 M. Smith, op. cit., pp. 57, 61
12 'Aṭṭār, op. cit., p. 45
13 ibid., p. 47
14 Muḥammad al-Ghazālī, born in Tus, Khurasan 450/1058, died 505/1111
15 P. Hitti *History of the Arabs* Macmillan 1937, pp. 484–5
16 A.I. Othman *The Concept of Man in Islam in the Writings of Al-Ghazālī*

(Cairo 1960) pp. 183, xix
17 M. Smith, op. cit., p. 102
18 cf. I Corinthians 2:9
19 M. Smith, op. cit., pp. 104–5, from Al-Ghazālī, op. cit. IV p. 267
20 M. Smith, op. cit., p. 71
21 'Aṭṭār, op. cit., p. 47
22 ibid., p. 44
23 ibid., pp. 44–5
24 Othman, op. cit., p. 182
25 ibid., p. 66
26 *Qur'ān* 89:27–30 Dawn
27 M. Smith, op. cit., pp. 44–5
28 M. Paul *Loving God for Himself Alone, An Appreciation of the Prayers of a Muslim Mystic, Rābi'ah of Basrah*, SLG Press (Oxford 1975) p. 7
29 M. Smith, op. cit., p. 27, from Al-Ghazālī, op. cit., IV, p. 353

Notes for Chapter 6 (pages 68–75)

Title page:

R. Burton *Arabian Nights* (Lady Burton's Edition) (London 1886) p. 24.
S. Ikramullah *Behind the Veil* Karachi 1953, p. 4
1 P.K. Hitti *The Arabs, A Short History* Macmillan 1948, p. 90
2 *Encyclopaedia of Islam* New Edition, Vol. I, p. 898
3 Bayard Dodge, ed. and trans. *The Fihrist of Al-Nadīm, a Tenth Century Survey of Muslim Culture*, Columbia University Press (New York 1970) 2 vols.
4 A. Wormhoudt, trans. *The Dīwān of Abū Nuwās al-Ḥasan ibn Hāni al-Ḥakamī* William Penn College (Pennsylvania 1974) p. i
5 M.M. Ali *A Manual of Hadith* (London and USA 1978) p. 205
6 E.W. Fernea and B.Q. Bezirgan *Middle Eastern Women Speak* University of Texas 1977, pp. 3–6; R.A. Nicholson *Literary History of the Arabs* Cambridge 1930, p. 126
7 N. Abbott *Two Queens of Baghdad* (Chicago 1946) pp. 104–6. For the names mentioned in the following pages, see the Biographical Index of *Al-Fihrist* Vol. II, pp. 931 et seq.
8 *Al-Fihrist* Vol I, p. 198, Vol II, p. 993. She was Lailā bint 'Urwah ibn Zaid
9 *Al-Fihrist* Vol. I, pp. 103–4
10 ibid., Vol. I, pp. 12–13
11 Al-Khatīb al-Baghdādī *Ta'rīkh Baghdād* (Cairo 1931) 14 vols.
12 M. Rahmatallah *The Women of Baghdad in the Ninth and Tenth Centuries, as revealed in the History of Baghdad of al-Hatīb* MA thesis,

University of Pennsylvania, 1952, published Baghdad 1963, p. 4
13 N. Abbott, op. cit., p. 148
14 Abul-Faraj al-Isbahānī *Kitāb al-Aghānī* (Cairo 1931) 9 vols.
15 N.R. Keddie "Problems in the Study of Middle Eastern Women" *International Journal of Middle East Studies* Vol. 10, 1979, p. 227
16 *Al-Fihrist* Vol. II, pp. 712–3, 720–4
17 ibid. Vol. II, p. 714
18 M.I. Gerhardt *The Art of Story Telling, A Literary Study of the Thousand and One Nights* Brill 1963, p. 355
19 J. Kritzeck *Anthology of Islamic Literature* Pelican 1964, p. 314
20 R. Burton, op. cit., p. 24
21 Fatma Moussa Mahmoud *The Arabic Novel in Egypt 1914–1970* (Cairo 1973) p. 57

Notes for Chapter 7 (pages 76–89)

Title page:
John R. Hayes, ed. *Genius of Arab Civilisation* Phaidon Press 1976, p. 21, Ibn Qutaybah, encyclopaedist and critic, died 276/889
Ashraf Abu Turab and Zia Sardar *A Time to Speak, Anecdotes from Sadi Shirazi* Islamic Foundation (Leicester 1976) p. 27
A.J. Arberry *Aspects of Islamic Civilisation* Allen and Unwin 1964, p. 396
1 Carl Brockelmann *History of the Islamic Peoples* (London 1949) p. 199
2 A.J. Arberry, op. cit., pp. 165, 167–8
3 J. Schacht and C.E. Bosworth, ed. *Legacy of Islam* 2nd edn. (Oxford 1974) p. 362
4 A.J. Arberry, op. cit., pp. 173–4
5 R.C. Broadhurst trans. *Travels of Ibn Jubair* Broadway Travel Series (London 1952) p. 348
6 A.J. Arberry, op. cit., pp. 178–9
7 R.C. Broadhurst, op. cit., p. 311
8 ibid., pp. 320, 325
9 E.M. Jamison "The Sicilian Norman Kingdom in the Mind of Anglo-Norman Contemporaries", *British Academy Proceedings* 1938, Vol. xxiv, pp. 20–22
10 R.C. Broadhurst, op. cit., p. 341
11 ibid., p. 360
12 ibid., pp. 128, 131
13 ibid., pp. 137–8
14 ibid., p. 191
15 Aida Tibi: thesis on Al-Maʿāfirī *Biographies of Famous Women*; (unpublished) Oxford 1974, p. 22

16 R.C. Broadhurst, op. cit., p. 190
17 B. Spuler *The Muslim World*, Part I: The Age of the Caliphs, Brill 1960, pp. 95–6
18 R.C. Broadhurst, op. cit., pp. 189–90
19 'Izz al-Dīn Kilij Arslān ruled 1156–1192; he was the son of Rukn al-Dīn Mas'ūd, ruled 1116–1117; Spuler, op. cit., p. 118
20 R.C. Broadhurst, op. cit., p. 240
21 ibid., pp. 192–3
22 ibid., pp. 207–9
23 ibid., p. 193
24 ibid., p. 231
25 ibid., pp. 239–40
26 ibid., p. 246
27 'Umar Ridā Kahhāla *'A'lām al-Nisā'ī* (Damascus 1958) Vol. ii, p. 155
28 Muḥammad ibn Sālim ibn Wāsil *Mufarrij al-kurūb fī akhbār banī ayyūb*, ed. Jamāl al-dīn al-Shayyāl, Vols. 1–3 (Cairo 1953) ed. H.M. Rabī'a, A.F. 'Āshūr, Vol. 4, 1972, Vol. 5, 1977
29 C. Waddy, Ph.D. Thesis on Ibn Wāṣil *Mufarrij al-kurūb fī akhbār banī ayyūb*, University of London, 1934, p. 12
30 M. Rowlatt *A Family in Egypt* Robert Hale 1956, p. 107

Notes for Chapter 8 (pages 90–98)

Title page:
Firishta: quoted by M. Smith *Rābi'a the Mystic* (Cambridge 1928), p. 185.
1 See Chapter 10, p. 112
2 *Encyclopaedia of Islam* Vol. iv, pp. 515–17 sv Ṣulaiḥī
3 H. Ingrams *The Yemen* John Murray 1963, pp. 29–30
4 H. Scott *In the High Yemen* John Murray (London 1942) pp. 100–1
5 R.W. Stookey *Yemen* Westview Press (Colorado 1978) p. 63; from *'Omārah's History of Yaman*
6 H.C. Kay ed. and trans, *Yaman, Its early Mediaeval History* by Najm ad-dīn 'Omārah al-Ḥakamī, (India Office, London 1892) pp. 21–2
7 ibid., pp. 30–7
8 ibid., pp. 38–48
9 ibid., p. 55
10 ibid., p. 64
11 ibid., p. 267
12 ibid., p. 76

Notes for Chapter 9 (pages 99–107)

Title page:
Muḥammad Asad *The Road to Mecca* (Tangier 1974) pp. 129–130

1 H.A.R. Gibb *Arabic Literature* 2nd edn. (Oxford 1963) p. 107
2 Lailā ʿAlī Ibrāhīm *The Status of the Egyptian Woman through the Ages*: unpublished paper for seminar organised by the Centre for Egyptian Civilisation Studies, Cairo, for Harvard University Center for Middle East Studies, 1976, p. 4
3 F. de Jong "Cairene Ziyārah Days" *Die Welt des Islams*, Brill 1977, Vol. xvii, 1–4, pp. 26–43
4 ibid., p. 37
5 A. ʿAbd ar-Rāziq *La Femme au temps des Mamlouks en Egypte*, Institut Français d'Archéologie Orientale du Caire 1973, p. 207; L.A. Ibrahim, op. cit., p. 8
6 M. Devonshire *Rambles in Cairo* Schindler 1931, pp. 46–7
7 *Encyclopaedia Britannica* 1911 edn., Vol. 21, p. 717
8 See below, Chapter 10, p. 112
9 Trans H.A.R. Gibb *The Travels of Ibn Baṭṭūṭa*, Hakluyt Society, Cambridge 1958, p. 357; Abd ar-Raziq, op. cit., pp. 60, 119
10 M. Lings and Y.H. Safadi *The Qur'ān, A British Library Exhibition* World of Islam Festival 1976, Nos. 25 and 26, p. 30
11 ibid., p. 56, nos. 79, 80, 82, 83, Plates xii, xiv, xv
12 L.A. Ibrahim, op. cit., p. 8
13 *Encyclopaedia of Islam*, Vol. I, p. 818, s.v. Cairo
14 Ed. Charles Schefer *Sefer Nameh, Relation du voyage de Nassiri Khosrau* (Paris 1881) p. 133
15 Ibn Baṭṭūṭa *Travels in Asia and Africa 1325–1354 AD* translated and selected by H.A.R. Gibb (London 1929) Broadway Travellers Series, p. 50
16 Ed. John S. Badeau et al. *The Genius of Arab Civilisation* Phaidon Press (Oxford 1976) p. 159
17 M. Rowlatt *A Family in Egypt* Robert Hale (London 1956) p. 34
18 *Qur'ān* 3:15 ʿImrān, and elsewhere

Notes for Chapter 10 (pages 108–113)

Title page:
Trans. H.A.R. Gibb *The Travels of Ibn Baṭṭūṭa*, Hakluyt Society (Cambridge 1958) Vol. I, pp. 1–2

1 Ibn Baṭṭūṭah *Travels in Asia and Africa 1325–1354AD* translated and

selected by H.A.R. Gibb, Broadway Travellers (London 1929) p. 46
2 F.G. Gies "To Travel the Earth" *Aramco World Magazine* Jan–Feb 1978, Vol. 29, No, 1, p. 18
3 He ruled from 713/1313 to 742/1341. See p. 104 above
4 Ibn Baṭṭūṭah, op. cit., pp. 148 et seq.
5 ibid., pp. 244–5
6 ibid., pp. 243–4
7 ibid., p. 244
8 ibid., p. 330: M. Smith, *Rābi'a the Mystic*, Cambridge 1928, p. 129
9 Ibn Baṭṭūṭah, op. cit., p. 320–1
10 A. 'Abd ar-Rāziq *La Femme au temps des Mamlouks en Egypte*, Institut Français d'archéologie orientale du Caire 1973, pp. 39–41
11 M. Smith, op. cit., p. 154
12 ibid., pp. 185–6; Ibn Baṭṭūṭa, op. cit., p. 230
13 Ibn Baṭṭūṭah, op. cit., pp. 146–7
14 Halide Edib Adivar *Turkey Faces West*, Yale 1930, p. 6; T. Taşkıran, *Women in Turkey*, Istanbul 1976, p. 18
15 Ibn Baṭṭūṭah, op. cit., p. 136, and note p. 356
16 Alkan Akat *Bursa* Publications of Bursa Museums and Historical Monuments 1976
17 Emine Foat Tugay *Three Centuries, Family Chronicles of Turkey and Egypt* OUP 1963, p. 134

Notes for Chapter 11 (pages 114–121)

Title page:
Ed. A. Upham Pope *Survey of Persian Art* (Oxford 1939) Vol. ii, p. 1141
P. Sykes *History of Persia* Macmillan 1951, 3rd Edn., Vol. ii, p. 155
1 Pope, op. cit., Vol. ii, p. 1124
2 British Museum, MS Or 1359, folio 452b, Sharaf al-Dīn Yazdī, Zafarnāma, dated 959/1552. For the author, see E.G. Browne *Persian Literature under Tartar Dominion 1265–1502* (Cambridge 1920) pp. 363–5
3 J. Munro "Islam in Russia" *Aramco World Magazine* Jan–Feb 1976, pp. 6–12
4 These were published two hundred years later, in Oxford, in Latin, translated by John Greaves, Savilian Professor of Astronomy. The catalogue of the Bodleian Library lists three separate printings of Latin translations from Ulugh Beg in 1648 and 1650. The *Tabulae* were published in 1665, with notes by Thomas Hyde. Translations appeared in 1853 (French), 1917 (English) and 1918 (Russian).
5 M. Lings *The Quranic Art of Calligraphy and Illumination* (London

1976) Plates 81, 82, 83
6 Pope, op. cit., Vol. xiv, p. 3134
7 R. Byron *The Road to Oxiana* (London 1950) 2nd edn., p. 220
8 B. Spuler *The Muslim World* Brill 1960, Part ii, p. 69
9 *Journal of the Bengal Asiatic Society* 1834, quoted by R. Byron, op. cit., p. 91
10 S.P. Seherr-Thoss *Design and Colour in Islamic Architecture* (Washington 1968) Plate 60, p. 134.
11 Pope, op. cit., Vol. ii, p. 1122
12 F. Bémont *Les Villes de l'Iran* (Paris 1969) Vol. 1, p. 179. See above, Chapter 4
13 P. Sykes, op. cit., Vol. ii, p. 155
14 R. Byron, op. cit., pp. 219–224 for the whole story
15 Pope, op. cit., Vol. ii, p. 1136
16 ibid., Vol. ii, p. 1120
17 M. Smith *Rābi'a the Mystic* (Cambridge 1928) pp. 155–6. See also Aziz Ahmad *Islam in India* Edinburgh 1969, p. 42, where the Qādiriyyah leader Muḥammad Mīr is named as the preceptor of Dārā Shukoh and Jahān Ārā

Notes for Chapter 12 (pages 122–133)

Title page:
Aida Tibi "A Study of Al-Ma'āfirī's *Biographies of Famous Women in Early Islam*" unpublished D.Phil. thesis (Oxford 1974) p. 42
Halide Edib Adivar *Memoirs* John Murray 1926, p. 147
W.S. Walker, A.E. Uysal *Tales Alive in Turkey* (Harvard 1966) p. 234
1 *Encyclopaedia Britannica* 11th edn., 1911, vol 12, p. 764, s.v. Gynaeceum
2 Tezer Taşkıran *Women in Turkey* (Istanbul 1976)
3 ibid., pp. 18–19
4 A Persian word meaning "palace". It passed into English as "seraglio", French "serail"
5 P.K. Hitti *The Arabs, A Short History* Macmillan 1948, p. 196
6 L.A. Ibrahim "Status of the Egyptian Woman through the Ages" unpublished paper, Cairo 1976, p. 11
7 N. Penzer *The Harem* (Philadelphia 1937) p. 186
8 S. Skilliter "Three Letters from Safiye to Elizabeth I" in S.M. Stern *Documents from Islamic Chanceries* OUP 1965, pp. 139, 150–1
9 B. Lewis *Istanbul and the Civilisation of the Ottoman Empire* (Oklahoma 1963) p. 105
10 N. Abbott *Two Queens of Baghdad* (Chicago 1946) p. 255

11 M. Levey *World of Ottoman Art* Thames and Hudson 1975, p. 61
12 ed. R. Halsband *The Complete Letters of Lady Mary Wortley Montagu* Vol I, 1708–1720 (Oxford 1965) p. 400
13 M. Smith *Rābi'a the Mystic* (Cambridge 1928) p. 158; L.M.J. Garnett *The Women of Turkey and their Folklore* (London 1891) Vol. 2, p. 538
14 R. Halsband op. cit., pp. 327–8
15 ibid., p. 321
16 ibid., p. 343
17 ibid., pp. 347–8
18 ibid., pp. 349–52
19 R. Halsband *Life of Lady Mary Wortley Montagu* (Oxford 1956) p. 84
20 Halsband *Letters* p. 381
21 ibid., p. 382
22 ibid., pp. 338–9
23 *Encyclopaedia Britannica* 11th edition 1911, p. 249
24 N. Barber *Lords of the Golden Horn* Macmillan 1973, p. 109
25 H. Edib Adivar *Memoirs* John Murray 1926, p. 332
26 Cerdet Kudret *Türk Edebiyatinda Hikâye ve Roman* 1859–1959, Vol II (Ankara 1967) pp. 62–3; Şükran Kurdakul *Şairler ve Yazarlar Sözlügü* (Istanbul 1971) pp. 10–12
27 H. Edib Adivar op. cit., pp. 71–3

Notes for Chapter 13 (pages 134–140)

Title page:

Tezer Taşkıran *Women in Turkey* (Istanbul 1976) pp. 57–8
Robert Shaaban, quoted in Ali A. Jahadmy *Anthology of Swahili Poetry* African Writers Series, Heinemann 1977, p. 14
1 Dr Nimet Taşkıran "Florence Nightingale and some documents relating to her from the Turkish State Archives" *Haseki Tıp Bülteni* (Haseki Medical Bulletin) Vol. 13, No. 3, 1975, offprint
2 Kenneth Clark *Civilisation* BBC and John Murray 1969, p. 33
3 Halide Edib Adivar *Turkey Faces West* (Yale 1930) p. 229
4 Arianne Stassinopoulos *The Female Woman* Davis Poynter 1973, pp. 7, 11
5 Interview 1978

Notes for Chapter 14 (pages 141–156)

Title page:

Ḥāfiz Ibrāhīm wrote nationalistic poetry in the classical style of the Abbasid poets, especially elegies on famous Egyptians of his time such as Muḥammad 'Abdūh and Sa'ad Zaghlūl. M.M. Badawi *A Critical Introduction to Modern Arabic Poetry* (Cambridge 1975) p. 46

A.M. Said *Arab Socialism* Blandford Press 1972, p. 122

1 C.C. Adams *Islam and Modernism in Egypt* (London 1933) p. 13

2 Laila Ali Ibrahim "The Status of the Egyptian Woman through the Ages", unpublished paper, Centre for Egyptian Civilisation Studies (Cairo 1976) pp. 14–15

3 P.S. Ali *Status of Women in the Muslim World* (Lahore 1975) p. 91

4 M.A. Zaki Badawi *The Reformers of Egypt* The Muslim Institute, Croom Helm 1978, p. 90

5 L.A. Ibrahim, op. cit., note 39

6 Fatma Moussa Mahmoud *Women in the Arabic Novel in Egypt* (Cairo 1976) p. 13

7 Aziza Hussein "The Role of Women in Social Reform in Egypt" *Middle East Journal* Vol. 7, No. 4, 1954, p. 440

8 E.W. Fernea and B.Q. Bezirgan *Middle Eastern Muslim Women Speak* (Texas 1976) p. 199

9 Baheega Sidky Rasheed et al. *The Egyptian Feminist Union* Anglo-Egyptian Bookshop (Cairo 1973) p. 9

10 Baheega Arafa *Social Activities of the Egyptian Feminist Union* (Cairo 1973) pp. 10, 12

11 R.F. Woodsmall *Moslem Women Enter a New World* American University of Beirut, Social Science Series, Allen and Unwin 1936, pp. 214, 404

12 Mona M. Mikhail *Images of Arab Women* Three Continents Press (Washington DC 1979) pp. 30–2

13 Interview, April 1972

14 B. Arafa, op. cit., p. 7

15 *The Listener* 18 August 1977, p. 196

16 ibid., loc. cit.

17 ibid., loc. cit.

18 A.M. Said, op. cit., p. 122

19 Professor Faṭma Moussa Mahmoud, Interview, 1978

20 B. Arafa, op. cit., p. 20

21 ed. A. Dearden *Arab Women, Minority Rights Group*, Report No. 27 (London 1975) p. 6

22 Interview, 1977

23 B.S. Rasheed, op. cit., p. 25

24 Amīnah al-Sa'īd, Lecture delivered in Beirut, 12 December 1966, published in *Les Conférences du Cénacle* Vol. 21, nos. 11–12, 1967, translated by E.W. Fernea and B.Q. Bezirgan, op. cit., pp. 379–81

Notes for Chapter 15 (pages 157–170)

Title page:

All Pakistan Woman's Association, *Silver Jubilee Report* (Karachi 1974) p. 23

Welcome Peace and Development Pamphlet, General Federation of Iraqi Women, 1977 p. 15. Jamil Ṣidqī al-Zahawī (1863–1936), Iraqi thinker, politician, social reformer and prolific poet, was dismissed from the Law School in Baghdad in 1908 for publishing an article "In Defence of Women". His most effective social poems deal with women's rights. M.M. Badawi *A Critical Introduction to Modern Arabic Poetry* (Cambridge 1975) pp. 48, 53

1 Parveen Shaukat Ali *Status of Women in the Muslim World* (Lahore 1975) pp. 59–60

2 ibid., pp. 60–1

3 K.A. Nizami *Sir Syed Speaks to You* (Aligarh 1968) p. 39

4 K.K. Aziz *Ameer Ali, His Life and Work* (Lahore 1968) pp. 97–112, 161–85; reprinted from *Nineteenth Century* September 1891 and May 1899

5 K.K.Aziz, op. cit., pp. 111–2

6 Nawab Sultan Jahan Begam *An Account of My Life* Vol. II, trans. A.S.Khaṅ (Bombay 1922) pp. 151–3

7 ibid., pp. 265–6

8 R.F. Woodsmall *Moslem Women Enter a New World* American University of Beirut, Social Science Series, No. 14 (London 1936) p. 164

9 P.S. Ali, op. cit., pp. 65–6

10 APWA *Report*, 1974, op. cit., p. 23

11 P.S. Ali, op. cit., pp. 67–8

12 ibid., pp. 65–8

13 S. Ikramullah *From Purdah to Parliament* (London 1963) pp. 93–5

14 P.S. Ali, op. cit., p. 212

15 ibid., p. 69

16 APWA *Report*, op. cit., pp. 23–4

17 ibid., loc. cit.

18 Kay Miles *The Dynamo in Silk, A Brief Biographical Sketch of Begum Raana Liaquat Ali Khan* (Rome 1963) Second edn. (Karachi 1974) p. 15

19 op. cit., p. 21

20 B.S. Rasheed et al *The Egyptian Feminist Union* (Cairo 1973) p. 32 (picture)
21 APWA *Report*, p. 26
22 S. Ikramullah, op. cit., p. 86
23 ibid., p. 166
24 P.S. Ali, op. cit., pp. 69–70
25 ibid., p. 185
26 S. Ikramullah, op. cit., pp. 167–8
27 P.S. Ali, op. cit., pp. 71–3

Notes for Chapter 16 (pages 171–184)

Title page:
From two interviews: 8 and 15 January 1971, by Walīd ʿAwaḍ for *Al-Ḥawādith*: reprinted in E.W. Fernea and B.Q. Bezirgan *Middle Eastern Muslim Women Speak* (Texas 1977) pp. 251–61
1 Mary Borden *Journey Down a Blind Alley* (New York 1946) pp. 273–5
2 Fernea and Bezirgan, op. cit., p. 252
3 Letter from Mrs Sarah Jamāli, Tunis, September 1979
4 Frantz Fanon *The Wretched of the Earth* English translation Penguin Books 1967
5 David Caute *Fanon* Fontana 1970, pp. 51–3
6 Ed. Ann Dearden "Arab Women" *Minority Rights Group Report* No. 27 (London 1975), p. 9
7 Anwār Sadāt *In Search of Identity* Collins 1978, p. 5
8 Muḥammad Asad *The Road to Mecca* (Tangier 1974) pp. 165–6
9 Juliettes Minces *L'Algérie de Boumedienne* Collection Terre des Autres, Presses de la cité (Paris 1978) p. 75
10 Dearden, op. cit., pp. 11, 18
11 André Pautard *Bourguiba* Editions Média (Paris 1978) p. 82
12 Nādiah Abū-Zahrah "On the Modesty of Women in Arab Villages: A Reply" *American Anthropologist* October 1970; "Material Power, Honour, Friendship and the Etiquette of Visiting" *Anthropological Quarterly* (Washington DC) January 1974; "Baraka, Material Power, Honour, and Women in Tunisia" *Revue d'histoire Maghrebine* (Tunis) January 1978, based on D.Phil. thesis, Oxford 1968
13 MEED *Arab Report* (London) July 18 1979
14 Dearden, op. cit., p. 5
15 MEED *Arab Report* May 5 1979
16 Farīdah Allāghī and Zakiyah El-Sahlī "On Libyan Women" *Mission of the Libyan Arab Jamahiriya to the United Nations* Libyan Papers 8, 1978, p. 25

17 Amal Sharqī, *Progress of Women in Iraq* Iraq Cultural Centre London 1978, p. 13
18 Carla Makhlouf *Changing Veils* Croom Helm 1979, p. 20
19 Dearden, op. cit., p. 19
20 ibid., p. 14

Notes to Chapter 17 (pages 185–194)

Title page:
Muḥammad Asad *The Road to Mecca* (Tangier 1979) pp. 165–6 "Azayyiz" is an affectionate diminutive of Aziz.
1 P. Shaukat Ali *Status of Women in the Muslim World* (Lahore 1975) p. 134
2 This and other information given in this chapter is derived from an interview graciously granted by Her Majesty Queen 'Īffat to the author, Paris, February 1979.
3 Interview, BBC Woman's Hour, repeated 22 April 1979
4 Ed. R. Dunipace et al., *The Kingdom of Saudi Arabia,* Stacey International, London 1977, p. 196
5 Madame Nouha Alhegelan "Women in the Arab World" *Irish Arab World* Summer 1978, p. 12

Index